'Everatt and Denston  –
troversy with this aut' :–
ful and informative – g
detailed accounts of r it
of the theories of dy d
intervention. I found y
illuminating. Not enough has been written about this a.
This book benefits from the authors' lengthy experiences, their
academic insights and their sound awareness of best practice in this
field. This is a must buy for all involved in this area and will surely
become one of the seminal texts in this field.'

Gavin Reid, Chair of British Dyslexia Association Accreditation Board,
Former Senior Lecturer, University of Edinburgh, Scotland, UK

'Many texts on dyslexia provide in-depth information on a few
select research topics, or go to the other extreme, providing a
superficial overview of topics that requires more explication. *Dys-*
lexia: Theories, Assessment and Support provides a welcome contrast. Everatt and Denston have provided an accessibly written, yet
comprehensive and well-considered overview of classic as well as
current research related to dyslexia and related reading difficulties.
They explore standard cognitive and linguistic processes influencing word recognition and comprehension and are careful to
include critical contextual factors such as teaching practices,
experience, interest and self-concept. This book will provide a
welcome resource to university students in reading courses, teachers, as well as researchers who are looking for a comprehensive
update.'

Charles W. Haynes, EdD, CCC-SLP, Department of
Communication Sciences and Disorders, MGH Institute of Health
Professions, USA

DYSLEXIA

Dyslexia: Theories, Assessment and Support offers a broad perspective on dyslexia, providing a range of views from theory to practice which help explain the continued controversy surrounding the condition. Offering a framework on which to understand the concept of dyslexia, the book considers procedures that can both identify the condition and help support those with it. With a focus on self-concept, the authors highlight ways to positively influence both literacy acquisition and individual well-being.

This book is ideal reading for those taking courses on dyslexia or literacy learning difficulties within education, psychology and related disciplines. It will be of great interest to specialist teachers, special education staff, educational psychologists and those in related occupations.

John Everatt is a Professor of Education at the University of Canterbury, New Zealand.

Amanda Denston is a post-doctoral researcher in Education at the University of Canterbury, New Zealand.

DYSLEXIA

Theories, Assessment and Support

John Everatt and Amanda Denston

Routledge
Taylor & Francis Group

LONDON AND NEW YORK

First published 2020
by Routledge
2 Park Square, Milton Park, Abingdon, Oxon OX14 4RN

and by Routledge
52 Vanderbilt Avenue, New York, NY 10017

Routledge is an imprint of the Taylor & Francis Group, an informa business

British Library Cataloguing-in-Publication Data
A catalogue record for this book is available from the British Library

Library of Congress Cataloging-in-Publication Data
A catalog record for this book has been requested

ISBN: 978-1-138-63625-5 (hbk)
ISBN: 978-1-138-63626-2 (pbk)
ISBN: 978-1-315-20608-0 (ebk)

Typeset in Bembo
by Wearset Ltd, Boldon, Tyne and Wear

Printed in the United Kingdom
by Henry Ling Limited

CONTENTS

FIGURES

1
INTRODUCTION TO THE SKILLS OF READING AND WRITING

Background to the book

The aim of this book is to provide the reader with an understanding of the basics of dyslexia. It is mainly aimed at those studying the field (maybe as part of an education or psychology qualification), but hopefully it will be of interest to the general reader who want to know more about the background to research and practices related to dyslexia. Note that there are more general books, written over the last couple of decades, that the reader may want to consider (for example: Doyle, 2002; Fawcett & Nicolson, 1994; Miles & Miles, 1999; Osmond, 1993; Reid, 2009; Reid & Green, 2011; Selikowitz, 1993; Shaywitz, 2003; Snowling, 2000; Thomson, 2009). All have a specific focus that will interest the reader: some are targeted more at teachers, others at parents or individuals with dyslexia, for example, so it is possible to find the right book for the specific interest.

The current book also has a focus. One of the aims of this introductory part is to provide the reader with a background to understand the book's focus. It will discuss theory and research more than most general readership books, given that it is targeted at students of the subject, but it also takes a specific perspective on the cause of dyslexia and its likely outcomes, which may be of interest to dyslexia practitioners as well.

The book aims to provide a range of references and background information, along with a general framework for thinking about dyslexia, which should allow the reader to develop their knowledge of the subject through a consideration of the points presented and further researching of the literature. It should also allow the reader to understand some of the controversies surrounding the concept of dyslexia and what we do know from about 100 years of research on the topic and what we don't know. The latter will require some discussion of the complexity of the subject, though we will try to avoid too much technical jargon in explanations, or try to use the terminology in a way that makes them as clear as possible.

As a basic starter for understanding some of the key terms, we will touch on words such as phonology, which is usually used to refer to the study of language sounds – or, a bit more formally, it is the study of how speech sounds are organised in a language, and thus in the mind of the language user, in order to convey meaning. For our purposes, the important part is that it refers to sounds within a language. This is important because a word can be considered a whole sound or as made up of parts: the word 'phonology' has four syllables represented by 'phon-o-lo-gy', for example. However, each of these syllables could also be split up into basic sounds – the first syllable is made up of an initial sound which, in English, is represented by 'f' in 'fish' – the second sound is the sound usually represented by the letter 'o', as in the sound represented by 'o' in 'dog' – and the final sound is the usual sound represented by 'n' in English. Each of these sounds is called a phoneme; hence, phonemes are considered the basic units of sound in a language. We will also come across the term phonological processing, which is usually used to refer to the processing of phonological units such as syllables and phonemes. Processing here refers to identifying or recognising sounds, storing sounds in memory or manipulating sounds in some way, such as adding them together to form a word, as well as linking them to other forms, such as their corresponding letter. In terms of work on dyslexia, the phonological processing deficit viewpoint is that dyslexia is caused by problems processing units of sound in the language. The phoneme is seen as the most important for the purposes of discussing dyslexia since linking letters or groups of letters with their corresponding phonemes is a useful skill in learning to read, and the basis of the alphabetic principle. Phonological awareness is then used to refer to the ability of the individual to recognise these different units of sounds within the language.

Written text also has its own terminology. The basic unit of text is not a letter, rather it is called a grapheme. This allows us to consider 'ph' in phonology as a basic unit of written text – a grapheme. Hence, linking graphemes and phonemes is an important part of recognising the link between a language and its written form. The rules (or conventions) that make up a writing system are referred to by the term orthography – though this is also used as synonymous with the general idea of a written form: the written form of the English language is referred to as the English orthography, for example. Hence orthographic rules determine how letters or groups of letters go together and, therefore, link with their corresponding sounds or provide the basis on which to understand syntactic relationships and hence meanings within written text. Orthographic awareness, then, relates to an understanding of how orthographic units go together within the system of writing that the individual is using.

Meaning also has its own set of terms. Vocabulary is an obvious one: a store of word meanings, a bit like an English dictionary. However, in research, a store of words is also referred to as a lexicon. This can sometimes be useful to allow research to refer to a phonological lexicon (a store of information about the sounds of words) and an orthographic lexicon (a store of information about written words). A third lexicon would then be the semantic lexicon, which is a store of information about the meaning of words – the term semantic referring to meaning. However, basic units of meaning are referred to as morphemes: the word 'disagreeable' has a base morpheme 'agree', which is then modified by the 'dis' morpheme to mean the opposite of the base form, and change in function by the 'able' morpheme in order for it to have the right syntactic form to fit with the meaning of a sentence. Morphemes often relate to the origins of words, and this can be a useful guide to spelling: 'phonology' is a good example, as using 'ph' instead of 'f' at the start of this word relates to its Greek origin. Greek words in English have regularly been used to refer to scientific ideas, so expect to see spellings related to Greek origins in more scientific texts. Dyslexia is another good example. It was not chosen to frustrate those with difficulties spelling, even though it can. Rather, it was a word that also alludes to the Greek-science background. The 'lexia' part is to refer to words – and we will see later how, in the field of reading research, a lexicon is used to refer to a store of words (either spoken words or written words). The 'dys' part is to refer to difficulties. Hence, the term gives a science-basis (with its Greek origins) to the idea of someone having difficulties with words. (See also Joshi, Treiman, Carreker & Moats, 2008, for some interesting ideas about how word origins can help with understanding spelling rules.) Hence, morphemic awareness may support an understanding of spelling rules based on word origins as well as an understanding of how morphemic units go together. (And see Denston, Everatt, Parkhill & Marriott, 2018, for a discussion of using morphemes in intervention methods aimed at students who are struggling with literacy learning.) Additional terms will be explained as we progress through the book; however, this will have to be relatively brief explanations, given space limitations, but further readings will provide additional material to further understand such terms.

Such terminology will only be used when necessary to support an understanding of the field, since this is the aim of the book. However, this aim at understanding the field of dyslexia will be based primarily on providing a framework for dyslexia. This will require us to consider theories/perspectives that have been proposed to explain the cause, features and manifestations of dyslexia. These will also provide a basis on which to discuss some of the main research findings in the literature, and some of the key authors in the field. Of necessity, the theory/perspective parts of the book will be fairly research (and reference) heavy, but it will provide the reader with material to develop their own ideas about the topic. Furthermore it will provide the basis on which to consider practices that have been used to identify and support those with dyslexia. The discussion of methods used in the identification of dyslexia will consider ways that have been used to distinguish a learner with dyslexia from those who seem to be showing no difficulties with learning, as well as those with other types of learning difficulties that may be associated with poor educational achievement. A discussion of these identification procedures should help the reader develop an appreciation of the main characteristics associated with dyslexia and some of the issues related to the assessment of educational achievement. Knowledge of theoretical viewpoints and identification practices will also provide a basis on which to recognise the range of methods used to overcome dyslexia-related problems. An awareness of a range of intervention procedures will give a sense of how different practices can be tailored to the individual, taking into account their strengths and weaknesses; though we will also consider some of the problems associated with practices associated with dyslexia work. The book will cover both current and historical perspectives, so that the reader can grasp how ideas about dyslexia have developed and changed over time – and understand some of the controversy linked to the topic. Before we discuss these theories and practices, however, we need to consider the background to the main feature of dyslexia: i.e. problems with reading and writing/spelling.

The skill of reading and writing

The aim of this introductory part of the book is to provide a summary on the acquisition of literacy, focusing mainly upon reading, but it will also cover some of the issues related to writing/spelling. This should provide the reader with the background knowledge to understand the following parts that focus on dyslexia. We will focus on the processes (or skills/abilities, if these terms seem simpler to use) that distinguish a skilled reader from a beginning reader. As part of this, we will discuss some of the ideas related to the development of reading/spelling, and touch on how reading and writing might be taught, particularly as it relates to the development of the skill. Given the framework presented in the book, that an learner with dyslexia has difficulties in acquiring word reading and spelling, an understanding of how reading and writing are expected to develop, as well as the typical processes and methods of learning involved, will allow an appreciation of what may be the basis of difficulties with learning. This will allow us to consider those reading/writing problems that have most often been associated with dyslexia.

A general view of reading and writing will be taken, and based on a consideration of the research evidence. Again, more detailed information about reading and writing can be found elsewhere (e.g. Cain, 2010; Ellis, 1984; Funnell & Stuart, 1995; Gillon, 2018; Kamhi & Catts, 2012; Oakhill & Garnham, 1988; Perfetti, 1985; Rayner & Pollatsek, 1989; Snowling & Hulme, 2005; Underwood & Batt, 1996). Instead, this section is as an introduction to dyslexia work, rather than an explanation of reading and writing itself. This current section will focus on reading rather than writing. This is because reading is the more researched of the two skills; though reference will be made to writing skills (and particularly spelling) to explain similarities and differences compared to reading. Reading and writing are both complex but learnt skills. Although reading can often be taken for granted, when we study the skills needed in detail, we find ourselves in a complex world of learnt operations and mental processes. Many of the mental processes involved in reading will have developed for other abilities (such as spoken language) but which the acquisition of literacy seems to refine (e.g. an appreciation of phonemes, or basic language sounds, seems to develop with reading). This complexity is best summed-up by Huey, who was one of the first influential researchers in reading:

> to completely analyse what we do when we read would almost be the acme of a psychologist's achievements, for it would be to describe many of the most intricate workings of the human mind, as well as to unravel the tangled story of the most remarkable specific performance that civilisation has learned in all its history.
>
> *(1908, p. 6)*

Despite the increase in understanding of the processes involved in reading, and writing, this statement is as true today as over 100 years ago.

Reading and writing are learnt skills, as can be seen if we consider the relatively brief history of writing systems: such systems seem unlikely to have existed for more than 10,000 years given that the earliest known written artefacts date from about 5000 to 6000 years ago. Reading and writing are relatively new skills in terms of human evolution. This relatively recent development of what we would consider a writing system means that the brain could not have changed enough to provide a dedicated reading/writing brain area – and that there cannot be a simple reading/writing gene. Although both reading and writing will depend upon innate abilities/processes (the obvious one is the ability to process verbal language in which a range of genes and areas of the brain do seem to specialise), the skill itself is not inherited. Therefore, if there are innate processes which are important for reading and writing, they must have evolved for reasons other than the ability to read itself. Hence, when looking at the biology of reading and writing (and hence dyslexia), we have to remember that this biology (genetic dispositions and brain areas) exists because of other human behaviours, not in order to read and write. We have to learn to read and write – we don't have biological systems set up to allow acquisition.

It is also the case that reading and writing have been the province of a select few (scribes and priests, administrators, or the relatively rich) for much of the period that we have been using writing systems. For example, in the UK, the 1870 Education Act brought reading and writing to many children who would not have had the opportunity to learn to read before this. Hence, until very recently, the vast majority of people did not have the opportunity to be taught reading/writing, and therefore could not read or write. Instances where large numbers of individuals will have been identified as having a specific difficulty in acquiring reading and writing skills (the primary feature of dyslexia) would be rare prior to the point of more universal tuition. A focus on the need for all to have the opportunity to learn to read and write is even more recent in many parts of the world: there are still countries with high levels of illiteracy due to lack of educational opportunity. In those countries with high levels of illiteracy due to education policies, the need to identify dyslexia is less likely to be a focus of educational practice. Hence, it may not be surprising that most of the work on dyslexia (research, theories and practices) has been conducted over the last 100 years or so. It may not be too surprising to find a relative lack of work on dyslexia in languages where universal literacy policies are more recent developments, though this has been changing over the last decade or so (we will return to points about dyslexia in different languages later in this book as it is a newer, and potentially exciting, feature of work in the field).

Reading and writing development

Given that a child does have access to literacy tuition, and that reading and writing are learnt skills, the focus moves to how the child acquires reading and writing, and what do educationalists need to do or note to support this acquisition. How does reading and writing develop or change to become skilled? One way to consider this is in terms of 'reading readiness'. It may be that certain skills or ability need to develop prior to reading and writing being acquired. This may be particularly important to consider in terms of dyslexia, since it may be that those with dyslexia are not ready to learn to read. Although this is not the position of this book, it is worth considering since it may give some ideas of why difficulties with literacy acquisition may occur; and a clue to the biological foundations of dyslexia. For example, it has been considered that some level of intelligence is needed for the child to be ready to learn to read. Hence, intelligence has been considered a factor when discussing dyslexia (we will return to this point when we consider different perspectives about dyslexia). However, when referring to work on dyslexia, intelligence is more often discussed in terms of differences between intelligence and the ability to read: a dyslexic student has in the past been seen as someone whose reading ability is much lower than their intellectual ability. Indeed, the field of dyslexia provides a clear indication of how such abilities as reading can be dissociated from intelligence (see Ferrer, Shaywitz, Holahan, Marchione & Shaywitz, 2010) and there is ample evidence that those with very low scores on an assessment of intelligence (an intelligence quotient or IQ) can be taught many of the basic skills associated with reading (see discussions in Gillon, 2018).

A second area that may be useful for beginning to learn to read is visual attention, given that we learn a visual form of writing. Therefore, it may not be too surprising to find that many initial perspectives on dyslexia focused on visual memory or visual word processing problems (we will discuss these further in the following part of the book). However, although, it may be useful, again we can find instances where those with very severe levels of visual problems can learn to read: braille readers are an obvious example. Although, this has required the learning of a very different form of written text, it does argue against the necessity of the visual part of the focusing of attention in order to learn a complex task such as reading. Therefore, it may be better to assume that focused attention is important, rather than visual attention. We will discuss visual deficit theories of dyslexia, though, later in the book, so this should not be dismissed entirely.

A third possible factor that may be influential at beginning of learning to read and write relates to the fact that written text is a representation of oral language. Hence, language may have to develop to a certain level before literacy (the term used for reading and writing in this book) can be acquired. This is consistent with one of the main propositions of the framework for dyslexia covered in the book; i.e. that dyslexia is a difficulty with acquiring reading and spelling skills due to a problem with processing certain aspects of language. The precise language deficit related to dyslexia is likely to be problems with processing sounds within the language; typically referred to as phonological processing deficit (see specific discussions in Gillon, 2018; Snowling, 2000 – though we will discuss this perspective on dyslexia throughout this book). The Report of the National Early Literacy Panel (see Lonigan & Shanahan, 2008) identified a number of variables that were predictive of later literacy performance (after controlling for intelligence and socioeconomic status). These included:

1 alphabet knowledge, such as letter names, and an understanding of the association between letters (graphemes) and sounds (phonemes), as well as concepts about print (e.g. what a book cover looks like, what looks like written text);
2 phonological awareness, or the meta-linguistic ability to reflect on and analyse the sound structure of language, such as a knowledge of syllables and phonemes;
3 rapid naming of items (such as objects or colours, and digits or letters with educational experience) which can sometimes be a useful one for predicting fluency of reading;
4 the ability to write one's own name, or letters in isolation or a simple letter sequence;
5 phonological memory, which refers to the ability to hold speech information briefly in memory;
6 oral language, or the ability to produce or comprehend spoken language, including a knowledge of vocabulary.

Each of these is related to language processing to some extent, or the relationship between text and language. Hence, it may not be surprising to find that those with early language problems show evidence of later literacy difficulties (Bishop & Leonard, 2000; Catts, 1993; Gillon, 2018; Snowling, Adams, Bishop & Stothard, 2001; Stackhouse & Wells, 1997). We will return to most of these areas described in the report over the course of the book, as they also relate to issues associated with dyslexia.

Once some basic abilities are available, developmental models suggest that the child will go through a series of stages in the development of skilled reading/writing (see, for example, Ehri, 1995; Frith, 1985; Marsh, Friedman, Welch & Desberg, 1981; Seymour, 1990). Traditional stage models (e.g. Marsh et al., 1981) saw children having to go through a series of stages in a set order, but those that are probably more relevant to the current discussion (e.g. Frith, 1985) emphasise some of the strategies that an individual can use to try to support reading/spelling development. For example, the use of some salient visual aspect of a word or some meaningful information around the word (a picture or another known word) may be used to guess at the word's meaning, which in turn may allow the child to access its pronunciation via a developed spoken vocabulary. In Frith's model, this was referred to as a logographic stage, and is exemplified by the sort of errors that early learners make, such as the written word 'bath' being read as 'bed', since they both begin with a 'b', or the written word 'Alex' being read as 'Max' since they both end in an 'x', or the written word 'bay' being read as 'dog' since they both have the same overall shape. The assumption is that the individual elements of writing are not clear to the beginning reader – a word is seen like a logograph with a salient visual feature that links to meaning: a bit like an emoji in texting.

However, teaching the beginning reader to focus on salient visual features of words is a questionable strategy except maybe as a way of gaining initial attention. Potentially more useful is the use of sounding-out strategies since these can relate a letter string with a spoken form, which can allow access to meaning and pronunciation via verbal language. These strategies are part of Frith's alphabetic stage, and should show the ability of the early reader to make links between text and language, which does make sense from a teaching perspective if conducted appropriately. Indeed, as we will discuss over the course of this book, appropriately administered engaging phonics-based teaching methods that aim to make links between graphemes and phonemes, are amongst the more successful ways of teaching reading and spelling skills. One problem with such methods in the past is that they have been used as relatively boring drill-based methods of teaching reading and spelling skills. Clearly, any teaching method that is boring is going to be less successful in most learning contexts.

However, a simple process of linking letters and sounds (or grapheme and phonemes) is not the end point in the reading development model of Frith. More experienced readers will use additional strategies that may focus on pronouncing a word because it has a similar spelling to another word ('bantish' may be pronounced like the start of 'banter' plus the morpheme 'ish'), or by learning more complex rules that leads to a variation in pronunciation, such as when an 'e' is found at the end of a word. The use of these more complex features of the writing system was referred to as the orthographic stage by Frith. This point is where the reader builds an orthographic lexicon, i.e. a store of written words, rather than relying on accessing a word via its spoken form. This will develop with experience and practice, just like many other aspects of a learnt skill, but is vital if we are able to understand the meaning of words such as 'piece' versus 'peace'. If we accessed meaning only via the spoken form of a word, then these two words in isolation would be indecipherable. That experienced readers know the different meanings of 'piece' versus 'peace' or 'pair' versus 'pear' indicates that they have a written words store, much like a spoken word store, which can be used to recognise familiar words in the form in which they are presented.

However, another point about these strategies (which have often been explained as part of development, as in the Frith model), particularly those associated with the final, skilled stage of reading/spelling, is that they may not be that simple to learn/use. In addition, the learning of relatively complex features of reading and spelling may relate to some of the features often associated with dyslexia, but may be more a consequence of lack of practice needed to learn them, rather than as aspects of an underlying, neurological deficit. A lack of understanding or use of an orthographic rule need not be due to an underlying orthographic deficit, but to less than optimal levels of practice needed to learn the rule. For example, the direction of writing is relatively arbitrary – in English we go from left-to-right, whereas in the Arabic orthography, the direction is right-to-left. This directionality needs to be learnt, just like most aspects of reading and writing, meaning that a lack of practice may lead to errors. Hence, reversal errors (e.g. reading 'saw' instead of 'was'), often considered as a feature of dyslexia, may not be due to the underlying cause of dyslexia, but rather a feature of lack of practice (Vellutino, 1987) – we will return to this point in the next part of the book. The point here is that practice is a vital component of learning a new skill – particularly a complex skill. However, it is likely that an individual with dyslexia will practise less than an individual with no difficulties in literacy learning. After all, if you are struggling with something, why would you practise it? Hence variations in development may be due to a lack of practice caused by feelings about the task as much as a feature of the processing deficits that lead to dyslexia. Issues in self-concept (confidence and self-efficacy) relate to such problems, and we will touch on these later in the book. However, practice is one of the key features that we need to take account of when we consider dyslexia – both in terms of its characteristics and when we aim to support an individual with dyslexia. This is one reason why early identification and intervention are likely to be highly worthwhile. Catching up on a lack of practice, and the development of skills that this leads to, will be harder than avoiding the problem in the first place.

Reading processes or skills

Stage theories have not stood the test of time that well. One problem is that there is evidence that children need not go through the stages in a specific order (e.g. Stuart & Coltheart, 1988). Some of the strategies associated with specific stages in developmental models are more a function of teaching experiences than a process of development. The positive point of this is that it suggests that teaching influences the development of a skill as much, if not more so, as development determines the way we teach, which offers the potential for appropriate teaching and/or learning experiences to overcome a developmental difficulty such as dyslexia. This will form the basis of discussions about how to support individuals with dyslexia in the final general part of the book.

Before focusing on dyslexia, though, a basic understanding of the features of skilled reading (and writing) would be useful. Again, the focus will be on reading (rather than writing), given that it has been more thoroughly researched. The aim in this part of the book is to build a model of the skills that go into reading, with a focus on those areas proposed by at least one influential theory as a cause of dyslexia. Although this may not be a complete model of skilled reading, it provides the basis to understand some of the points made in this book (see Figure 1.1).

We will start with a very basic idea about reading. Given the link between the written form and spoken language (as suggested throughout this book), and the fact that a reasonable amount of spoken language will have been acquired prior to learning to read (and spoken language has its own specific areas of the brain to support acquisition within the right environment), then skilled reading may simply be recognising a written word, and performing some translation process to allow the spoken language system to understand the meaning of the word and those around it in text. Skilled reading could be reduced to word recognition and comprehension (the central squares in the model). Indeed, there is a fairly useful general model of reading called the Simple View of Reading (Gough & Tunmer, 1986; Hoover & Gough, 1990; Tunmer & Chapman, 2012) that argues for something similar. This model suggests that a simple way of looking at reading comprehension is by considering the processes that go into the decoding of letter strings (or word recognition in Figure 1.1) and the processes that go into linguistic

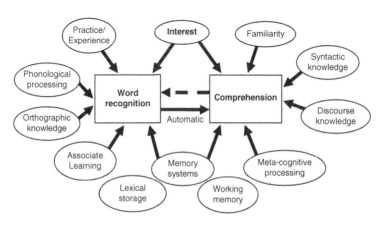

FIGURE 1.1 A basic model of reading processes

comprehension (i.e. the ability to understand language, which is part of the comprehension box in Figure 1.1). For successful comprehension of written text, both components are required.

Therefore, in terms of the Simple View of Reading, difficulties in reading will occur due to problems with word recognition/decoding or language/linguistic comprehension, or problems in both components. This explanation has been relatively successful in describing students with different types of reading difficulties (see, for example, Catts, Kamhi & Adlof, 2012). Dyslexia is associated with word reading and spelling difficulties. Hence, in this model, we are looking for difficulties among those processes or skills that support decoding or recognising words. However, we will also find students without word decoding difficulties, but who have problems with reading comprehension due to difficulties within the linguistic comprehension system. Such groups of students are identifiable and separable from those who we would consider as dyslexic (Catts et al., 2012; Nation, 2001). Children with specific reading comprehension difficulties will not show the same problems with reading or spelling individual words as their dyslexic peers. If we give them a word they have never seen before, they should be able to use grapheme–phoneme conversion strategies to make a reasonable attempt at pronouncing the new word – in contrast to those with dyslexia who often struggle with such a task (see later assessment section in Part 4 of this book). Rather, children with specific reading comprehension problems show difficulties in deriving the meaning of connected text (see also discussions in Cain & Oakhill, 2007; Cornoldi & Oakhill, 1996; Nation & Snowling, 1998). Consistent with this, such children have been found to show deficits in processing language, when given vocabulary or verbal reasoning tasks, for example. Therefore, this model provides a potentially simple way to view different types of reading problems and also suggests where we should look for difficulties. The central part of Figure 1.1 is a slightly simplified version of the Simple View of Reading.

The Simple View of Reading is also a useful framework to consider typical reading ability, as measuring the two general skills of word decoding and linguistic comprehension can predict reading comprehension levels in children to a large degree (see, for example, Lonigan, Burgess & Schatschneider, 2018). The model (and models derived from it) has also been found to be applicable to orthographies other than English (see Florit & Cain, 2011; Joshi, Tao, Aaron & Quiroz, 2012) and a writing version of the model has also been proposed (Berninger et al., 2002). Another advantage is that it allows us to conceptualise the potential for difficulties within the word recognition system to be compensated to some extent by the language understanding system. Although this may not be optimal, given that both systems support learning, it may be useful practice to consider such compensatory strategies when working with older students with word recognition difficulties. Strategies such as using sentence context to support word identification, or using the general gist of a passage to infer meaning, may be a feature of dyslexia (see discussions in Fidler & Everatt, 2012; Nation & Snowling, 1998). Additionally, the relative contribution of the recognition/decoding aspects and the language/linguistic comprehension component changes over time (Catts, Hogan & Adlof, 2005): among a general ability sample (i.e. typically developing readers), decoding processes will be more important for early reading development, but once these skills have developed to a reasonable extent, then different levels of reading comprehension are better explained by variations in linguistic comprehension skills. Again, this may help us understand the specific characteristic of the reading behaviours of students with dyslexia. Although continued poor levels of word decoding will clearly impact on later reading comprehension, compensatory strategies may overcome some of these challenges, particularly with experience and some educational support with decoding strategies. Again, this is a point that we will return to in later parts of the book.

A further feature of this model is that it allows us to consider the relationship between word recognition and linguistic comprehension. Understanding text may be the element that we want to put all our thinking into, so it would be advantageous to make the word recognition part as effortless as possible – to make it automatic, so that it occurs without us having to think about it too much (hence, in Figure 1.1, the arrow from word recognition to comprehension has automatic written next to it). Making word recognition effortless will allow us to concentrate on deriving the meaning of the written message. Consistent with this, skilled word recognition does seem to possess many features of an automatic process. Skilled readers do not have to think about a familiar word – and often familiar words are read automatically even if this may not be the desired outcome. Attempting to proofread something that we have written ourselves is a good example of how we may read words automatically – it can often lead to us reading what a word is supposed to be rather than what it is: spolling [spelling] mistakes and grammatical errors is [are] obvious examples – and all skilled readers/writers make such errors.

Maybe a better example though is the interference that a written word can produce on another task. Anyone who has experienced the Stroop effect will understand how difficult it is to avoid reading words when you are a skilled reader of a language. This word interference effect was originally devised by Stroop in 1935, and has been an interesting phenomenon in psychology ever since. The basic idea is to ask a native speaker/reader to name colours. First these are presented as colour blocks (red, green, blue, yellow) repeated several times in an array: e.g. six instances of each colour randomly presented on a sheet of paper. This is often a fast, simple task. However, then the same colours are presented in the form of words that represent a different colour name: the word 'red' is presented in green, blue and yellow ink. The task now is to still name the colour, but you now have to ignore the written word. Even if the two tasks are presented in exactly the same way, except for the inclusion of written words, there is a noticeable difference between the two. When presented as a written word, naming a colour is harder if the written word does not correspond to the colour: the time to name colours is slower, there are more hesitations in naming and sometimes errors. This seems to be because a skilled reader cannot help but read the word and the name of the word gets in the way of naming the colour. (MacLeod, 1991, discusses some interesting examples of this effect – see also http://imbs.uci.edu/~kjameson/ECST/MacLeod_TheStroopEffect.pdf.)

The point in Figure 1.1 is that it is a good idea to make word recognition automatic as this will allow us to focus on meaning. Typically, practice will make a skill effortless, fast and error free (automatic). Problems with making word recognition automatic, therefore, will lead to effortful/difficult reading. We will return to this point when we discuss automaticity deficit viewpoints related to dyslexia (see later theory part of this book). Hence, one theory might be that dyslexics cannot make word decoding processes automatic.

The opposite relationship, from comprehension to word recognition, is also important (this is represented by the dotted arrow). Indeed, a number of reading models see the skills involved in processing text as interactive, which will be consistent with the ideas of compensatory strategies mention above (see the interactive compensatory model proposed by Stanovich, 1980). Hence, we need to think of a primary route from decoding to comprehension, but we may also want to think about the idea of a route from understanding to word identification (i.e. arrows in both directions). As explained above, the route from comprehension back to word recognition may not be optimal for learning to read, but it may explain some reading behaviours, particularly of adults. For example, Fidler and Everatt (2012) found that the adult dyslexics who they were working with were slow readers. However, this slow reading behaviour was not because of an underlying speed of processing deficit (again a theory of dyslexia that we will discuss later in the book) but because they were slowing reading down in order to support decoding: slow reading was a compensatory strategy. Reading the text several times allowed these dyslexic adults to get the main ideas from the text and then use this to support inferring the meaning of words that they could not read/decode. Clearly, this will not work if you cannot read a large number of words in the text; meaning is unlikely to be derived from only a small proportion of words. Similarly, it may not help with reading new or unfamiliar words since sentence context is rarely constraining enough to support such decoding (we will return to this point when we discuss teaching methods in the intervention part of this book), but it may be a strategy that some older dyslexics use to improve comprehension levels above that expected by word recognition weaknesses.

The framework that we will work on in this book argues that word recognition or decoding will be the primary area of difficulty for students with dyslexia. This will explain the early difficulties in learning to read experienced by children with dyslexia. It will also explain why dyslexic students have poor reading scores on measures of word reading or decoding (see Part 4 on identification). Therefore, if we consider Figure 1.1, we are looking for difficulties in one of the processes that has an arrow into the word recognition box. We have already discussed how a lack of practice or experience of reading can impact on word recognition. As indicated above, this will also impact on how automatic single word processing becomes since it is practice that makes a skill automatic: riding a bike or driving a car are good examples of how aspects of these skills become unconscious/effortless with extended practice. Similarly, interest is a vital component of learning any skill. The more interesting and motivating that we can make learning, even for someone who is struggling, the more likely that acquisition will take place – and that practice will be ongoing. Although interest is not a specific feature of dyslexia, it is vital to consider when supporting a learner – particularly when they may have had bad experiences of learning a skill previously. We will return to this point when we consider self-concept and intervention strategies in a later part of this book.

Additionally, we have also seen how the processing of sounds within words (phonological processing in Figure 1.1) is an important skill in literacy development/acquisition; and how phonological skills are an early predictor of later reading ability or disability. Recognising sounds within words may be particularly important when linking written text with language. If you have difficulties recognising sounds within words, you may not be able to associate sounds with their corresponding written form – or you may confuse links between phonemes and graphemes. However, recognising text itself is also an important aspect of literacy acquisition. Hence, in the model both phonological processing and orthographic knowledge are presented as key elements in word recognition. (Both phonological processing and orthographic knowledge have been considered as elements in models of dyslexia, so again we will return to these processes in the theory part of this book.) Furthermore, these two elements need to be associated: the reading needs to make associative links between verbal language and written text (between phonology and orthography in the terms used in Figure 1.1). Hence, a further element is the ability to learn associations. This may be related to intelligent behaviour, since the ability to make links between things is considered an aspect of intelligence. However, it may be the only element of intelligent behaviour needed for simple word recognition processes to occur – though we will come back to ideas related to intelligence later in the book. Again, though, the point in including this in the model is to show that learning is necessary; that the associations between orthography and phonology do not exist as innate structures in the brain, nor as obvious/intuitive connections. The framework behind the arguments in this book proposes that these associations will need some level of explicit teaching; and that this level of explicit teaching may need to be greater for those who find that making the links is difficult, such as those with a phonological deficit. Again, we will return to this throughout the discussions in this book.

However, there is a final system that needs to be considered in Figure 1.1. Learning also involves storing learnt material for later use. Hence, the efficient storage of written and verbal material will be necessary for comprehension. As we discussed above, the storage of words is often referred to in terms of a lexicon (hence the idea of lexical storage in Figure 1.1). We can see this as comprising one storage system that included everything about a word, but recognising the differences between verbal and written forms may be best represented by considering different, but interacting lexicons – three would seem to be the most useful (see discussions of the tri-lexicon model in Snowling, 2000). A semantic lexicon would hold information about the meaning of words. A phonological lexicon would hold information about how words are pronounced and maybe the phonological elements in that word (its syllables, phonemes, etc.). An orthographic lexicon would then hold information about the written form of the word. Separating these out means that we can think about one developing later than another: an orthographic lexicon would not start developing before written words are experienced, but language exposure would lead to earlier development of phonological and semantic lexicons. A skilled reader is likely to have a well organised orthographic lexicon. This means that written words will be accessed by entries in this lexicon. This can be considered as a sight vocabulary – we see a word and recognise it through its entry in this orthographic storage system. This is how we can determine that 'pear' and 'plum' are fruits, but 'pair' and 'plumb' are not. Skilled readers recognise written words directly via its entry in the orthographic lexicon, which would then connect to the semantic lexicon to access the word's meaning.

However, a beginning reader does not have such a well organised orthographic lexicon. Reading a new word and accessing its meaning can only come via the language lexicons already developed. Hence, the idea proposed as part of the framework in this book is that this is best achieved by teaching the links between letters and sounds (graphemes and phonemes). If these links exist, then parts of the word can be recognised (maybe in the orthographic system) and these will link with the phonological system. Given that accurate links are available, and that some process of combining phonological forms can also be used, then a spoken word form should be accessed in the phonological lexicon that will then connect to the semantic lexicon to access the word's meaning.

This argues for two routes to meaning. A direct route from the written form (an orthographic entry) to meaning (the semantic lexicon), and a more indirect route from orthographic elements to corresponding phonological forms and some assemble process to produce a whole word, then to meaning. This idea has a long history in explanations of word recognition processes and is often referred to as a dual route model (see Coltheart, Rastle, Perry, Langdon & Ziegler, 2001; Coltheart & Leahy, 1996; Ellis, 1984). Such dual route models have led to views that there may be several types of dyslexia: one where there are problems in the indirect route (a phonological deficit, for example, which we would refer to as phonological dyslexia) and one where there are problems in the direct route (an orthographic deficit, which has been referred to as surface dyslexia). Again, we will cover this idea later in the book.

The other part of the memory system is something called working memory. Again, this is something that now has close links with theories about dyslexia, though the theories are relatively under-developed compared to some others. The basic premise of working memory theories is that the memory system is made up of passive stores (such as the lexicons discussed above) but also systems that need to work with the information in those stores – the working memory component. Exactly how the working memory component works with the passive information varies across theories, but maybe the easiest to follow is the theory proposed by Baddeley and colleagues (see the original model in Baddeley & Hitch, 1974, with subsequent modifications in Baddeley, 1986, 2000, 2003; though see alternatives discussed in Cowan, 2005). This proposes a central executive system and a set of passive stores. The central executive is the system where attention is focused on certain aspects of the material that is contained in the more passive storage systems, which will lead to that material being manipulated to support the achievement of task goals. For example, Baddeley (1996) argued that the central executive as a system that controls encoding and retrieval of stimuli input and monitors attention changes, and is responsible for controlling and manipulating information stored in a number of passive short-term storage systems, one of which is for verbal/phonological information. Therefore, the central executive is basically the working part of this working memory model, which may make the distinction between simple storage systems and a working system easier to follow.

One of the functions of working memory, therefore, may be to focus the processing of material for a certain purpose. This would include verbal and written material. Hence, if decoding a written word is the task, and accessing its verbal equivalent the goal, then information may be stored in the passive stores (such as the sounds that the letter represents in a phonological store), but the executive system might be responsible for ensuring that the right material is accessed (such as the phonological equivalent of a grapheme) and that this is combined appropriately to achieve task goals (i.e. an appropriate pronunciation). If this is the case, then working memory may be a point of difficulty for those with word reading problems. Indeed, there are assumptions by some within the dyslexia field that the overloading of the working memory system is a feature of dyslexia – possibly the cause of many problems that students with dyslexia face with reading and other tasks (e.g. McLoughlin, Leather & Stringer, 2002). Overloading may occur because most models of working memory consider that there is a limited amount of information that can be stored and processed by the working memory. This relates to the origins of working memory theories in terms of short-term memory. Whereas the lexical system referred to above is mainly a long-term store, the passive storage systems associated with working memory are short-term stores. Information in these passive stores is retained for a short period of time so that it can be processed appropriately for task goals. However, the capacity of short-term memory is limited. In terms of verbal short-term memory, most adults can retain about seven pieces of verbal information at a time. This may be perfectly adequate in many situations but it may be limiting in others, and if an individual's capacity is smaller than normal, then limitations may be greater.

In terms of theories related to dyslexia, this is exactly the potential problem: i.e. those with dyslexia have more limited working memory systems. Measures of verbal short-term retention often show differences between those with dyslexia and those without (we will discuss this further in the following parts) and this may lead to individuals with dyslexia being unable to perform tasks that require working memory processes as efficiently as other individuals. In terms of decoding, working memory limitations may make translating from a letter to a sound more difficult. For example, if you need to store the sounds associated with 'd' and 'o' while processing 'g', but limited capacity means that the sound for 'd' is lost while you are processing 'g', then decoding 'dog' will be harder. However, there is little evidence that a limited short-term memory will lead to problems of this sort. Indeed, much of the research on working memory has focused on more completed task processing, including comprehending text rather than decoding words (e.g. Cain, Lemmon & Oakhill, 2004; Daneman & Carpenter, 1980). We will return to the point about short-term memory capacity when we consider interventions, but, for now, the functioning of the general working memory system may support decoding, but would seem to be more involved in making inferences from text, inhibiting unintended meanings and monitoring comprehension goals.

Although processes involved in comprehension are also vital for reading success, they are less relevant to the current focus on dyslexia, so we will not cover in detail except as a way of introducing some of the ideas that may be relevant when we think about teaching methods and learning strategies – the teaching of comprehension skills may be as important as teaching decoding, particularly for older/adult students. As with learning any skill, interest is important for supporting reading comprehension development, just as we have discussed its role in the acquisition of word recognition skills – examples of comprehension strategies will be easier to learn if the material is of interest to the student. Furthermore, understanding will be supported when material is not only interesting but also relatively familiar. Obviously, this does not mean the same material as before, as this will decrease interest, but building the meaning of what is written on already existing ideas or knowledge will support comprehension. For example, understanding the context of a crime novel will support comprehension of statements such as 'I bet it was the butler who did it'; but equally, a background knowledge of what a butler is would aid understanding. Therefore, when considering materials for learning, making them relevant to the background of the reader is particularly useful. Taking into account the background or culture of the learner may be useful, particularly for someone from a different background from the teacher (e.g. a student from an immigrant family or studying overseas). Cultural relevance also would likely be of interest to the individual and possibly those around them. Similarly, a background understanding of the form of discourse used by a writer may help. Understanding the difference between the text in this book and that in a fictional story would help in understanding what to expect from the text. Knowledge about the form of the discourse (how a specific type of text is structured) can allow predictions about what certain sections of the text will include – and how one section will relate to another.

An appreciation of the syntactic structure of text (how words go together) can also be useful aids to understanding. For example, the notice 'Alcohol free zone' would be interpreted very differently from 'Free alcohol zone'. Such phrase or sentence structures will also relate to grammatical and morphological features of words, which may support interpretation, as we have discussed previously in this introductory part of the book – though we will return to ideas about morphology later as well. The range of strategies, from understand phrase structure to working out aspects of familiarity, which can support understanding, may be best considered under the general term 'meta-cognitive' strategies – and again these have been part of the discussion of how to support those with dyslexia (see Leather, 2018). These relate to the idea of thinking about how to work something out – in this case, an understanding how one processes text, or at least some of the strategies that can help. Basically, interacting with the text, asking questions of the text, working out what the gist is and/or the objective, will all support comprehension. Hence, this part of reading should be the more active part of the process. Clearly, being able to decode individual words is vital as part of reading – and making this decoding process less active may be a good idea to allow the majority of the active interaction with the text to be at the level of comprehension – but practising both will support acquisition. This will be as important for a student with dyslexia as any other student. Hence, although the focus of much of this book is on issues related to the word-level difficulties experienced by those with dyslexia, these comprehension strategies are still important. Indeed, meta-cognitive strategies that can support text processing by a student with dyslexia just as well as they can for any student (see Fidler & Everatt, 2012). Such understanding of, and interaction with, text will also support writing (see the teaching ideas for spelling and composition skills in Berninger et al., 2002).

Overview of the rest of the book

Up until now, we have considered a range of views about what skilled reading (and spelling/writing) might look like. We have mentioned issues related to visual processing and focused attention, language development, skilled learning and automaticity, memory storage and working memory, text processing and comprehension. We have also discussed issues related to prior knowledge and interest, as well as a range of theories of reading: dual route, tri-lexical, working memory and the simple view. As indicated at the start of this background part of the book, many of these ideas were selected because they have influenced dyslexia research and/or practice. The aim was not to try to cover everything related to literacy research, but rather to prime the subsequent discussions of different perspectives about dyslexia. By now the reader should have a basic understanding of the complexity of reading and writing, plus the reasons for the need for continued research in the field; e.g. we still do not fully understand the role of working memory in reading. Hopefully, there is now a basis on which to understand the differing perspectives related to dyslexia that will be covered in the remainder of the book.

Although this background aims to provide a basis on which to consider dyslexia as related to difficulties in acquiring reading and spelling, the following part of the book suggests that we may need to look for more than simply poor scores on a measure of reading (or spelling) in order to identify dyslexia. There are situations where poor reading test scores may not be considered as dyslexia: a lack of opportunity to learn to read is a good example. This potential dissociation between dyslexia and poor scores on measures of reading has been the basis of many differing perspectives about dyslexia; specifically who should and who should not be included in a definition of dyslexia. This basic idea should provide a foundation on which to understand some of the differing perspectives on dyslexia proposed over the last 100 or so years (a similar historical discussion can be found in Miles & Miles, 1999). It should also help explain why differing numbers of students are said to have dyslexia: those who want to consider dyslexia as only one type of reading difficulty will refer to a smaller number of students who have dyslexia (say an incidence of 5 per cent within a population) compared to perspectives where all students with reading problems are considered to have dyslexia (maybe 10 to 20 per cent depending on the inclusiveness of the perspective). However, we will also see how the aspects of reading discussed above are intertwined with definitions of dyslexia, sometimes with the aim to distinguish dyslexia from some other types of poor reading, such as those with reading comprehension deficits. An understanding of the potential types of reading problems predicted by a Simple View of Reading would explain different types of poor readers – and help us determine when dyslexia may focus on decoding problems or when it may be combined with problems understanding text. Equally, an understanding of second language development should help explain the type of reading difficulties that a multilingual reader may encounter, which for many would be best distinguished from dyslexia – though it may also be necessary to be considered in conjunction with dyslexia (i.e. a dyslexic student learning to read in a second language).

The introduction to dyslexia in the next part of the book will start with some of the initial influential works in the field that were conducted in the late twentieth and early twenty-first century. It will then follow work through the mid-1900s, and through the debates and controversies that characterised the field through the 1980s/1990s and up to present times. An awareness of the many characteristics that have been associated with dyslexia should become apparent through this background discussion. As part of our discussions of these differing perspectives on dyslexia, we will cover some of the controversy surrounding the term: for example, definitions that associate dyslexia with intelligence, which have often led to arguments against the usefulness of the term dyslexia, but which still influence policy and practice in many parts of the world. However, use of the term dyslexia itself varies between groups, often due to differing theoretical frameworks. As suggested in the last paragraph, if you use dyslexia in a more focused way, then it need not cover all those with a literacy learning difficulty. In some theories (including the framework proposed in this book), reading comprehension deficits without word reading weaknesses would fall outside the focused definition of dyslexia (see Nation, 2001). However, an alternative argument/perspective might be that it is better to use terms that describe all (or most of) those with reading problems: for example, specific reading disabilities. The development of the criteria for reading and writing problems in the fifth version of the *Diagnostic Statistical Manual* (DSM-V; see discussions in Tannock, 2013) is a good example of the issues surrounding the best way to categorise literacy-related difficulties. However, currently, probably the best known argument about the usefulness of a restricted use of the term dyslexia (and hence the usefulness of the term itself) is the book, *The Dyslexia Debate* (Elliott & Grigorenko, 2014) – though see the more two-sided debate between Elliott and Nicolson, *Dyslexia: Developing the Debate*, which can be found at www.bloomsbury.com/uk/dyslexia-9781474233736/. Many of the issues about the usefulness of the term dyslexia revolve around the issue of intelligence and its historical (and in part of the world continued) use as an identifier of dyslexia. Rather than going into these arguments in detail, we will briefly touch on them in order to develop a framework for dyslexia that will be used as the basis of the rest of the book. This framework will help the reader understand the position taken in the subsequent parts on practice.

Before we focus on practice, however, we need to cover a number of theories for the cause of dyslexia, as well as some of the consequences that may occur if support is not provided for those struggling with reading and writing. The framework proposed in this book argues that the reading and spelling problems most often associated with dyslexia are due to specific problems with language processing, and that these are most likely related to difficulties with reliably/efficiently processing sounds within words. This is the phonological deficit hypothesis and we will look at some of the features of this perspective. Although this is the dominant theory in the field (the vast majority of theories about dyslexia incorporate this perspective either as the only cause of dyslexia or as one of two or more causes), some of the problems considering this as the only cause of dyslexia will be considered. This will include a focus on discussing dyslexia across different languages as the variability in the relationships between written symbols (graphemes) and language sounds (phonemes) has been used to question the universality of the phonological deficit perspective.

Therefore, alternative theories for the cause of dyslexia will be considered. It may be that one or more of these alternatives will help understand some of the instances where a child is struggling with reading acquisition but does not seem to show a clear pattern of phonological processing deficits. The framework proposed in this book is that the majority of children with dyslexia will have a phonological deficit that can be supported through methods that target these skills, but that some children will have other difficulties with reading and writing that will need alternative methods of support. These latter children may be better considered as having another learning difficulty or as showing negative consequences of poor learning experiences, which will need alternative or additional methods of support – and, for some, these alternative difficulties may co-occur with the primary features of dyslexia. Following the discussion of the dominant theory related to phonological processing, visual deficit theories will be considered, given the historical association between dyslexia and the concept of word blindness. Theories related to working memory, motor coordination or automaticity deficits will also be touched upon in the following pages. A consideration of their potential advantages and problems should provide the reader with an understanding of the relative complexities and controversies in the field, as well as an appreciation of some of the issues related to dyslexia that require further study.

We will also consider some of the potential consequences of dyslexia, particularly those which may occur if the condition is not identified and appropriate action taken. For example, word-level reading difficulties will result in poor comprehension of connected text, making accessing a curriculum difficult and, consequently, poor levels of educational attainment. Poor performance can lead to avoidance strategies, including challenging behaviour, and a lack of practice. Low levels of reading experience will further interfere with literacy acquisition but can also impact on vocabulary development. Finding school work a struggle can manifest as emotional and behavioural difficulties, and low educational attainment is related to poor employment prospects and has the potential to increase the incidence of anti-social behaviour. All of this can lead to feelings of low self-worth and poor self-concept, and negative perceptions of the self can lead to major problems for psychological well-being and poor health outcomes. Although not all dyslexics will experience these problems, negative feelings about ability (self-doubt and consistent experiences of failure) can be a major barrier to intervention work. Therefore, a final part of the book will concentrate on the link between self-concept and educational outcomes as this may be one of the main consequences of dyslexia that practitioners will need to deal with.

The fourth part of the book will cover issues related to the identification/assessment of dyslexia, many of which are based on ideas about the characteristics or causes of dyslexia. Hence, the range of procedures covered should be seen to build on the ideas discussed in the previous parts of the book. As part of this discussion, we will consider ways to identify those with dyslexia from individuals with no evidence of a learning difficulty. However, a key feature of the framework proposed in this book is that not all those with reading problems should be considered as having dyslexia. Therefore, we will also need to consider ways to differentiate dyslexia from those with other types of learning difficulties that may affect reading achievement and educational attainment. Such distinctions, as well as similarities, between different types of learning difficulties will also provide the basis on which to understand the intervention procedures covered in the final parts of the book. We may need to take into account other types of difficulties in intervention practices, for example, if a child with dyslexia also has additional difficulties related to another learning problem. Many consider that dyslexia and motor coordination problems (sometimes referred to as dyspraxia) co-occur, which means that we may need to take both into account when determining an educational plan for the individual.

Although general assessment procedures of the past have focused on measures of reading and measures of intelligence or IQ, methods have also been developed that assess the hypothesised underlying cause of dyslexia. These include assessments of various language skills (e.g. phonological awareness), memory systems (e.g. recalling or repeating speech), visual processing (eye movements through text) and motor coordination (balance or hand–eye coordination). We will touch on each of these in the following discussion. Screening measures, questionnaires and interviews, along with standardised skills assessment will form part of the discussion, which should provide a basis on which to understand the differing aims of varying practices. Also in this part of the book, we will present data from a large number of individuals with dyslexia from early primary school through to late primary and early secondary years, and up to adulthood. These data will be presented in the form of graphs of average performance of the individuals with dyslexia across a range of quantitative assessment measures. These graphical presentations will be used to discuss what a profile of performance of a typical group of individuals with dyslexia looks like and how this can change over time with increasing age and experience, which will need to be taken into account in assessment procedures. These data can also be used to clarify some of the potential consequences of dyslexia and how these might overlap with other conditions: e.g. relationships between dyslexia and those with emotional/behavioural problems may be more due to the consequences of the educational problems that those with dyslexia face rather than a common underlying cause with another condition.

We will also see how further work on identification methods is needed. Dyslexia is a problem related to processing language information, and, by this stage, the reader will have recognised the reoccurring themes on associations between reading/spelling difficulties and problems with phonological processes. However, the potential that reading development and literacy difficulties may vary with language (or orthography) leads to problems for assessment practices. Therefore, there is still a need for assessment practices to be developed that are appropriate for use across languages and with those from multilingual backgrounds. Multilingualism is more prevalent today than being monolingual, and assessment procedures need to be developed to take this into account. The position argued will be that dyslexia occurs across all languages and writing systems, most likely due to deficits in specific aspects of processing languages; however, the way dyslexia manifests is dependent on aspects of both language/cultural experience and features of the relationship between the language and writing system.

We will then discuss a selection of support, intervention and remediation procedures that have been associated with dyslexia. Again, the historical and theoretical perspectives covered in earlier parts of the book will provide a basis from which to understand the range of ideas proposed to 'cure' dyslexia, or as support procedures and strategies that can be used with, and by, individuals with dyslexia. This part of the book will also consider the complications that can be created by an individual experiencing more than one learning difficulty (e.g. comorbidity of dyslexia with conditions associated with attention or behavioural problems) and will discuss some of the evidence for combining intervention procedures.

The major teaching and support strategies used to assist individuals with dyslexia will be covered. Again, the focus will be on learning to read and write: the major defining feature of dyslexia proposed in the framework used within this book. Methods specifically developed for individuals with dyslexia will be covered, plus those devised for other reasons (e.g. for groups with other types of learning problems), but which have at least some data to argue for their potential effectiveness. The need for good teaching practice and effective support needs to be emphasised here, and we will cover this idea when we consider Response to Intervention methods. However, this needs to be a consideration for all methods, along with the aim of the method and its underlying rationale. We will consider these in the discussions of each method to provide the reader with examples of what to look for in an intervention practice.

The primary methods considered will be those that focus on phonological awareness training. However, the importance of linking this with the teaching of reading and writing will be emphasised. There will also be a discussion of multisensory strategies since these are often used with children with dyslexia, though an emphasis on the link between written symbols and language sounds are as important with these techniques as the previous phonological training methods. Although there will be an emphasis on techniques aimed at developing word-level skills and phonological awareness, we will also discuss the development of comprehension and resilience in the final two parts of the book since both will be vital for older learners with a background of difficulties related to dyslexia. Reading comprehension should be the focus of interventions aimed at older individuals, particularly adults at college (see also Fidler & Everatt, 2012), as this is the area of literacy that specifically supports their current learning needs. Methods assisting individuals to build resilience, and an awareness of how best to deal with problems, has the potential to reduce the negative consequences of difficulties (even perceived failure) in the future.

Many of the intervention and remediation methods that will be covered have been developed to target an underlying deficit argued to be the cause of dyslexia, which will build on our discussion of the causal theories and perspectives of dyslexia in the earlier parts of the book. A range of methods will be outlined, followed by a discussion of their theoretical basis and the evidence for and against their potential usefulness. Overall, the framework in this book argues that methods targeting the behavioural manifestation of dyslexia (i.e. that target literacy) have clearer evidence for their effectiveness than those that claim to 'cure' dyslexia through targeting underlying biological or cognitive causes. However, this discussion will also consider whether some of the methods discussed might be more appropriately applied to individuals with conditions other than dyslexia and, therefore, could be useful when considering comorbidity between conditions (i.e. the chance that a child may have dyslexia along with another learning difficulty): a child with dyslexia and an attention deficit may require different procedures from one with dyslexia alone, for example. This leads to a discussion about whether a range of methods may be necessary to support individuals with dyslexia. This may also be important when considering individual differences, since some may have a more severe form of dyslexia and, therefore, may need more intensive intervention. This discussion should provide the reader with a basic understanding of challenges associated with dyslexia practice. However, in all cases, the framework of dyslexia which is the basis of this book, will lead to the need to emphasise supporting the acquisition of reading and writing in addition to strategies that may target skills deficits or problems associated with conditions other than dyslexia (e.g. targeting weak spoken language skills or attentional/emotional problems). Despite the framework presented, further research focusing on the complexity of combinations of learning difficulties and individual differences is needed to inform best practice.

2

A BACKGROUND AND FRAMEWORK TO UNDERSTAND DYSLEXIA

Introduction

This part will focus on an overview of dyslexia, including some of the more influential individuals, theories, practices and research. The discussion will include a brief historical perspective through which to discuss the range of views that have been influential in the field of literacy learning difficulties and dyslexia. This will of necessity be brief and selective, but a more comprehensive history can be found at https://dyslexiahistory.web.ox.ac.uk/home (which was last retrieved by the authors in May 2019 – this site is regularly updated, hence the date). The brief historical overview is important because it should give the reader an insight into some of the reasons for the controversies surrounding the concept of dyslexia. For example, a range of disciplines (from education to psychology, social work, linguistics, and to medical or biological sciences and neurology) have been involved in work on the dyslexia over the years. This has led to the use of varying terminology to describe similar things, as well as a focus on differing characteristics associated with dyslexia. Such differing backgrounds has led to very different perspectives about dyslexia and the practices used to support those with dyslexia. This introduction should therefore provide a background to understand many characteristics that have been associated with dyslexia. In addition, this background will provide a basis on which to discuss some of the definitions of dyslexia that have been used over time, which will again give the reader an insight into why the concept is still relatively controversial. It will also provide an opportunity to look at some of the common aspects of these definitions, which will then be used to provide the current perspective on dyslexia used as a framework for the rest of the book.

The background discussion will start with ideas related to visual deficit perspectives on dyslexia, given the association of dyslexia in history with the term 'word blindness', before moving on to considering perspectives that have a much more language focus. The latter will lead to a discussion of one of the most commonly agreed theories of dyslexia: that dyslexia is related to some sort of phonological deficit, which will be covered in the following part. However, this part will also consider those perspectives that may have fewer supporters, but which have influenced educational policy and assessment practices (for example, associating dyslexia and intelligence). This will allow subsequent parts to consider issues for practice in terms of identification and intervention, since most practices have been influenced by views about dyslexia.

This part will provide the basis on which to develop an understanding of the more common characteristics associated with dyslexia. These will revolve around reading problems, but will also include difficulties with spelling, and a focus on literacy at the word level: i.e. single word reading and spelling. This is important to consider as there are potential differences between word reading and text reading that may be important when considering support practices for those with dyslexia. We will also focus on another common characteristic, that of phonological deficits: i.e. problems with the processes that allow an awareness of the sounds within spoken words that can be related to written text, and which are often seen as the basis of the alphabetic principle which can support the development of decoding strategies and independent reading/spelling. The part will also provide the basis on which to recognise potential consequences of dyslexia – particularly those which may occur if the condition is not recognised and appropriate action taken. For example, word-level reading difficulties will lead to problems comprehending connected text, which can lead to problems accessing a curriculum and poor levels of educational attainment. Poor performance can lead to avoidance strategies, including misbehaviour, which leads to lack of practice – and low levels of reading experience can impact on vocabulary development. Furthermore, difficulties in education, and the feelings of failure with which a lack of being able to access text is sometimes associated, can lead to poor self-esteem, low levels of self-worth and self-efficacy, which can lead to related emotional and behavioural difficulties. Poor educational attainment also often leads to poor employment prospects and has the potential to increase the incidence of anti-social behaviour. An understanding of these potential consequences may help explain the range of characteristics that have been associated with dyslexia over the history of the field, but will often be important to take into consideration when determining support procedures.

Reading/learning disability and dyslexia

As suggesting above, if we consider the history of dyslexia work, we will see that a range of disciplines has been involved in research and theory development. This has led to differing terminology, from reading or learning disabilities, to specific reading or learning difficulties, to developmental dyslexia, or simply dyslexia. The framework for thinking about dyslexia that is covered in this book has similarities to the conditions described by these varying terms. For example, the term learning disability (sometimes reduced to LD) is widely used around the world (and particularly in North America) to describe children with difficulties learning to read and spell words, which would be consistent with the use of dyslexia in this book. However, learning disability may also be used to describe children who have difficulties with acquiring mathematics skills either with or without reading/spelling problems. Hence, the term will be inclusive of dyslexia as described in this book, but would include others without dyslexia. The opposite could be said when specific reading disability is used. Again, this would be fairly consistent with dyslexia as used in this book, but would not necessarily include those who show improvements in reading but still struggle with spelling – a characteristic of many adult dyslexics who have had a reasonable level of reading support or reading experience.

There also needs to be a distinction between acquired dyslexia and developmental dyslexia. The term 'acquired dyslexia' is typically used for (mainly) adults who have learnt to read but following some brain injury have lost the ability to read or who have lost some aspects of the processing of written words. In contrast, dyslexia has been mainly used as the short form of developmental dyslexia, which refers to individuals who have struggled in learning to read and write. There may be some interesting overlaps between acquired and developmental forms of dyslexia, but there is an assumed difference in terms of the point when problems are experienced (during or following acquisition of the skill) and the two diverge in terms of the neurological features of the condition: in acquired dyslexia, there will be measurable neurological damage, whereas for individuals struggling to learn to read and write, neurological signs of 'damage' are not obvious.

A brief history of dyslexia

These differences are best understood when one considers the history of dyslexia. For example, the perspective that some individuals (both adults and children) have problems learning to read has been around for over 100 years. This initial work was mainly performed by those in the medical sciences. For example, Adolph Kussmaul (1877) talks of patients who 'were incapable of translating [written] words into spoken words' and who had 'lost entirely the power to read printing and writing'. Kussmaul referred to these individuals as 'word blind'. Although there were a range of scientists discussing this topic at the end of the nineteenth century (including another German professor, Rudolph Berlin, who in 1887, seems to have been the first to publicly use the term dyslexia), the person who many see as conducting the more comprehensive study of this condition is William Pringle Morgan. Pringle Morgan (1896) refers to children who despite being intelligent have 'great difficulty [learning] to read', and explains many of the issues that we have come to associate with dyslexia in statements such as 'In spite of … laborious and persistent training, he can only with difficulty spell out words of one syllable'. The term 'word blindness' is again used in these writings, along with the view that the condition was 'due to … some congenital deficiency of the visual memory for words'. This focus on visual memory, and the use of the word 'blind', meant that dyslexia has been associated with visual processing differences throughout its history. The references to intelligence by these early authors have also stayed with the field for a long time; although both need to be considered within the context of the time, rather than as necessary features of the condition that they were studying. Intelligence was considered the prerequisite for intelligent behaviour, which would include learning – and a work on verbal language deficits was also developing, so a distinction between the verbal and written language was likely.

Early in the twentieth century, the field was probably best represented by the work of James Hinshelwood. Hinshelwood (1917) studied what he called 'congenital word blindness' which he felt was not a rare condition: 'rarity is … accounted for by the fact that when they occur they are not recognised', which for the time seems a highly insightful comment. In the UK, where Hinshelwood was based, the Education Act of 1870 aimed to teach reading and writing to all, at least in terms of the reading of religious texts (the Bible). Therefore, the potential for recognising the condition increased; though the point that a lack of looking for it will mean that many may be missed is still something that we need to consider. Hinshelwood (1917) further discussed the societal (and to some individual) consequences that he saw related to literacy problems: he referred to the true nature of the problem needing to be recognised 'otherwise they may be treated as imbeciles … or punished'. This has a resonance with later accounts by dyslexic individuals themselves: for example, the actress Susan Hampshire, in her 1981 book, talks of her personal experiences of dyslexia,

> just knowing that I was not mentally retarded or lazy, or backward, or emotionally disturbed … would have made all the difference. … I assumed that no one could like someone as stupid as me. … Nothing has changed: the doubts of childhood remain.

A lack of recognising the difficulties that individuals may face with learning to read and write, and the reaction of those around the individual, can have major consequences – and we will return to this when we consider self-concept and its potential relationship to learning difficulties.

Probably the next major influence in the field was Samuel Orton (see Orton, 1937), who referred to word blindness in the 1920s. Orton argued that the condition was physiological and ran in families, but suggested that the term 'congenital ... [will] underemphasize ... environmental factors ... such as methods of teaching'. He, therefore, preferred developmental to congenital, which may have helped the change of focus from a neurological study of the condition to a consideration of the educational practices needed to support children with the problem. This is likely Orton's major contribution to the field: the idea that we can change education to help overcome problems associated with dyslexia – and is one of the reasons for the relative success of the Orton Society in the USA (established in the late 1940s), which later became the International Dyslexia Association. In contrast to his contribution that educational practices should be a focus within the work on dyslexia, Orton's theories about its cause were much less helpful. One of the main characteristics that he saw in the work of children with dyslexia was what he called a twisting of words (or 'strephosymbolia'), and he used this concept as part of the explanation of the 'visual' errors that he saw children making. The most quoted of these were what we now refer to as reversal errors. This is a characteristic of dyslexia that leads to letter or word order problems: for example, 'sad' may be spelt as 'sab' (the 'd' being written as a 'b' which can be seen as reversals of each other); or 'was' read as 'saw' (the letter order being the opposite of the written order); or 'enemy' pronounced 'emeny' (with the 'm' and 'n' said in the wrong order). Orton argued that these were due to the underlying cause of dyslexia and related these problems to crossed laterality and left-handedness. In his thinking about this, he suggested that mirror images of visual forms were projected to the left and right hemisphere, such that if the 'wrong' hemisphere processed the images, then a reversed imaged would be experienced. Given the understanding of the time that language processing was a left hemisphere process, then if the right hemisphere processed written language information, an image the reverse of what it should be will be processed. This might be related to cross-laterality – the right hemisphere performing language processing rather than the left. It could also be related to left-handedness, since the left hemisphere is associated with motor functions on the right side of the body and the right hemisphere is associated with motor functions on the left side of the body. An over-reliance of the right hemisphere may lead to left-handedness and cross-laterality. However, many of these theoretical ideas have been shown to be flawed in many respects. For example, the hemispheres do not produce mirror images – and neither do dyslexia: 'was' is not a mirror image of 'saw', it is just that the letters are in the wrong order. Similarly, the types of errors associated with reversal errors are produced by most children when they are learning to read, since the direction and order of writing is fairly arbitrary for early learning (see discussions of this in Vellutino, 1987). Following a reasonable amount of experience with text, these direction/order errors diminish. For those who have less experience with text, which may include many dyslexics, these errors may be prolonged. Hence, what Orton was likely seeing was evidence of lack of practice with text, rather than a cause of problems with learning text. Despite this, many of the ideas related to reversal errors, left-handedness, laterality and brain hemispheres are still features of more modern theories about dyslexia (see the range of views in Geschwind, 1982; Galaburda, Rosen & Sherman, 1990; Stein, 2001). And Orton will have a place in intervention work because of the idea of multisensory learning – see Part 5 on intervention in this book.

Dyslexia and intelligence

The work of Orton and others led to the increasing recognition of dyslexia and the formation of groups/organisations dedicated to advocate for and support the learning experiences of those with dyslexia. This led to the need to determine what dyslexia is. The use of word blindness had to some extent focused ideas away from language and education, and a number in the field moved to using the term dyslexia: e.g. Critchley's *The Dyslexic Child* (1970). Therefore, when one of the first attempts to produce a consensus definition was undertaken in the late 1960s, by the World Federation of Neurology (1968), it referred to dyslexia as 'A disorder in children who, despite conventional classroom experience, fail to attain the language skills of reading, writing and spelling commensurate with their intellectual abilities'. This has been an influential perspective since then to the present day. It emphasises the problems with reading, writing and spelling, but positions these as 'language skills'.

It also indicates that conventional classroom experience is needed as part of the criteria for identification, but it also associates dyslexia with intellectual abilities: dyslexia is apparent when literacy does not develop to a level commensurate with (or equivalent to) intelligence. This latter point has been one of the reasons why measure of intelligence (typically an intelligence quotient or IQ) is still used in assessment of dyslexia. The point here is that this definition is interpreted as meaning that a child who has a reading level that is consistent with their intelligence level is not dyslexic. If a ten year old child reads like a seven year old child, they are not dyslexic if their IQ is also equivalent to a seven year old child. Dyslexia only occurs if there is a discrepancy between the level of reading ability and the level of IQ – this has therefore often been referred to as a discrepancy method of identifying dyslexia. This interpretation has meant that for a long time assessors have been required to measure reading (and maybe spelling/writing) and assess intelligence to decide whether someone is dyslexic or not. Those who are dyslexic will get one type of support, whereas those who have the same ability in reading, but who have an IQ at about the same level as their reading ability, will not receive dyslexia-type support. This has been one of the major controversial aspects of dyslexia.

Given that many historical publications from medical scientists referred to problems with reading despite being intelligent (see above), it is not that surprising that intelligence formed part of a consensus view developed from a group within a neurology organisation. What may be more surprising is that this idea has lasted as long as it has, given the evidence to question is usefulness to allocate support. One of the problems with the idea from the start was determining what level of discrepancy should be used to identify dyslexia. Given that reading ability and IQ both vary, then the difference between them will also vary. If we say dyslexics are those with two years' discrepancy between reading age and IQ age, then we will find far fewer dyslexics than if we require the discrepancy to be only one-and-a-half years: a bigger discrepancy will identify fewer individuals. Hence, there is not a simple division between those who are dyslexic and those who are not – it is an arbitrary cut-off. This caused potential problems, not only because it seemed unfair, but also because different organisations took different cut-off points. Hence, a child could be dyslexic in one street, move to a near-by street under a different education authority and then become non-dyslexic, simply because the two authorities used different cut-off points. The joke 'how do you cure dyslexia – move states' was often mentioned at conferences in the USA – and clearly, this cannot be a useful way of determining something that may have long-lasting educational and social problems (as suggested by Hinshelwood, Orton and the experiences of Susan Hampshire). However, arbitrary cut-offs may not have been the major problem. Other concepts, such as obesity, are also based on such cut-offs and the level of risk associated with different cut-offs. Therefore, if a consensus could have been developed to determine levels of risk associated with different discrepancies, and these had been used to determine the level of support needed, then there may not have been a problem.

However, there were other problems with the simple IQ–reading assessment procedures. For example, definitions of intelligence have varied to a great extent over the years and, therefore, so have measures of intelligence. One measure of intelligence might lead to a discrepancy being identified, whereas another measure of intelligence may not. This may be related to the fact that some assessments in an intelligence test may require use of the very skills with which an individual with dyslexia may struggle precisely because of their dyslexia. An extreme version of this would be to require a dyslexic to read items on an intelligence measure – an intelligence score would therefore be lower because of the individual's dyslexia and because intelligence is low, it is unlikely to be discrepant with levels of reading. Another example may be a task that is influenced by reading experience. For example, vocabulary (word knowledge) will be influenced by the amount an individual reads – there are many words that we rarely experience in verbal conversation but which we will find in books. Hence, a lack of reading (as would be the case with most dyslexics) would potentially lead to low scores on a vocabulary measure in older dyslexic individuals. This again would lead to a measure of intelligence being less likely to be much lower than the measure of reading. The same argument has been made about items on IQ tests that require the recall of information – this may specifically disadvantage the dyslexic because of their dyslexia. Similarly, measures of reading may determine identification. Many adults with a history of dyslexia show evidence of reasonable reading accuracy, but remain slow readers and inaccurate spellers. Hence, a single measure of reading accuracy may miss the features associated with dyslexia in adults.

A further problem with the simple IQ–reading assessment procedure is the theoretical viewpoint underpinning the idea. The position is based on the idea that learning is based on intelligence – that you will learn something well or not so well depending on your level of intelligence: those with high intelligence will learn well, those with low intelligence will learn poorly. In order to say that intelligence is determining the level of reading, then we need to show that those with high intelligence will learn to read well, whereas those with low intelligence will learn to read poorly. Given that we associate dyslexia with problems in the initial stages of learning to read (i.e. problems with individual word reading), then we need to show that word reading levels are related to intelligence (they are correlated). However, the relationship between measures of intelligence and reading vary considerably depending on the reading task required; and the relationship between intelligence and the ability to read individual words accurately is not good at all, suggesting that factors other than intelligence are likely to predict who is a good word reader and who is not. This is also related to outcomes. If we contrast poor readers with low intelligence scores and with poor readers who have high intelligence scores, and then look at outcomes based on different teaching or intervention methods, there is very little difference between the two (Ellis, McDougall & Monk, 1996; Share, 1996). Similarly, both these groups of poor readers show evidence of similar levels of weaknesses in measures of phonological processing, which, as we will see, is the most likely cause of dyslexia (Shaywitz, Escobar, Shaywitz, Fletcher & Makugh, 1992; Stanovich, 1988; Stanovich & Siegel, 1994). These lack of differences make it questionable whether the discrepancy method is that useful in determining the likely cause of the problems and the ways to support the individual. The current finding, therefore, indicates that intelligence is not a cause of dyslexia, and that it also is an insufficient identifier of dyslexia. It is probably, therefore, sensible to see variations in intelligence in a population of dyslexics as similar to variations in intelligence in a population of non-dyslexics. One of the additional arguments that this suggests is that many skills will vary similarly between dyslexic and non-dyslexic populations: we may find high and low levels of ability in a range of skills across both groups, except where the skill is related to the specific features of dyslexia.

Perspectives and definitions

Such problems with the IQ-based perspective of dyslexia lead to alternative views about how to conceptualise the term. An alternative approach was based on the idea that relating dyslexia to IQ was basically saying what dyslexia was not: i.e. dyslexia was not low IQ. Rather than saying what it was not, maybe it is better to say what it was. This led to a range of views about the characteristics of dyslexia and hence a range of different definitions, which we will come on to shortly. In contrast to the IQ-discrepancy idea, some perspectives consider that subcomponents of IQ tests can be used to identify dyslexia (see Kaufman, 1994). One such method became known as the ACID test of dyslexia. This identifies dyslexia by low scores on certain sub-tests of the Wechsler Intelligence Scale for Children; i.e. poor performance on the measures of Arithmetic, Coding, Information and Digit Span (see Vargo, Grosser & Spafford, 1995). However, the ACID viewpoint has also been criticised as not indicative of the performance of many students with dyslexia (see Frederickson, 1999), and alternative groupings of measures from the same IQ battery have been proposed as indicative of dyslexia (such as replacing the coding measure for the vocabulary sub-test), with some even considering such methods to be biased towards male rather than female learners (see discussions in Zabell, 2003). The positive feature of such methods is that they argue for dyslexics to have good scores on some aspects of the IQ battery despite poorer scores in others: i.e. a profile of strengths and weaknesses, which may be better for self-esteem than a list of failed assessment scores. However, the variability across these different attempts to classify all dyslexics suggests that one set of poor scores on measures taken from an IQ battery, which after all was not intended as a way of identifying a literacy learning difficulty, is unlikely to be successful as an assessment practice. For one thing, IQ tests rarely include a measure of the reading/spelling problems that are one of the main features of dyslexia. Hence, although these perspectives might give us ideas of areas of strengths and weaknesses related to dyslexia (i.e. some of the potential characteristics), they are unlikely to provide us with a definitive set of criteria on which to define and identify dyslexia.

The use of IQ batteries as the basis of identifying dyslexia remains popular, though this may be more to do with the measures being well standardised and available to trained professionals: i.e. we are determining what dyslexia is based on those measures that we feel most confident in using, which seems the wrong way round when you write it down on paper. An alternative is to study what dyslexic students do and base the characteristics on these observations. Maybe the best example of this method was the work of Tim Miles. Miles (1993) argued that it might be better to see dyslexia as a syndrome, with a range of what we might call symptoms. Just as a diagnosis of a medical problem would be determined based on a set of symptoms, some of which an individual would have, but others they may not, then Miles argued that we can identify dyslexia based on a set of characteristics that he had observed over many decades of working with students with dyslexia. These characteristics/symptoms included (i) problems with reading/spelling/writing, (ii) difficulties in verbal language tasks, (iii) weaknesses in certain aspects of maths, (iv) orientation (mistaking left and right) and/or sequencing (e.g. letter ordering) confusions, (v) not being very good at processing things at speed, (vi) poor digit spans (i.e. low scores on measures of short-term memory) and (vii) an incidence of dyslexia (or the symptoms) within immediate family (indicative of the genetic/biological basis for dyslexia). Intelligence might also form part of the assessment, but these sorts of characteristics/symptoms were the thing to look for. The Bangor Dyslexia Test (see discussions in Miles, 1993) is based on attempting to identify these areas of difficulty. As with a medical diagnosis, it may be that certain individuals will not experience some of the symptoms, or some will be more severe than others. The point here is that the work of Miles argues for identifying the features, rather than only a discrepancy between reading and intelligence. Although some of these characteristics may be questionable (e.g. what problems with certain aspects of maths really means across a population of those with dyslexia – contrast the current discussion with the work on dyscalculia, such as in Chinn, 2015) and such a method of identification will lead to questions about how many features mean dyslexia, many of the ideas presented by Miles would still be recognised as relevant to current identification practices. The framework within this book is not that dissimilar from many of the ideas presented in these characteristics – language problems may be replaced with phonological problems – but there is certainly still a lot to be learnt from the work of Miles and colleagues.

This idea of explaining dyslexia in terms of characteristics coincided with the growth of groups that were formed to support individuals with dyslexia. Given that educational systems were potentially not recognising and supporting those with dyslexia, due to potentially varying criteria for deciding who did and who did not have dyslexia, it is maybe not surprising that there was a rise in organisations whose primary aim was to advocate for those with learning difficulties. These are most evident in the UK and USA, but there are similar organisations around the world now. However, these organisations not only advocated for dyslexia recognition and support, they also presented their own perspectives (definitions) on dyslexia. For example, the Dyslexia Institute in the UK (which now no longer exists in its previous form) had a focus on assessing students for dyslexia. To support this aim, in 1989 (see Pumfrey & Reason, 1991) it came up with the definition that dyslexia was 'organising or learning deficiencies which restrict the student's competencies in information processing, in motor skills and working memory, so causing limitations in some or all of the skills of speech, reading, writing, essay writing, numeracy and behaviour'. Although this may help with understanding the range of problems that a dyslexic individual may face, such a wide-ranging set of features/characteristics did little to avoid criticisms that the field did not know what it was looking at. A similar problem could be directed at the New Zealand Ministry of Education's working definition from 2007, which suggests that dyslexia is a

> spectrum of specific learning disabilities and is evident when accurate and/or fluent reading and writing skills, particularly phonological awareness, develop incompletely or with great difficulty. This may include difficulties with one or more of reading, writing, spelling, numeracy and musical notation. These difficulties are persistent despite access to learning opportunities that are effective and appropriate for most other children.

(See working definition in the 2008 report at www.inclusive.tki.org.
nz/assets/inclusive-education/resource-documents/About+Dyslexia.
pdf, which also has some good support ideas.) Although a little less
over-inclusive than the 1989 Dyslexia Institute statement, it could be
interpreted as suggesting that a good reader is dyslexic if they can't read
music.

Additionally, such organisations change their definition. Again, an
example from the UK. In 2000, the British Dyslexia Association (see
Smythe, 2001) argued that dyslexia was:

> a combination of abilities and difficulties which affect …
> reading, spelling, writing and sometimes numeracy/language.
> Accompanying weaknesses may be identified in areas of speed of
> processing, short-term memory, sequencing, auditory and/or visual
> processing, spoken language and motor skills. … Dyslexia occurs
> despite normal intellectual ability and conventional teaching; it is
> independent of socio-economic or language background.

Then, in 2009, this was revised to (see discussions of different references, including this one, in Mather & Wendling, 2012):

> Dyslexia is a specific learning difficulty which mainly affects the
> development of literacy and language related skills … characterised
> by difficulties with phonological processing, rapid naming, working
> memory, processing speed, and the automatic development of skills
> that may not match up to an individual's other cognitive abilities
> … resistant to conventional teaching.

(Further information about the British Dyslexia Association can be
found at www.bdadyslexia.org.uk/.) The 2000 definition refers to a
large range of potential difficulties – again, presumably to make sure that
we do not miss something when supporting a child with dyslexia,
though at the risk of making the definition seem non-specific. And
although the 2009 definition may be more specific, the 'automatic
development of skills' statement is also potentially wide-ranging, and
the changes within a decade may lead some to conclude that there is a
lack of consensus even within organisations – though, equally, it could

be argued as evidence for revising perspectives based on emerging evidence.

The alternative to trying to encompass everything within a definition is to restrict it to only the primary feature or features. This can be found in the field also. For example, the Health Council of the Netherlands focused on 'Dyslexia is present when the automatization of word identification (reading) and/or spelling does not develop or does so very incompletely or with great difficulty' (Gersons-Wolfensberger & Ruijs-senaar, 1997). The British Psychological Society (1999) followed soon after with the view that dyslexia is evident when 'accurate and fluent word reading and/or spelling develops very incompletely or with great difficulty' – though they also suggested that dyslexia 'focuses on literacy learning at the "word level" and implies that the problem is severe and persistent despite appropriate learning opportunities'. However, these may suffer from the potential problem of not indicating what the cause of the reading/spelling problems might be – for example, a child who has learnt English as a second language may struggle with aspects of English reading until their English language skills improve, but they are surely not dyslexic prior to the English language improvements? This can be contrasted with the 2002 International Dyslexia Association definition which does attempt to specify the cause as related to phonological processing deficits: dyslexia is

> a specific learning disability that is neurological in origin. It is characterized by difficulties with accurate and/or fluent word recognition and by poor spelling and decoding abilities. These difficulties typically result from a deficit in the phonological component in language that is often unexpected in relation to other cognitive abilities and the provision of effective classroom instruction.

(See https://dyslexiaida.org/definition-of-dyslexia/ for the definition.) Indeed, if we were to go for a definition from the past that seems to still encompass many of the features that more modern research data have established, then the International Dyslexia Association 2002 definition is arguably the best.

A framework for dyslexia

If all of the above perspectives on dyslexia are considered, then there are some common themes across the majority, which if we combine these with a framework produces the following key aspects of dyslexia. The remainder of the book will take this framework as its basis for discussion. (Though see also Tunmer & Greaney, 2010, for a similar framework to the one proposed here.)

First, most views of dyslexia talk about difficulties with word reading and writing: though it may be more specific to say spelling rather than writing in general. The more focused definitions used a statement along the lines of dyslexia occurs when 'accurate and/or fluent reading and writing/spelling develop incompletely or with great difficulty'. This seems a useful way of seeing dyslexia. It indicates that the common feature will be reading and spelling problems, but that problems can emerge in accuracy and/or fluency – as indicated above, many adult dyslexics may be slow readers, which seems to be captured by using fluency as well as accuracy. However, saying that they develop incompletely or with great difficulty avoids the interpretation that a dyslexic cannot learn to read or spell. This is important if we are to consider that educational support or interventions will make a difference – which, as we will see, they can. This statement may also be important for acknowledging that some hard work may be necessary for both the dyslexic and those who support them. But it may also be important to avoid problems with a lack of engagement and feeling that it is not worth trying; i.e. which can lead to problems with self-worth and learnt helplessness. It is difficult, but it is not impossible. Finding ways of experiencing success in learning will be as important for the dyslexic child as any child to maintain motivation and self-worth.

All of the definitions suggest at least one caveat to the reading/spelling problems statement. This is that if the child has not had the opportunity to learn, then they are not necessarily dyslexic. This may be best summed up by the statement that dyslexia is 'persistent despite access to learning opportunities that are effective with most individuals'. This also suggests that something will need to change in terms of the learning opportunity. This does not mean a need for a radical change in teaching – it may mean more intensive support, for example – but it does indicate the need to do something and focuses the issue on learning.

Many of the definitions also indicate problems are unexpected in some way compared to other abilities. However, we have seen that simply relating this to intelligence may not be helpful as it may lead to the interpretation that a specific level of intelligence needs to be reached before dyslexia is identified. On the other hand, not indicating that dyslexia may only influence reading and spelling has the potential to leave it open to interpretation that the dyslexic may not be able in a range of skills. Given the impression that a dyslexic can be great at mathematics or at poetry or sport can maintain self-esteem and engagement in learning. Therefore, a statement in a definition that makes the area of difficulty more specific may well be worthwhile. For current purposes, we will suggest that dyslexia is likely to be 'unexpected in relation to typical development in non-literacy areas'. So, those with dyslexia may struggle when literacy skills are expected, but they are likely to perform as well as their non-dyslexic peers when the task (including a school assignment) does not require literacy skills.

The final point is to suggest a reason for the difficulties experienced. For the rest of this book, the assumption will be that dyslexia is related to 'problems related to language, particularly the phonological component'. This is consistent with the International Dyslexia Association's viewpoint, but the phonological deficit hypothesis is probably the dominant theory in the field. It has the majority of evidence supporting it, and it focuses support on procedures that have the most evidence of success with the majority of individuals. It also positions dyslexia as a problem related to language processes, though potentially only one aspect of language processing, and with skills that seem to predict levels of reading and spelling across a range of learners: i.e. it fits with current models of reading and spelling.

Finally, we need to acknowledge that dyslexia can be related to other areas of difficulty. However, these may be better viewed as consequences of dyslexia rather than defining characteristics. Hence, if word-level reading problems are not overcome to some extent, these will lead to text reading problems – with time, many with dyslexia will show poor text comprehension. The same may be true of writing: poor spelling may lead to poor writing practice and incoherent text production. Poor text reading will make reading course text books difficult, which may lead to poor learning in most areas of the school curriculum. Less than coherent writing (and in some places, bad spelling) may lead to poor results in assignments. Problems with accessing the curriculum, and poor assignment results, are likely to lead to poor educational qualifications, which can impact on employment prospects. Failure in school work may also lead to feelings of frustration that can lead to negative behaviours or conduct problems, which may increase the chance of school exclusion and the individual and societal problems with which exclusion is associated: high levels of exclusion are related to anti-social or criminal behaviour. Poor ability in class can lead to feelings of anxiety and stress – reading out loud in class may be something that a child has to avoid either by hiding at the back or disrupting class activities. Poor school work may also impact on self-concept, leading to an individual feeling stupid and worthless. This can have a major negative impact on well-being. Many of the negative effects above can also lead to health problems. If these consequences are considered against many of the problems highlighted in the definitions, then it becomes clearer where the range of characteristics in the definitions came from. However, treating these as consequences, rather than a definitional feature of dyslexia, indicates that they should not be considered as a necessary feature of dyslexia – indeed, many dyslexics will show none of these additional problems, and the more extreme consequences (such as criminal behaviour) will only occur within a few cases.

3
THEORIES OF DYSLEXIA

Introduction

In this chapter we will focus on a discussion of some of the main theories about the cause of dyslexia. An understanding of these theories should give an idea of the origins of some of the major assessment and intervention practices associated with dyslexia, which we will cover in following parts. This part will start with the currently dominant theory, the phonological deficit viewpoint, following on from previous discussions related to definitions of dyslexia (see the earlier perspectives section in Part 2). However, this part will also consider those theories that may have fewer supporters, but which have influenced intervention/remediation methods – those which practitioners in the field are likely to come across. As part of this discussion of theories, we will also touch on explanations for cross-language issues related to dyslexia. For each theory, this part will consider their basic ideas/premise, but we will also highlight their potential advantages and problems. As with previous parts, we will cover the basic ideas associated with the theory, but provide references for the reader to explore these ideas in more detail.

Phonological processing and dyslexia

As suggested above, during the second half of the twentieth century, there was a move from considering dyslexia as something akin to 'word blindness' and a medical issue to more of a focus on the connection between verbal and written language and the need to consider educational answers to the difficulties experienced by children with dyslexia. This was particularly evident in work conducted in the 1970/1980s when research questioned visual causal explanations of dyslexia and focused more on language-related causal explanations (see Vellutino, 1987, for an example of how the focus was changing). However, despite this move, visual theories of dyslexia still exist (we will discuss these in the next part). Indeed, the last 30 or so years of dyslexia research has led to a number of theories on what causes dyslexia, some of which we will touch on in the rest of this part (though see an interesting perspective on this in Frith, 1999). Given the change in perspective towards a language explanation, and its relative dominance as the most likely cause of dyslexia, we will start with the view that phonological processing deficits lead to the problems with reading and spelling that learners with dyslexia experience.

The initial dyslexia feature that teachers report focus on problems with word reading accuracy. As discussed before, word reading development is dependent on two basic processes that provide the ability to recognise letters (graphemes) and an awareness of the basic sounds (phonemes) within a language. The importance of letter knowledge is unsurprising – without a good level of experience, and recognition, of the units of the writing system, literacy learning would be difficult, if not impossible. Furthermore, both letter recognition and phoneme awareness are important for the phonological decoding of words – i.e. the translation of graphemes within a word into their corresponding sounds (see discussions in Adams, 1990; Duncan, Seymour & Hill, 1997; Ehri, 1987; Muter, Hulme, Snowling & Taylor, 1998; Wagner et al., 1997). Therefore, it may be not too surprising to find that these two skills (letter recognition and phonological awareness) are among the better early predictors of reading problems (e.g. Puolakanaho et al., 2007; Scarborough, 1998; Simpson & Everatt, 2005).

Phonological processing is an aspect of language processing – and develops along with language (see Goswami, 2000). Therefore, it also has the promising feature that it can be assessed prior to reading experience. However, the development of phoneme awareness is likely dependent on some level of experience of written text as well, with phonological awareness at the level of larger units than the phoneme (such as syllables and rhymes) being easier to measure with pre-readers (see discussions of phonological awareness in Gillon, 2018). Hence, for pre-readers, assessment of being at risk of future reading and spelling difficulties may be better associated with the slower acquisition of efficient processing of different levels of phonological awareness. The theoretical perspectives that have focused on phonology, therefore, often consider the assessment of phonological processing at a range of levels: from word, to syllables and rhymes, and to phonemes. Therefore, we will refer to this as the phonological deficit viewpoint and relate this to the idea that dyslexia is related to deficits in the phonological component of language (see the International Dyslexia Association, 2002, definition).

The evidence for the phonological deficit viewpoint comes from a range of sources (see discussions in Bruck, 1993; Gillon, 2018; Goswami, 2000; Joanisse, Manis, Keating & Seidenberg, 2000; Kamhi & Catts, 2012; Liberman, Shankweiler, Fischer & Carter, 1974; Lundberg, 1989; Olson, 2004; Ramus, Pidgeon & Frith, 2003; Snowling, 2000; Stanovich, 1988; Vellutino, 1987). However, the findings can be focused around three general conclusions. First, phonological awareness, and the associated phonological decoding skills, are good predictors of English literacy levels: children with good phonological skills show good levels of reading ability at both the word and text level of processing. As discussed previously, it has been clear for some time that phonological skills form an integral part in the acquisition of word-level literacy (e.g. Bryant & Bradley, 1985). Second, measures of phonological processing typically distinguish those with dyslexia from those without; hence, along with measures of reading and writing, they are the more likely measures to be found in assessment procedures designed to identify those with dyslexia – we will cover these in the assessment section in Part 4 in this book. For example, even though there is a reciprocal relationship between literacy learning and phonological skills (Lukatela, Carello, Shankweiler & Liberman, 1995; Morais, Cary, Alegria & Bertelson, 1979), difficulties in phonology can distinguish between dyslexics and non-dyslexics matched for age and reading level (Rack, Snowling

& Olson, 1992; Snowling, 2000); i.e. dyslexics and non-dyslexics who have the same reading age are likely to show differences in phonological skills, which suggests that these differences are not simply a function of reading experience. These difficulties in the processing of phonological forms have been associated with dyslexia throughout development and into adulthood (Beaton, McDougall & Singleton, 1997; Bruck, 1993; Elbro, Nielsen & Petersen, 1994), which suggests that they are not transient differences. Finally, many successful intervention procedures include phonological awareness training, though the language skills of phonological processing need to link to literacy (i.e. decoding needs to be part of the training) for them to show major benefits for reading and spelling acquisition (we will discuss this in greater detail in the intervention Part 5 of this book). This wealth of research evidence over the last 30+ years has made this viewpoint the most often quoted in the research literature and as part of evidence-based practice.

The basic premise of the phonological viewpoint is that weaknesses in the efficiency with which basic sounds are processed by the learner with dyslexia leads to problems with making connections between basic sounds in the language and letter forms in the written script. Given that making the link between phonemes and graphemes is an important part of learning to read and allows more independence of decoding new words, then those who are having problems with making these connections will be less independent readers (they will be more reliant on others telling them the pronunciation of an unfamiliar written words) and potentially less accurate or less fluent readers. The same will be the case for spelling. The lack of links between what is heard and what is written will make accurate spelling harder to acquire. Indeed, the features of the English script may mean that accurate spelling is harder to acquire than accurate reading if the stored links between sounds and characters are fussy; as a relatively simplistic example, you have to recall a spelling but might be able to make reasonable guesses to support the recognition in reading. Additionally, the more complex the links between letters and sounds, the more likely that problems processing sounds clearly and efficiently will lead to difficulties. For example, a fairly complex made up word (non-word) such as 'sploodet' requires the processing of a relatively complex set of sounds to form the sounds associated with 'spl' in the non-word, as well as the avoidance of confusions between sounds associated with 'd' and 't', and then it requires the recognition of a likely syllable boundary. Combining these decoded sounds into a whole word is also likely to be reliant on efficient processing of language at the phonological level – as is splitting the whole word up into basic sounds in order to attempt a likely spelling. Each element requires some efficient processing of sounds for accurate spelling and reading, but there will also be a dependence on the experience of linking sets of letters, such as those found in 'sploodet', with a pronunciation to determine the more likely pronunciation. Problems with processing sounds will lead to problems making a reasonable attempt at reading this non-word, but they will also restrict experience of linking groups of letters with sounds, which will also make reading and spelling more error-prone. This will likely lead to a reciprocal relationship between the two: experience of linking letters to sounds is as vital as accurate processing of those sounds.

However, the phonological deficit hypothesis is not without its potential difficulties – and there is still ongoing research to specify exactly its influence (e.g. is the problem with processing phonology, storing phonological forms precisely or translating between phonological and orthographic forms?). Some have questioned the idea of a phoneme (see discussions in Uppstad & Tønnessen, 2007) since the boundary between one phoneme and another is often fairly arbitrary in spoken language and can vary depending on the sounds around it. Although this is more of a linguistic argument, it can lead to questions about how we teach something that is not a precise construct. Similarly, there has been disagreement as to the key features of phonology that are essential to early word reading. The ability to hear sounds in words develops (Goswami, 2000), as discussed above. Hence, there is a debate whether children should progress through the different levels of phonological skills, from word to syllable and onset-rime levels, prior to being explicitly taught to recognise sounds at the phoneme level, or whether they should be taught to work at a phoneme level immediately upon starting the process of learning to read (see discussions in Bryant, 1998; Hulme, Muter & Snowling, 1998; Goswami & Bryant, 1990; Muter et al., 1998). This might be particularly pertinent to those who are struggling with phonological awareness. Should the developmental process be followed even if reading seems to be related to linking letters to phonemes rather than syllables and rhymes? We will come back to this question in the intervention part of the book, but the evidence seems to indicate that teaching the link between basic sounds (phonemes) and the letters that those sounds represent as early as possible leads to good outcomes for many of those struggling with reading and spelling. Hence, although there may be questions about the exact description of what a phoneme is, and there may be cases where problems with phonological processing may be so severe that a focus on phonemes may not be possible, these problems with the phonological viewpoint may be less of a concern in practice.

There are also questions about what exactly should be included in a phonological-based theory. The ability to translate between written symbols and phonological forms, the ability to store these phonological forms and manipulate them, as well as the ability to produce verbal labels quickly and accurately, have all been associated with phonological processing. However, such processes involve a range of skills, and many add independent variance to literacy suggesting that they have differential influences on reading/spelling, which is more consistent with separate constructs rather than a single process (see Wagner & Torgesen, 1987). Indeed, difficulties experienced by dyslexics in some of these processing areas have been presented as evidence for alternative causal theoretical viewpoints. Differences in rapid naming tasks (i.e. the speed of access of phonological or verbal labels) have been used as evidence that dyslexics have a speed of processing deficit (see evidence and discussions in Denckla & Rudel, 1976; Spring & Capps, 1974; Wolf & Bowers, 2000; Wolf & O'Brien, 2001) – we will return to a discussion of naming speeds and their relationship to dyslexia when we discuss the Double Deficit Hypothesis below. Similarly, finding that short-term recall of phonological information is a characteristic of dyslexia may be consistent with a phonological deficit, but it may also be due to a working memory deficit, which has also been proposed as the cause of dyslexia (see discussions in Hulme & Mackenzie, 1992; Mann & Liberman, 1984; McLoughlin et al., 2002; Swanson, 2015). Various studies (e.g. Gathercole & Baddeley, 1993; Wimmer, Mayringe & Landerl, 1998) have argued that difficulties with retaining sounds for short periods of time (a working memory process) are related to the acquisition of vocabulary and linking letters with sounds. Working memory has also been proposed as an important component in reading and listening comprehension (Daneman, 1991; Daneman & Carpenter, 1980; Gathercole, Willis, Emslie & Baddeley, 1992) and Catts (1989) suggested that dyslexics have greater than expected difficulties with the short-term recall of letters, words, digits and sentences. However, the direction of causality between working memory deficits and poor reading has yet to be established unequivocally (Hulme & Roodenrys, 1995). Furthermore, dyslexics can show similar levels of performance to non-dyslexics on measures of short-term recall, particularly if the task does not require the processing of verbal information (see Everatt, McCorquodale et al., 1999; Gathercole & Pickering, 2001) – though, again, we will return to this viewpoint when we consider working memory intervention work in the final part of the book.

However, because the rapid naming task involves phonological labels and the specific memory deficits relate to phonological forms, these alternative causal theories have often been subsumed under the one phonological deficit position. Clearly, though, the same findings can be related to different theories. Therefore, in many ways, what constitutes a phonological deficit often depends on the theoretical position of the researcher/practitioner. From a parsimony point of view, subsuming these different factors into one explanation seems attractive and avoids potentially unnecessary sub-typing when it comes to decisions about support. However, it may be that future research does indicate the need for dyslexia to be split into differing sub-types related to phonological awareness and accuracy of reading and spelling, versus, for example, those with a speed of verbal processing difficulty which leads to a lack of fluency in reading and writing. For present purposes, the framework around a single phonological cause may be the easiest with which to work.

Differences in dyslexia across languages and orthographies

A final potential problem for the phonological perspective is that different orthographies have different rules for relating letters/graphemes and sounds/phonemes. This is often talked about in terms of orthographic transparency, with the relationship between written script and verbal language being more transparent in some orthographies than others. Some orthographies are more regular in their correspondence between letters and sounds, whereas others are more opaque and may require the learning of more complex rules based on larger groups of letters or an understanding of morphological units or word origins. Therefore, the importance of the decoding processes that support processing of unfamiliar words (Rack et al., 1992) as one of the main explanatory features of the phonological deficit viewpoint may vary across orthographies. This may mean that the influence of phoneme or phonological awareness may also vary across orthographies. It presents the possibility that a phonological deficit in one language may be less of a problem for learning to read in another language. This is particularly pertinent given that English is considered as one of the less transparent (more opaque) orthographies (Share, 2008). In English, the relationship between letters and sounds (or graphemes and phonemes) is more complex than in many other languages (Smythe et al., 2008; Ziegler et al., 2010), yet much of the history of dyslexia has involved studies of English speakers. It may be that this has skewed explanations of dyslexia to a phonological viewpoint, whereas in other languages/orthographies phonological decoding is less of a problem even for those with phono-logical deficits. Indeed, the peculiarities of the English orthography has led some theorists in the field to view English as a 'dyslexic' ortho-graphy (Spencer, 2000) or, perhaps less controversially, as an outlier in comparison to other alphabetic-type orthographies (Share, 2008).

In contrast to English, languages such as French and Greek (Bruck, Genesse & Caravolas, 1997; Harris & Giannouli, 1999) have been argued to be more regular in their letter–sound correspondences for reading, though less so for spelling. A relatively simple example in French is the final consonant of a word, which is typically pronounced with the initial vowel of the following word. Hence, although the word space is obvious for reading, it is not the case in its audible form (Bruck et al., 1997). In the case of Greek, the written form has changed relatively little over time in contrast to the spoken form (see Mazi, Nenopoulou & Everatt, 2004). The spelling of a Greek word, there-fore, reflects its historical background rather than its modern spoken form, meaning that a child learning Greek may need to assimilate some key morphological rules in order to spell words correctly.

Further along the transparency continuum, German, Spanish and Italian are relatively transparent for both reading and spelling in contrast to English. These orthographies that have some exceptions from the normal association of letters and sounds (e.g. the length of vowel representations in German), but they may include relatively consistent rules for deducting more complex letter–sound relationships or a relatively small number of exception words compared to English. There are languages that have a consistently transparent orthography: Finnish and Hungarian are good examples: see the research of Smythe et al., 2008, and Ziegler et al., 2010. However, many orthographies with consistent relationships between letter and sounds are relatively new orthographies and so will not have experienced the level of language change during the period of use of the orthography that often leads to exceptions. The revisions of some orthographies, such as Turkish, can provide interesting, relatively modern examples of the regularisation of an orthography.

Arabic is an interesting exception to the above. Consistent with most Semetic languages (such as Hebrew), it has a highly regular/transparent orthography (the marked or vowelised form of the writing system), but it is based on a highly derivational morphological system, the emphasis on which leads to a reduction in the importance of the relationship between letter and sound except as a means of initial learning. Once learning of the basic association between written and verbal form has taken place, the emphasis of the written form is on meaning, which is primarily conveyed by morphological components. Hence, despite languages such as Arabic and Hebrew having a highly regular orthography when fully marked (vowelised), this form of the orthography is rarely used in literature read by the more experienced reader. Once beyond initial schooling grades, the Arabic or Hebrew child experiences mainly non-vowelised text, which is highly opaque in its relationship between letters and sounds, leading to a large number of homographic words (i.e. words that look alike but which represent different concepts and are often pronounced very differently). Such non-vowelised text needs to be read 'in context'. This means that an adult or child experiencing such writings needs to recognise the context within which a word is written, such as the meaning of words around the homograph or the general theme of the passage, to be able to understand the meaning of the word and even pronounce that word correctly. Hence Arabic goes from a relatively transparent form in early learning (consistent with languages such as German, Spanish and Italian) to a relatively non-transparent form, more akin to English, once initial learning has occurred. An understanding of learning to read and write in Arabic, therefore, may require an understanding of learning to read and write across the orthographic transparency dimension.

The potential importance of orthographic transparency can be seen in cross-language comparisons of reading ability that contrast scripts varying in the transparency dimension. In the majority of such studies, the rate of literacy learning, particularly word reading/decoding, has been found to increase with the level of orthographic transparency. This has been found in comparisons of different language groups (see the Cost A8 work reported in Seymour, Aro & Erskine, 2003), although differences in terms of the cultural importance of literacy learning or variations in educational practice could also explain these effects. However, similar results have been found amongst bilinguals learning two orthographies of differing transparency (Everatt et al., 2010; Geva & Siegel, 2000; Veii & Everatt, 2005). Typically, these findings point to word recognition and non-word decoding processes developing faster in the more transparent orthography. For theories of literacy development, such data have been discussed in terms of less transparent orthographies potentially requiring several processing systems (a sub-lexical route for words that can be decoding via letter–sound correspondences and a lexical route for words that are exceptions to these correspondence rules), whereas languages with a relatively transparent orthography can rely on letter–sound or sub-lexical procedures for word recognition. Such dual-route perspectives have been influential in cross-language theorising (see, for example, Coltheart et al., 2001) and are closely related to the Orthographic Depth Hypothesis (Katz & Frost, 1992), which argues for differences in literacy acquisition, and lexical and sub-lexical influences, across languages of different orthographic transparency (though see Baluch & Besner, 1991; Barry & Bastiani, 1997; Oney, Peter & Katz, 1997; Raman, Baluch & Besner, 2004; Taouk & Coltheart, 2004). In terms of dyslexia research, the dual-route position argues for more transparent orthographies being associated with primarily with one sub-type of dyslexia, usually referred to as phonological dyslexia (and consistent with the dominant phonological deficit perspective discussed in this part). In contrast, less transparent orthographies may be more associated with orthographic processing deficits (sometimes referred to as surface dyslexia), in addition to phonological deficits. However, the basis of this sub-typing method has been questioned (see Manis, Seidenberg, Doi, McBride-Chang & Petersen, 1996; Stanovich, Siegel & Gottardo, 1997) and the predicted sub-types have not been found in a number of studies across different languages (e.g. Gonzalez & Santana, 2002; Zabell & Everatt, 2002). Although such sub-typing perspectives are still controversial, they do argue for further research to assess the possibility of a range of potential underlying causes of reading problems across orthographies.

Furthermore, there is ample evidence to show a relationship between literacy acquisition and phonological awareness in more transparent orthographies (Abu-Rabia, Share & Mansour, 2003; Bentin & Leshem 1993; de Jong & van der Leij, 1999; Harris & Giannouli, 1999; Patel, Snowling & de Jong, 2004; Sprenger-Charolles, Siegel & Bechennec, 1997; Wimmer, Landerl & Schneider, 1994). Indeed, the link between phonological skills and literacy has been derived from a number of cross-language comparisons (for example, Geva & Siegel, 2000; Goswami, 2000; Katz & Frost, 1992; Smythe et al., 2008; Ziegler et al., 2010), including research focusing on European Latin-based scripts (see Ziegler & Goswami, 2005) as well as non-Latin-based scripts, such as Arabic (Elbeheri & Everatt 2007; Taibah & Haynes, 2011) and Chinese (Ho & Bryant 1997; Newman, Tardif, Huang & Shu, 2011). Such findings argue for common underlying processes influencing literacy acquisition across languages (see discussion in Frost, 2012; Share, 2008), and suggest that an awareness of sounds within words, and therefore the need to decode letters into sounds, may be a vital part of learning to read and write across languages/orthographies (see Ziegler & Goswami, 2005). Studies showing that early phonological training (together with suitable linkage to early orthography and literacy experience) improves word literacy and reduces the likelihood of literacy difficulties across a range of orthographies also support the cross-language generalisation of the phonological perspective (see Bryant & Bradley, 1985; Cunningham, 1990; Elbro, Rasmussen & Spelling, 1996; Olofsson & Lundberg, 1985; Schneider, Küspert, Roth, Visé & Marx, 1997). Hence, although differences across orthographies, and their relationship with language, exist, the findings have been more in support of the importance of phonological processing than against its application only to languages such as English.

Another problem for the phonological deficit perspective has been the reported cases of individuals who have experienced difficulties with reading, writing and spelling, without obvious evidence of an accompanying phonological deficit. These cases have been reported relatively infrequently in English (see Goulandris & Snowling, 1991; Howard & Best, 1997); however, such cases may be more frequent in other languages. For example, it has been argued that 50 per cent of Chinese dyslexics do not have a phonological awareness deficit as assessed by English derived measures (Ho, Chan, Tsang & Lee, 2002); instead such children often show evidence of rapid naming deficits. This takes us back to the argument of what should be included in the phonological viewpoint, but a lack of evidence for difficulties in measures of phonological awareness is more of a problem, suggesting that the rapid naming deficit is independent of the phonological awareness skills. However, the interpretation of these findings requires us also to consider some of the features of reading across orthographies as well as the manifestation of dyslexia.

Given that dyslexia is typically identified through problems with literacy, assessment of cross-language (possibly universal) deficits in literacy learning ability should inform procedures for identifying the individual with dyslexia, as well as theories of dyslexia that are based on the characteristic features of the learning difficulty. However, there is a need to determine the appropriateness of test measures and materials across language contexts (see Cline & Shamsi, 2000; Elbeheri, Everatt, Reid & Al-Mannai, 2006; Everatt, Smythe, Ocampo & Gyarmathy 2004; Geva & Siegel, 2000). Assessments of literacy-related learning difficulties require measures that take into account features of the language and script, as well as cultural and educational experience. Primary in the consideration of these cross-language assessment procedures is the view that although literacy learning shares common features across languages, there is evidence that the factors that predict literacy learning, and that distinguish the dyslexic from the non-dyslexic, may vary across languages. Everatt et al. (2004) found that although phonological awareness tasks could distinguish groups of Grade 3 children with and without literacy deficits in English, they could not distinguish similar groups of Hungarian children. The same reduction in the ability to distinguish between good and poor literacy learners has been found for decoding skills amongst German learners (see Wimmer, 1993). At the very least, these findings suggest the need to consider more than phonological awareness measures in dyslexia assessments across different languages.

Clearly, phonological awareness and phonological decoding measures are important predictors of literacy acquisition. However, other abilities, such as letter identification, expressive vocabulary, print concept knowledge and efficient rapid naming, have been found to play a predictive role (see, for example: Catts, Fey, Zhang & Tomblin, 2001; Lonigan & Shanahan, 2008; Scarborough, 1990; Simpson & Everatt, 2005). Even visual processes, which have been seen as the traditional alternative to the phonological viewpoint, may help explain variability in literacy skills if a cross-language perspective is considered. For example, Ho (1994) found that visual discrimination skills (especially constancy of shape) and visual memory skills at three years old were, along with phonological awareness, significant predictors of reading Chinese at four and five years old. Similarly, McBride-Chang and Ho (2000) have suggested that speed and phonological awareness are important predictors of Chinese character recognition, and that slow naming speeds are associated with poor visual attention as well as letter knowledge. Gupta and Garg (1996) found that dyslexic Hindi/English bilinguals produced poorer visual discrimination scores than non-dyslexic bilingual controls and a similar result was found by Everatt, Smythe, Adams and Ocampo (2000) with Sylheti/English bilinguals. As with much of this evidence, such groups of bilinguals also presented evidence of differences between good and poor readers in measures of phonological processing, but they do suggest the potential for other factors to influence literacy levels in addition to phonological processing, which may also suggest the need to consider more than phonological deficits in theories of dyslexia.

However, before interpreting such cross-language comparisons, a word of caution is needed about the methods and measures implemented in such work. In any comparative work of this nature, there is a need to ensure that only those language differences directly studied vary between the conditions in the study, and that comparable measures of performance are used across the languages tested. For example, in order to study orthographic transparency, other potential confounding factors will need to be controlled. Such confounding factors may include word familiarity, which may need to be controlled to ensure that the children in the different language cohorts are equally familiar with the words used in the tests. If familiarity varies across languages, then differences between the languages may be due to familiarity effects rather than transparency. Alternatively, there may be different cultural traditions in the use of rhyming words across the languages assessed. Cross-language differences in rhyme-based phonological tasks, therefore, may not be due to differences in processing of phonological forms but to these cultural factors. Similarly, in the design of test measures, simple translation across languages may not produce valid assessments of the factors under investigation. Most likely, it will be necessary to develop measures across languages so that the factor under investigation is assessed in all cases. This may require different assessment measures across those languages, which will necessitate careful validation and comparison procedures. For example, assessments of letter–sound decoding often incorporate non-word reading tasks. Non-words are made-up strings of letter that have no meaning and are unlikely to be familiar to the child tested. Such non-word reading tasks are used widely; however, difference in the orthographies tested may make non-word reading tasks very different across the languages tested. English non-words are very different from non-word items derived from Chinese characters. In both cases, the features of being made up and meaningless, but still pronounceable, are retained; however, the non-words themselves are very different in form, and it is arguable whether the two types of non-words are assessing exactly the same skills.

Rather than as a way of determining the potential usefulness of universal, cross-orthography explanations of dyslexia, studies of orthographic processing itself may be worthy of further research. As discussed above, the translation between graphemes and phonemes may be one of the most likely areas of processing difficulty for those with dyslexia. In the phonological deficit viewpoint, the problems focus on the processing of phonemes. However, it may be that processing graphemes is an area of difficulty. Hence, the storage of orthographic representations has been a focus of research into reading problems. Some of the more interesting work along these lines has focused on studies of brain activation, and the mapping of areas of the brain to determine their likely function. Such studies (see discussions in Dehaene, Cohen, Sigman & Vinckier, 2005; Démonet, Taylor & Chaix, 2004; Shaywitz, 2003; Shaywitz, Mody & Shaywitz, 2006) suggest that there is a number of brain areas related to differences in performance, particularly in word processing tasks, between those with dyslexia and those without. One is a parietal-temporal area of the brain which is involved in language processing, including potentially the processing of phonological forms. Evidence for such an area showing differences between dyslexic and non-dyslexics has also been used to support the phonological deficit viewpoint (see also Tanaka et al., 2011). A second area, however, is further back in the brain compared to the language areas of the brain. This is an occipito-temporal area that seems to be involved in processing aspects of visual forms, and has been termed the 'Visual Word Form' area since it seems to be activated by orthographic patterns in readers. Differences in activation in this area between those with and those without reading problems or dyslexia (see also Specht et al., 2009) suggest that the efficiency of processing orthographic representations in the brain may be an additional area of processing difficulty to that proposed by the phonological viewpoints. Clearly, this area of the brain did not develop to process letters, so it should be involved in tasks that do not involve word/letter processing. However, determining the specific function of this area involves ongoing research. One possibility is that it processes relatively complex spatial relationships between basic shapes, which may be consistent with its involvement in processing letters, which are also complex patterns of shapes. However, further data are required before this area is understood well enough to make firm conclusions.

Given that this brain area may be involved in dyslexia, and that it is involved in representations of orthographic forms, then orthographic processing itself may be a feature of reading. Consistent with this, a number of researchers has claimed that measures of orthographic processing skill predict additional variability in word and/or text reading over and above that of measures of phonological skills (see, for example, Barker, Torgesen & Wagner, 1992; Elbeheri, Everatt, Mahfoudhi, Al-Diyar & Taibah, 2011; Hoien, 2002; Juel, Griffith & Gough, 1986).

Furthermore, there is evidence that those with reading disabilities have impaired orthographic processing skills compared to average readers in tasks that require the processing of whole word and sub-word orthographic features (Hultquist, 1997). In contrast, superior orthographic awareness in children with developmental dyslexia has been shown in a task where learners are required to select a non-word items that look more word-like (e.g. UWRT versus WRUT), as well as in spelling recognition tasks (Siegel, Share & Geva, 1995; Stanovich & Siegel, 1994). Also, there is a problem with many orthographic tasks in that they are confounded by reading achievement. Hence, any difference between good and poor readers on measures of orthographic processing will simply reflect the individual's level of reading experience. In the phonological viewpoint, measures of phonological processing can be separated from reading by being presented verbally and requiring a verbal or motor response. For measures of orthographic processing, separating the underlying skill from reading level is almost impossible – hence, the interest in studying the Visual Word Form area of the brain.

Accuracy versus speed and double deficit perspectives

The developmental model of Goswami and others (see Goswami, 1999, 2000; Ziegler & Goswami, 2005) has suggested that phonological processing skills develop along with literacy learning. However, this may also vary with the language or script that the child is learning. Goswami (1999) has presented evidence suggesting that the phonological units that correspond to the vowel and subsequent consonants of a word or non-word (e.g. /ink/ in 'think' or 'nink') were most salient to young English readers in comparison to young French readers, but were not salient to young Spanish and Greek readers who seemed to show more evidence of a sensitivity to phonemes. Based on these findings, Goswami (1999) concluded that children learning a relatively transparent orthography develop an awareness of phonemic units at a very early stage of learning to read, and much earlier than expected based on data from studies of less transparent scripts (see also Ziegler and Goswami, 2005). If this is the case, a poor reader with a weakness in phonological awareness (a dyslexic child under the phonological deficit viewpoint) may not be as disadvantaged when learning a relatively transparent orthography compared to their counterparts having to decode a less transparent orthography with a much more complex relationship between letters and sounds. A dyslexic child might be able to rely on relatively simple grapheme–phoneme association rules to support decoding. This simplicity of association may not task the weak phonological system as much as an orthography with a more complex and irregular correspondence between graphemes and phonemes.

Furthermore, given the reciprocal relationship between literacy learning and phonological skills, learning a more transparent language may lead to improvements in the phonological processing skills of the dyslexic (Everatt, Smythe, Ocampo & Veii, 2002). Hence decoding skills may be better developed in the dyslexic learning a more transparent language, leading to reading accuracy being relative good compared to that presented by dyslexics learning a less transparent orthography. Consistent with this, evidence suggests that word reading accuracy may be less of an identifier of dyslexia in more transparent orthographies. For example, Landerl, Wimmer and Frith (1997) compared the reading abilities of English and German dyslexics and found that English dyslexics made comparatively more word reading errors than their German counterparts. It may be that the relatively transparent German orthography may serve as a protective factor against the reading accuracy deficits associated with dyslexia because German children are able to rely on the high rate of consistency between grapheme and phoneme enabling them to decipher infrequent words and non-words more easily than their English counterparts.

In contrast, although the reading accuracy of poor readers from more transparent orthographies are usually found to be higher than those of poor readers from less transparent orthographies, Landerl et al. (1997) found that the German dyslexics presented evidence of slow reading speeds (see also Wimmer, 1993). This finding suggests that phonological decoding deficits can be overcome to some extent by a slow process of translating letters into sound. However, if reading is slow, again just as likely due to weak phonological decoding, then general reading efficiency may suffer, potentially leading to poor understanding of text (reading comprehension deficits), less experience of new words (lower vocabulary levels) and a lack of enjoyment of reading that may lead to de-motivation to improve reading and spelling skills (Everatt et al.,

2002; Snowling, 2000; Stanovich, 1986). Hence, the identification of dyslexia amongst children learning a relatively transparent orthography may have to rely on alternative measures to the word reading accuracy tasks typically incorporated in assessment procedures (see discussions in the following identification Part 4 of this book). The most likely alternative is reading rate; i.e. the number of words or non-words that can be accurately decoded in a set time. If phonological decoding weaknesses can be offset by slowing the decoding process, accuracy will be improved but the rate will still remain slow compared to expectancy levels.

However, a second potential reason why rate of reading may be a better identifier of dyslexia in a relatively transparent orthography returns to one of the problems with the phonological deficit viewpoint discussed above. Weakness in rate may not be due to phonological weaknesses, but rather to slow speeds of processing, particularly verbal information. This may lead to slow literacy learning, weak vocabulary and a lack of enjoyment in literacy – much the same as for those with decoding deficits due to phonological weaknesses. As such, dyslexia in some (or all) languages may be due to poor speed of processing rather than weaknesses in phonological decoding processes. This explanation is consistent with evidence of slow rapid naming amongst dyslexic individuals and those with weak literacy skills across a range of orthographies (for reviews see Bowers & Ishaik, 2003; Semrud-Clikerman, Guy, Griffin & Hynd, 2000).

Such rapid naming deficits have been found using a multitude of different stimuli: with colours, line drawings/pictures of familiar objects, digits, letters, words and non-words (Denckla & Rudel, 1976; Spring & Capps, 1974; Wolf & Bowers, 2000; Wolf & O'Brien, 2001). Longitudinal studies have shown that, not only are such measures predictive of later reading performance (Wagner, Torgesen & Rashotte, 1994), but that naming deficits can persist into adulthood (Felton, Naylor & Wood, 1990). Although it has argued that the importance of rapid naming measures may have been overemphasized (Hammill, 2004; Swanson, Trainin, Necoechea & Hammill, 2003), research suggests that rapid naming measures can be used to identify literacy deficits/dyslexia with a reasonable level of reliability, particularly when relatively transparent scripts are considered (de Jong & van der Leij, 1999; Di Filippo et al., 2005; Wolf, Pfeil, Lotz & Biddle, 1994). Wimmer (1993) found that amongst German speaking children, rapid naming of numbers was the largest predictor of variance in speed of reading text and non-word reading. Relatively slow rapid naming speeds were characteristic of German dyslexic children, even though they generally do well on reading accuracy. However, in a study by Landerl (2001), also on German speaking dyslexic children, it was found that rapid naming tasks showed a much stronger relationship with measures of reading speed, whilst phoneme tasks were mainly related to reading accuracy. Similarly, Saiegh-Hadded (2005) found that the strongest predictor of reading fluency in vowelised Arabic was letter recoding speed, which was itself predicted by measures of rapid naming, as well as phoneme isolation.

However, naming deficits can be found in the number of errors produced by dyslexic individuals as well as the speed with which names are produced. These naming errors are particularly evident when objects with low frequency names are used (Swan & Goswami, 1997). These findings suggest that poor naming performance may not be due to a speed of processing deficit but to poor representations of the verbal labels, an interpretation more consistent with a phonological deficit perspective (see Swan and Goswami, 1997; Ziegler & Goswami, 2005): poor phonological representations lead to naming errors with infrequent names and they may also slow accessing of names in general. Therefore, in order to explain problems specifically associated with phonological processing, and at the same time retain the speed of processing deficit perspective, Wolf and colleagues (Wolf & Bowers, 2000; Wolf & O'Brien, 2001) have proposed that there are distinct sub-types of dyslexia that are based on the occurrence of phonological and/or speed of processing deficits. Some poor readers are considered to have phonological processing deficits with no speed of processing problems, while others show the reverse symptomatology, and a third group show problems in both areas. The double deficit group is considered to show the most problems in literacy skills development. This model is consistent with Cronin and Carver (1998) who found that phonological and rapid naming tasks both predicted unique variance in reading attainment amongst first graders, suggesting that these measures should be considered as separate factors in the initial stages of reading development. Similarly, de Jong and van der Leij (1999) found that Dutch children, from kindergarten to second grade, showed independent influences of rapid naming of objects and phonological awareness on reading achievement. Finally, intervention programmes that train fluency in word identification strategies have been found to improve exception word reading skills in those with reading difficulties, particularly those with specific naming deficits (Lovett et al., 1994; Wolf, Miller & Donnelly, 2000). Although it still needs to be shown that these interventions specifically targeted speed of processing, and that it was the improvements in this area that led to the identified literacy gains, such findings point to potential advantages for strategies that may improve rapid accessing processes.

Such multiple causal views also present the possibility of differences in the factors associated with dyslexia across languages. Where phonological decoding may be key to literacy learning, phonological processing deficits may be the main identifiable characteristic of dyslexia. Where rate is the defining characteristic of poor literacy, naming speed may be a more reliable identifier of dyslexia. Hence, the features of the language or script that a child is acquiring may determine the influence of disabilities or weaknesses on the manifestation or identification of dyslexia.

Perceptual factors and visual processing deficit accounts

If phonological processing deficits have not accounted for all dyslexia-related learning difficulties across languages, alternative causal accounts may prove important for identification and remediation. Historically, the main alternatives to the language-based, or phonological, theories have been the visual processing deficits theories (see Everatt, 1999). These have taken many forms, but those most obviously independent of language-based phonological viewpoints are those that focus on visual perceptual processes (i.e. processes involved in the recognition of the visual stimulus – the letter string in the case of reading). The historical perspective that dyslexics have a problem with visual memory seems unlikely (see Vellutino, 1987). For example, dyslexics have been found to perform as well as non-dyslexics in a range of visual tasks, including those that require visual memory or storage of visual details (e.g. Winner et al., 2001). Therefore, alternative, more modern, visual perceptual theories related to dyslexia focus on why dyslexics can do some visual tasks but not others. These can be subsumed into three general types: (i) those that propose a dysfunctioning transient or magnocellular visual pathway (see Breitmeyer, 1993; Lovegrove, 1996), which are currently the most promising visual deficit accounts; (ii) those that have argued for poor control of the movements of the eye, or the centre of focus of the eye during text processing (Pavlidis, 1981; Stein, Riddell & Fowler, 1989); and (iii) those that view reading problems as deriving from sensitivity to certain wavelengths of light (Irlen, 1991; Wilkins et al., 1994). We will cover each briefly, mainly to show why the phonological viewpoint is still the most widely accepted.

The magnocellular pathway deficit idea covers a range of related theories that argue for problems in part of the visual system – for most, this is within the brain, rather than the eye. The magnocellular pathway has been the most often considered as the potential problem area. This pathway seems to be responsible for processing low-level visual information – shadows, outlines, etc. One of the reasons for its interest in the field is that differences in low-level visual processing in poor versus good readers have been found across a range of languages, which may provide a universal explanation of dyslexia to rival the phonological theories. However, these cross-language findings are not always consistent, making interpretation difficult (see, for example, Ben-Yehuda, Sackett, Malchi-Ginzberg & Ahissar, 2001; Eden et al., 1996; Farrag, Khedr & Abdel-Naser, 2002; Schulte-Korne, Bartling, Deimel & Remschmidt, 2004; Spinelli et al., 1997; Ygge, Lennerstrand, Axelsson & Rydberg, 1993). Some studies show deficits in the magnocellular visual system, while others present findings that argue for deficits in the parvocellular system, a visual pathway that is relatively distinct from the magnocellular system. The magnocellular system is thought to comprise large cells for the processing of coarse (general) details, and is often associated with processing information in peripheral vision (i.e. processing information outside the centre of sight, which may guide eye movements) and movement. The parvocellular pathway, on the other hand, comprises primarily small cells that process fine/precise details and may be more active in central vision (at the centre of fixation) and when processing stationary stimuli. In a study of Arabic readers, Farrag et al. (2002) argued that deficiencies in the parvocellular system lead to an inability to process high frequency/high contrast stimuli. Such parvocellular system processing efficiency may be particularly necessary to perceive the fine detailed features that discriminate one Arabic letter from another, consistent with the views of some researchers that Arabic is a visually complex orthography to process (Ibrahim, Eviatar & Aharon-Peretz, 2002). Such research suggests that letter features in the orthography may lead to certain languages being more prone to visual deficits causing literacy learning difficulties: basically, the more detailed the features, the more likely it is that a visual weakness will lead to poor literacy acquisition (though see also Hutzler, Kronbichler, Jacobs & Wimmer, 2006). However, these cross-language differences make it difficult to determine the exact nature of the visual deficit argued to be associated with dyslexia and currently no visual-based theory is able to explain adequately such differences across orthographies. Additionally, given that the dominant theories related to dyslexia focus on the influence of the magnocellular system, whereas the parvocellular system seems more appropriate for processing motionless, highly detailed visual stimuli found when reading, there is still a lot of explanation needed before we can regard this as an explanation of dyslexia.

Apart from the cross-language contradictions, visual-based perspectives suffer from additional problems in their explanations of dyslexia. One of the main problems is that many of the theoretical accounts of how visual deficits lead to dyslexia have been poorly detailed. The scotopic sensitivity viewpoint suffers most from this weakness since there is little that could be called a theory (though also look at Wilkins, 2005). Scotopic suggests vision in dim lighting conditions, rather than the problems with certain wavelengths of light that the intervention associated with this theory (i.e. the use of coloured lenses or filters) would suggest. And, clearly, individuals do not read in dim light. The link between the underlying explanation and the process of reading is not clear in most explanations, though Wilkins (2005) has suggested that over-activity of cells within the visual processing system (akin to that found with epilepsy) may be one explanation. However, this view is not specific to dyslexia: put simply, epilepsy is not a feature of dyslexia. Therefore, the theoretical rationale is difficult to follow. Additionally, as discussed in the intervention Part 5 of the book, the practices associated with the use of coloured lenses are also inconsistent with many of the explanations.

Furthermore, all visual-based viewpoints have problems explaining the sort of literacy deficits experienced by dyslexics over the life-span; such as the likelihood for adult dyslexics to show problems with spelling accuracy more than continued weaknesses in reading accuracy (Miles, 1993). For example, it is difficult to see why an eye movement deficit would lead to problems with long-term problems in spelling but not reading. Related to this, there is evidence that many individuals with dyslexia do not show deficits in non-literacy tasks that require the use of those processes associated with the theoretical cause: for example, some dyslexics with measurable literacy problems do not show transient/magnocellular processing deficits (Everatt, Bradshaw & Hibbard, 1999), and others do not show poor eye movement/focus control (Goulandris, McIntyre, Snowling, Bethel & Lee, 1998; Rayner & Pollatsek, 1989). The converse of this is that research has also indicated that some individuals show the same visual deficits as dyslexics, yet present little evidence of literacy acquisition problems (see discussions in Skottun, 2000; Vellutino, Fletcher, Snowling & Scanlon, 2004). These difficulties have led theorists in this area to suggest multiple causal pathways to literacy weaknesses and dyslexia (see Stein, 2001).

Stein's (2001) potential explanation of the evidence that not all dyslexics show a visual processing deficit has been to argue that dyslexia is produced by a temporal processing deficit that affects both visual and auditory perceptual systems. The origins of this perspective can be found in the work of Tallal and colleagues (Fitch, Miller & Tallal, 1997; Tallal, 1980) on children with speech and language difficulties. In this work, children with speech and language difficulties failed to discriminate auditory information that was separated by millisecond gaps or which could only be distinguished by the initial few milliseconds after their onset. These findings locate problems in the area of processing rapidly changing auditory information and are consistent with findings for deficits in the processing of rapidly changing visual information that have been used to argue for a transient or magnocellular deficit. These commonalities might explain the visual and auditory/phonological-related deficits identified in the literature – and the same framework may relate to the proposed timing deficits that have been argued as a feature of the cerebellum deficit viewpoint (Fawcett & Nicolson, 2001). However, although grand theories such as those proposed by Stein (2001) have been valuable in bringing together different findings, they often suffer from a lack of specification as to how the hypothesised cause leads to the identified behavioural difficulties. In this case, the question remains as to how the temporal deficit leads to the literacy problems associated with dyslexia and whether the theory can provide a testable set of hypotheses based on predictions derived from the proposed causal pathways. Why does one dyslexic have an auditory processing deficit and another a visual processing problem if both conditions derive from the same underlying dysfunction?

Indeed, the auditory deficit position also has its problems. The discrimination of most sound units within a language relies on the ability to perceive changes in frequency amplitudes and voicing onsets that occur within a very brief time span. A temporal processing deficit in the auditory system would potentially explain the relationship between dyslexia and poor phonemic awareness, and hence explanations of literacy-related difficulties based on the phonological deficit viewpoint can be encompassed by a temporal auditory processing deficit theory. However, although cross-language evidence of problems with speeded processing of auditory stimuli has been provided, as with the visual perceptual deficits, there is variability in such auditory deficit findings, which leads to inconsistency in theoretical interpretation (contrast: Laasonen, Service & Virsu, 2001; Meyler & Breznitz, 2005; Taylor, Batty, Chaix & Demonét, 2003). Furthermore, other studies have not found evidence in support of the temporal auditory processing deficit position (e.g. Marshall, Snowling & Bailey, 2001; van Beinum, Schwippert, Been, van Leeuwen & Kuijpers, 2005). These inconsistent findings have been obtained from studies of the same languages, suggesting that they cannot be explained by reference to any particular language feature. Rather, these diverse findings suggest that the theoretical models underlying the proposed deficits need further development. Indeed, the theories focusing on auditory deficits have been criticised for confounding temporal processing with sound/phoneme discrimination (Mody, Studdert-Kennedy & Brady, 1997; Studdert-Kennedy, 2002) and some models have explained the connection between auditory deficits and phonological weaknesses in terms of alternative sound features that are more consistent with a phonological viewpoint (see Goswami et al., 2002). Hence, the evidence for such perceptual factors explaining literacy learning difficulties is at best equivocal and further work is needed to provide evidence of consistency in findings and interpretations.

Motor and cerebellum deficit viewpoints

Another perspective that has a reasonably long history in work on dyslexia is that problems with learning are associated with deficits in motor movements or the development of movement processes from reflexes to coordinated and automatic skills performance (see discussions in Goddard, 1996). The more historical perspective has argued that interruptions in the development of motor skills interfere with the acquisition of skills such as reading and writing. This has been associated with a relatively controversial set of remediation procedures that require the training of either basis reflexive or baby-type movements, such as crawling. The idea is that these need to develop correctly for further movements to build on these basis skills. The developmental sequence starts with reflexive responses, which are not under conscious control, and progresses to highly skilled movements that are dependent on basic skills. More advanced skills involving hand and finger movements may be dependent on the development of early grasp reflexes and predetermined finger movements found with many infants. These hand/finger movements may include the ability to manipulate objects, as in handwriting. Handwriting will involve other skills, such as hand–eye coordination and directional movement, but these may also develop from basic skills and experiences. All of these need to be coordinated appropriately, which will require practice, and more conscious control. However, a problem for the general motor deficit perspectives is that children with major physical/motor problems from birth do not necessarily show literacy deficits. Therefore, theories need to explain which type of motor movements lead to dyslexia and which do not. For example, there has also been the suggestion that these basic reflexive movements are overactive or non-inhibited, leading to possible interference with learning new skills. Consistent with this interpretation, McPhillips, Hepper and Mulhern (2000) have argued that the training reflexive responses in children with evidence of a lack of appropriate reflexes (for example, the inhibition of the asymmetrical tonic neck reflex) has led to improvements in literacy levels in those with evidence of dyslexia and poor reading levels (see also McPhillips & Jordan-Black, 2007).

However, despite the history of motor training procedures for those with learning problems, and some research evidence (such as McPhillips et al., 2000; see also Wolff, Michel & Ovrut, 1990), there has been a relative lack of systematic research on motor deficits explanations specific to dyslexia and the theoretical basis is questionable. In most explanations, it is difficult to see why a motor problem would lead to reading problems, even if handwriting difficulties may be a more obvious link. Probably the simplest explanation is to consider this as related to the eye movement control explanations more often associated with visual deficit perspectives: motor problems lead to poor eye movement control, which in turn makes reading a problem. The problem is that linking this explanation to poor eye movement control means that it is subject to the same problems as eye movement explanations. For example, the reason why eye movements have been associated with dyslexia is because of the differences in eye movement patterns between those with dyslexia and those without. Those with dyslexia show prolonged fixations on words: fixations are when the eyes are relatively stationary over a stimulus that seems to be the focus of attention. Dyslexics also have more movements around the text, including movements back through the text, compared to those without dyslexia. However, prolonged fixations and larger numbers of movements back through text are evident in non-dyslexic readers when they are given something difficult to read. These features need not be evidence of poor control of eye movement, but of sensible eye movements when text is difficult (see Everatt, 2002; Kennedy, 1987; Rayner & Pollatsek, 1989). And the evidence that dyslexia is associated with poor eye movement control is questionable, with a number of studies finding no evidence of abnormal eye movement patterns in dyslexics when reading is not required (Adler-Grinberg & Stark, 1978; Olson, Kliegl & Davidson, 1983; Stanley, Smith & Howell, 1983).

If we cannot be confident of the eye movement explanation, then it is difficult to see how the motor perspectives relate to reading. Furthermore, there is also no obvious explanation for why a motor-based intervention would then lead to better reading performance – again, unless better eye movement control is proposed as the intermediate factor.

There is nothing in schooling that would suggest that those with better motor coordination would perform better in the tasks expected in a reading class, unless we assume that it is the inhibition of motor movements that allows for increased attention to classroom tasks. However, again, there is little in the general motor-based theoretical explanations that relates to the type of hyperactivity or conduct problems that can create problems for learning with those with Attention Deficit Hyperactivity Disorder (ADHD) or diagnosed Conduct Disorders. Reflexive movements do not occur all of the time such that they distract from learning. Indeed such explanation of behavioural problems may make theories of motor deficits more consistent with studies of these alternative conditions (for example, see Wimmer, Mayringer & Raberger, 1999). Therefore, although this area of explanation may be useful to consider problems that some children may experience in school (motor training interventions may be better suited to alleviate some of the problems experienced by children with dyspraxia, for example – see discussions of dyspraxia in Everatt & McNeill, 2014), it is difficult to see why it is an explanation of the specific problems associated with those with dyslexia.

An alternative to the simple motor deficit perspective is that dyslexics have an underlying difference in the way they learn, and this will include learning motor movements, and potentially coordinating or sequencing those movements (Needle, Nicolson & Fawcett, 2015). One of the most enduring, and at times controversial, viewpoints originated from the idea that those with dyslexia have problems making skills automatic. A well-practised skill will become effortless, efficient and relatively error-free. It can often occur without too much thinking about how it is performed: it may happen without too much conscious concentration on skilled performance, and hence will be referred to as automatic. Such well-practised skills can often be performed while doing other tasks. For example, practised bike riders can usually perform the task of riding a bike while doing something else like listening to music – they can maintain balance while reaching for a drink. Practised car drivers can often have a conversation while driving, particularly on a familiar road. They may only become aware of driving when something unusual happens. All these features are those of an automatic skill and making a skill automatic may allow the individual to concentrate on another task. If, however, skills do not become automatic (because of an automaticity deficit), then they will require conscious concentration for their performance – they will be effortful.

One of the earliest specific dyslexia theories along these lines was proposed by Nicolson and Fawcett. In some of their initial work, Nicolson and Fawcett (1990) asked groups of dyslexic and non-dyslexic children to perform tasks either on their own or in combination. The idea was that if one or both of the tasks could be performed automatically, then there would be no difference in the task alone and task together conditions. However, if the tasks could not be performed automatically, then task performance in the task combined condition would be worse than in the task alone condition. One of the more striking examples was a balancing task, where the two groups of dyslexics and non-dyslexics had to simply maintain balance. When this was performed on its own, the two groups showed similar levels of balance control. However, when the children were required to count backwards at the same time as maintaining balance, the children with dyslexia showed more balance problems than the children without dyslexia. This was interpreted by Nicolson and Fawcett as indicating that the non-dyslexics can balance automatically but the dyslexics could not. Hence, even simple motor skills such as balancing may not be performed automatically by a dyslexic – they may have to concentrate on such skills.

The use of motor-type tasks in both the research and subsequent assessment methods (e.g. Fawcett & Nicolson, 1996) has led to this theory being related to motor-based interventions (see Reynolds, Nicolson & Hambley, 2003) – we will return to this point in Part 5 on interventions related to dyslexia. The initial models proposed by Nicolson and Fawcett also related the problems to the functioning of the cerebellum (Fawcett & Nicolson, 2001), an area of the brain just above the spinal cord and often associated with coordinating task performance; and more recently to ideas about procedural learning (see Nicolson & Fawcett, 2011). Therefore, although this is a learning theory, it potentially explains some of the motor skills difficulties that have been associated with dyslexia. It also explains reading and writing problems based on the idea that these skills also suffer from not being automatic, at least in part. Whereas a non-dyslexic can read words automatically, a dyslexic student will require much more effort to read words, they will be less efficient in the reading (they are likely to be a slower reader) and they are unlikely to become error-free in their performance, particularly if concentration/effort cannot be maintained. The same would be the case for writing/spelling – both would be effortful, less efficient and error-prone.

The potential usefulness of such a theory is that it links dyslexia with a wider range of difficulties that can be tested outside the context of reading – any skill that, with practice, can be performed automatically by a non-dyslexic will show poorer performance by those with dyslexia. However, linking this theory to motor skills also associates it with problems of associations with other conditions: ADHD, for example (Wimmer et al., 1999) or dyspraxia (Everatt & McNeill, 2014). Wimmer et al. (1999) replicated the single versus combined task performance study of Nicolson and Fawcett (1990) and found that any differences between dyslexics and non-dyslexics in a combined task performance condition were confined to those dyslexics who also showed evidence of ADHD. When children with combined dyslexia–ADHD features were removed from the data set, there was no difference between those with dyslexia and those without. Hence, the problems in the combined task may be more related to the attentional problems of those with ADHD than with automaticity weaknesses among dyslexics. The controversial nature of a supposed cerebellum intervention has also led to doubts about the theory (see discussions issue of the journal *Dyslexia*, volume 9, pages 122–135 and 137–176, and volume 13, pages 78–109). Furthermore, those with dyslexia show evidence of Stroop-type interference effects of written words (see Everatt, Warner, Miles & Thomson, 1997; Jones, Snowling & Moll, 2016). If reading words was effortful for a dyslexic student, it seems odd that interference from a word would occur. Hence, although this is an interesting perspective, the evidence is not conclusive enough to make it specific to dyslexia.

Morphology and meaning

The development of language is a vital component of successful literacy acquisition, and problems in language development can predict subsequent weaknesses in language and literacy (Bishop & Snowling, 2004; Catts, 2017; Sparks, Patton & Murdoch, 2014). The goal of reading and writing is to convey meaning. This is usually achieved through accessing the meaning of individual words and combining these to derive the meaning of phrases, sentences and passages, with additional support coming from processes beyond the word level, such as the use of discourse knowledge and making inferences about the intended meaning of a section of text. Given that dyslexia is typically seen as a word-level deficit, and the deriving of text meaning is seen as involving more than word-level processing, the two areas have often remained separate. Those studies that have looked at text comprehension amongst dyslexics typically consider this from the perspective of problems with word-level processes (i.e. the ways in which word-level deficits lead to text comprehension weaknesses); although there are studies that have considered the possible compensatory influences of semantic context on word-level decoding (see Nation & Snowling, 1998; see also Bishop and Snowling, 2004; Everatt, 1997). However, word processing and the influence of individual word meaning have been considered in terms of dyslexia, albeit mainly in terms of morphological processing.

The term morpheme is usually used to refer to the basic unit of meaning in a language. Most words in a language represent one concept and, therefore, the written representation of that word is usually a morpheme. However, written words can comprise several morphemes. Add a plural to a word and an extra level of meaning, and hence a morphemic unit, has been added. Therefore, an appreciation of morphemic units within a language and its written form may support the reader's understanding of the text. Given this potential influence on literacy acquisition, it is surprising that morphemic awareness has not been studied as much as other factors argued to be related to literacy learning difficulties. Interestingly, in contrast to much of the evidence discussed in previous sections of this part, a larger proportion of studies has focused on spelling rather than reading. These studies suggest that children are capable of making use of morphology in their spelling development at a relatively early age (see Bowers, Kirby & Deacon, 2010; Nunes, Bryant & Bindman, 1997; Treiman, Cassar & Zukowski, 1994). In addition, there are also studies that have demonstrated an influence of morphological processing in reading, and variability in measures of morphological skills have also been found to contribute unique variance in explanations of literacy acquisition (see McBride-Chang, Wagner, Muse, Chow & Shu, 2005). However, there seems to be a reciprocal

relationship between literacy development and morphological awareness, and the development of morphological awareness processes may
be dependent upon phonological processing skills (see discussions in
Bryant, Nunes & Bindman, 1998; Casalis, Cole & Sopo, 2004; Ravid &
Schiff, 2004). As such, morphological deficits may be a feature of literacy development, rather than a cause of literacy learning difficulties,
or they may be another result of a phonological deficit.

Despite the potential for the influence of morphology to be determined by other language factors, it may still explain certain areas of
literacy acquisition where morphological processing may play more of
a principal role – these may be particularly important when considering languages other than English. For example, Bentin and Frost
(1995) have suggested that morphological analysis was necessary for
readers of the Hebrew language, particularly for morphologically
complex Hebrew words. Another example comes from the work of
Abu-Rabia (2002) who concluded that, for readers of Arabic, morphological analysis was necessary for reading comprehension. These
views are consistent with the position that morphological processing
in reading, at least, supports the accessing of a semantic lexicon.
Although such findings may be difficult interpretively (see discussions
in Morton, 1979), evidence derived from Hebrew speakers has suggested that lexical access to a word was better facilitated by other
words that shared the same root compared to words that were based
on similar orthographic patterns but which did not share the same
morphemic root (Frost, Foster & Deutsch, 1997); and similar evidence
has been presented for Arabic speakers when complex words were
used (Boudelaa & Marslen-Wilson, 2005). An influence of morphological processing has also been found in the processing of complex
English words (Rastle, Davis & New, 2004), suggesting that morphology may support the identification of a written word, particularly
when accessing the precise meaning of a word may prove difficult. If
this is the case, morphological understanding seems to be important
for word processing, but it may be an additional resource to use when
complex materials are encountered. Therefore, as complexity (most
likely morphemic complexity) increases across languages, so the
importance of acquiring the ability to process morphology would be
predicted to also increase. Although this prediction has not been

formally tested, due to a need to operationalise the complexity dimension, this may explain why research on Hebrew/Arabic is more likely to suggest that morphological processing skills are important for full literacy development (see discussions in Elbeheri et al., 2006).

Morphological awareness deficits have also been found amongst dyslexic children from different language backgrounds (Abu-Rabia & Taha, 2004; Arnbak & Elbro, 2000; Ben-Dror, Bentin & Frost, 1995; Bourassa, Treiman & Kessler, 2006; Carlise, 1987; Joanisse et al., 2000; Mahfoudhi, Elbeheri, Al-Rashidi & Everatt, 2010). Abu-Rabia and Taha (2004) found significant difference in the number of morphological errors produced in reading and spelling tasks between Arabic speaking dyslexics and a group of age-matched controls, but not between dyslexics and a reading-level-matched control group, suggesting that the dyslexics are lagging behind in the development of their morphological processing skills rather than presenting with an inability in the area of morphology. If this conclusion is correct, it becomes difficult to argue that the dyslexics' morphological deficits are an inherent feature of dyslexia, and it could be that with proper training, morphological processing may support word identification among dyslexic children. Consistent with this view, training in morphological awareness has been found to improve performance in reading and spelling of morphologically complex words (e.g. Arnbak & Elbro, 2000), and some studies have argued that dyslexics are able to make use of a morphological cue to support word recognition processes, when phonological decoding strategies fail (see Joanisse et al., 2000; Schiff & Ravid, 2004). Similar evidence has been reported for English speaking dyslexics. Bourassa et al. (2006) found similarities in the way morphologically complex words were spelt by dyslexics and younger normally developing spelling-level-matched children; again consistent with the lag hypothesis. However, it is the case that as normally developing spellers age, they became more capable of appropriately using such morphological skills in spelling, whereas dyslexic individuals still show evidence of inconsistent usage of these skills in their spelling. Although the dyslexic seems capable of using morphological skills in reading and spelling, they may be less secure in their use of those skills (at least without formal and appropriate instruction) than their normally developing peers.

Overall, while morphological processing is important in normal literacy acquisition, it may be of secondary importance to phonological processing, and its relationship with dyslexia is currently unclear, with some studies showing deficits in morphological processing amongst dyslexics, and others suggesting that morphological awareness may be used as a compensatory strategy for weak phonological awareness. Clearly further evidence is necessary here, with cross-language comparisons providing an ideal basis on which to provide such further data.

Conclusions

Although a number of theories about dyslexia have been proposed (and covered in this and previous parts of the book), those that seem to be best at explaining the features associated with dyslexia focus on language deficits, particularly in the area of phonological processing. Such theories are not without their difficulties, and further work is needed to develop these theories into a comprehensive explanation of dyslexia. Additional language-related perspectives on the importance of vocabulary, particularly for difficulties with reading comprehension, and maybe morphology as a way to support word reading and spelling development, would clearly be useful (see discussions in Bowers et al., 2010; Bowyer-Crane et al., 2008; Clarke, Snowling, Truelove & Hulme, 2010; Denston et al., 2018; Snowling & Melby-Lervåg, 2016). However, such phonological perspectives, coupled with our current understanding of the processes that support reading and writing acquisition, provide the basis on which to determine early identification and intervention practices (see also Snowling, 2013). This will be the basis on which we discuss ideas related to dyslexia practice in the remainder of the book, though this discussion will also consider alternative perspectives (such as visual attention, and motor coordination viewpoints) since these may provide opportunities for support procedures as well as provide the basis on which to consider dyslexia in contrast with other types of learning difficulties (such as attention deficits or dyspraxia). One reason why it may be important to consider these additional areas when trying to understand dyslexia is that they can co-occur with dyslexia: i.e. a student may have dyslexia and dyspraxia, or show evidence of phonological deficits along with attentional problems. Such comorbidity of learning difficulties needs to be considered for a better understanding of any one of the conditions (see discussions in: Adams, Snowling, Nehhessy & Kind, 1999; Caron & Rutter, 1991; Everatt, Weeks & Brooks, 2008; Kaplan, Dewey, Crawford & Wilson, 2001).

4

IDENTIFYING DYSLEXIA

Introduction

Normally, dyslexia assessments are used to determine that someone has dyslexia, and to inform an educational plan to support the individual with dyslexia – the same would be true of many assessment processes developed with a particular learning disability/difficulty in mind (see Reid, Elbeheri & Everatt, 2015). Such assessments are rarely used as a way to develop a skill, although curriculum assessments (which may be formative in focus and structure) may be used to compare individual performance against expected levels of ability, and some monitoring processes used as part of Response to Intervention procedures (we will discuss these further in the intervention part of the book) may be considered as supporting skills development. Therefore, assessments of dyslexia will have most often been developed with the aim to be used as an identification tool, rather than specifically for educational or training purposes. Their development will have focused on determining an area of difficulty, often consistent with a theory about dyslexia that specifies its characteristics and/or its causes. Therefore, previous coverage of theories of dyslexia is relevant to understanding the background to an assessment tool, and these different perspectives should be kept in mind when considering assessment practices. There is not the space in this book to cover all potential tools/resources that can be used for assessment/screening purposes: other sources, such as Reid et al. (2015), provide more coverage on such resources. Rather this part of the book provides a discussion of the issues related to the identification of dyslexia that can form the basis of an understanding of the sort of practices used in relation to dyslexia – hopefully, the reader will then be able to make up their own mind about tools that they come across in the literature. In addition to this background, this part of the book will also consider suggestions about identification that are related to the framework of dyslexia proposed in the book as a way to discuss such practices and the types of measures that this framework suggests.

Types of assessment methods

Dyslexia assessments can involve a range of methods to assess a skill or identify an area of difficulty or strength. These include:

- standardised tests, which will be used to precisely measure a skill and compare against expected or typical levels of performance (e.g. against children of the same age as the individual being assessed);
- curriculum or more informal measures of an ability to give additional information about educational level (are they at the level expected based on their school year?), and which might be used to monitor progress over time (again, Response to Intervention procedures are a good example to determining growth over the course of an intervention);
- observations of behaviour either in class or during test taking to determine the occurrence of negative behaviours that might interfere with task performance or strategies that might mask difficulties, as well as evidence for struggling with a task despite successful completion;
- student self-reports about a difficulty, which may be determined by interview or a questionnaire, and might be used to determine the history of the difficulties or to give an indication of the student's own perceptions about what is happening and feelings of self-worth;

- parent or teacher reports, which will help with determining the history of the problems, particularly for young learners, but which may also provide indications of the specific nature of any problem behaviours (e.g. do they happen during reading or are they a more general occurrence across situations or when the child is tired or frustrated?).

Each of these methods can be useful in its own way – and we will refer to several throughout the book. To start with, though, a distinction between screening and full assessment may also be useful. Any of the methods in the bullet points above can be used for screening purposes or as part of the processes used in identifying a condition to receive accommodations or support of some kind. For example, a questionnaire may be distributed to students entering a course to determine if there is a likelihood that an individual student may experience problems that might be related to dyslexia – or such a questionnaire may be found on a web page and used to recommend that someone should seek a more formal assessment of difficulties. These types of dyslexia-related questionnaires might be best referred to as a screening tool. It is likely to give relatively simple indications of there being no dyslexia-related risk factors or it may suggest that there are risk factors and suggest that further advice is sought. The aim of such a screener may be to avoid large numbers being assessed, which would require too much in the way of resources: a screener can help specify where the assessment resources are best applied. It may also be used to avoid unnecessary expense for an individual or organisation. As such, a screener does not specifically identify a problem, nor does it give detail on what to do about the problem – typically, it will suggest seeking further advice for identification and support purposes. Such identification and support recommendations are better decided through more detailed assessment.

An example may help with the distinction here. Smythe and Everatt (2001, see www.bdadyslexia.org.uk/dyslexia/how-is-dyslexia-diagnosed/dyslexia-checklists) put together a checklist for adults with dyslexia comprising a series of questions related to dyslexia. These were derived from a much larger number of questions based on a range of dyslexia theories (as per previous discussions in this book) and previously developed questionnaires about dyslexia (e.g. Vinegrad, 1994). A relatively large number of adults, many themselves dyslexic, were asked to answer this larger number of questions. The adults were also asked to indicate whether they were dyslexic or not, and this simple self-classification was used to determine the set of questions that best distinguished between those who self-reported dyslexia and those who did not. Note, therefore, that this is simply related to self-report – it is not an exact estimation of whether someone has dyslexia or not. The sort of questions cover a range of potential characteristics, from those related to reading (such as 'Do you confuse visually similar words when reading (e.g. tan, ton)?' and 'Do you lose your place or miss out lines when reading?' and 'How easy do you find it to sound out words (e.g. el-e-phant)?') and writing ('When writing do you find it difficult to organise thoughts on paper?'), to those focused more on language (e.g. 'Do you confuse the names of objects (e.g. table for chair)?' and 'Do you find it difficult to find the right word to say?') and areas associated with skills that may require verbal memory/labels, but may also be related to skills acquisition (e.g. 'Did you learn your multiplication tables easily?' or 'Do you have trouble telling left from right?') or even compensatory strategies ('How easy is it to think of unusual (creative) solutions?'). There are 16 simple questions and a scoring system for each question that when totalled produces an indication of how likely it is that the respondent has dyslexia. This does not aim to determine any specific area of weakness via an individual answer – nor does it attempt to determine exactly how likely it is that an individual has dyslexia. It is more of a guide to determine if further assessment would be recommended. As such, it may be used by an assessor, say in a college/university, as part of a system to determine if a full assessment would be recommended. Using the checklist as part of an interview that also included questions about specific current or past difficulties may help determine recommendations to the individual to pay for a full assessment. Given that full assessments are expensive, this may be worthwhile.

However, over the years of work on dyslexia, a certain amount of blurring between screeners and full assessments has occurred. For example, although they may not be as accurate as standardised measures, checklist-type questionnaires have been used in research on dyslexia. For example, Snowling, Dawes, Nash and Hulme (2012) developed an adult questionnaire (based on checklists, including Smythe & Everatt) that also asked questions about levels of reading difficulties and was associated with an assessment of dyslexia or scores on measures of reading. This questionnaire was developed in order to assess the potential level of family-related incidence of literacy learning problems. Such a tool could then be used in studies of genetic and/or environmental factors related to dyslexia, and may be used to help determine family risk of dyslexia: i.e. how much it runs in families (see also van Bergen, de Jong, Maassen & van der Leij, 2014). Similarly, a screening process may be used to determine basic support without a specific determination of the area of difficulty or a statement about dyslexia. Extra time in examinations may be one type of accommodation that may be provided following a screening process. If someone is struggling with reading, particularly fluency of reading, then extra time may provide a basis on which to allow a more accurate determination of knowledge. This accommodation may be provided while full assessment processes are ongoing, which will then determine a wider-ranging set of educational support procedures.

The Dyslexia Screening Test of Fawcett and Nicolson (1996) is another good example of where the distinction between a screener and a tool used for identification (or diagnosis) and educational plan has blurred. Despite the name, this screener is often used in schools to identify those with dyslexia in order to consider accommodations. However, whether a screener should be used for these purposes may be questionable. One of the confusions is that tools such as the Dyslexia Screening Test cover a range of skills that fit with a theoretical model of dyslexia and, therefore, may be indistinguishable from other tools that do not use the term 'screener' and which argue that they can be used for identification purposes. If we contrast the Dyslexia Screening Test with the Bangor Dyslexia Test (Miles, 1993) or the Cognitive Profiling System (Lucid Creative Ltd: see www.lucid-research.com), as examples, we will see that although they derive from different theoretical perspectives about dyslexia, they all test a number of similar skills (e.g. related to literacy and memory). The same comparison can be made with the Turner and Smith's (2004) Dyslexia Screener (see www.gl-assessment.co.uk/dyslexia). All may be seen as providing the same level of identification reliability, and all provide some advice on educational support as part of the materials associated with the tool. However, a report from such a tool is unlikely to fit with the requirements of an educational organisation to access resources. Hence, they may be useful in-house, but may not be seen as providing a full diagnostic/assessment report required by external organisations. The distinction between a skills assessment test and a questionnaire-based self-report scale also cannot be used to determine which can be used for identification and which cannot. For example, Weedon and Reid's (2003) Special Needs Assessment Profile (SNAP) includes mini-tests and self-reports, as well as questions for teachers, which together aim to provide a diagnostic assessment and profile of a child's strengths and weaknesses. Again, this can be useful for those within a school trying to identify a potential problem and find solutions to that problem, but such a tool may not meet the requirements of a funding source or regulatory body (such as an education system or employment organisation). Policies related to additional resources or formal organisational recognition of a problem are determined by other bodies than those producing tests. Hence, when selecting a tool to use as part of supporting students who may have dyslexia, or dyslexia-related difficulties, an understanding of the aim of the tool is vital: just because it is called a screener or test or an assessment battery or profiling system, for example, may not be a simple guide to its purpose, nor what it is meant to tell the user. Also, once the purpose is to determine, it is necessary for the user to determine their purpose in using the tool. If it is for regulatory purposes, then the tool, or procedures required by the regulatory body, may need to be used. For example, in some parts of the world it is still necessary for an assessment process to provide an IQ as part of determining access to resources (see discussions in Elbeheri & Everatt, 2009), despite the research evidence that this may not be useful as part of an assessment of needs related to dyslexia.

Assessment procedures and evaluation

It is also necessary to understand the procedures for using a screening/assessment tool. This applies to questionnaires as much as standardised tests. Both require some level of practice to administer and interpret. This will be particularly the case if the tool has to be administered by an individual, but can also apply to a computerised method. The latter will require the administrator to understand when/where the computer can be accessed and how the computerised procedure should be performed: e.g. are others allowed to help? – is quiet concentration important? – are headphones or such like necessary? – how long will the method take? – can the individual take part and return to complete the rest later? If applying the method via pencil and paper, then the administrator will need to know how to do this: is there a specific procedure necessary? – do methods need to follow a specific order? – can questions be answered? – can praise be given? Errors in administration will most likely lead to errors in outcomes – and human behaviour is always subject to error, so it does not need any help in making the level of error worse. Therefore, understand the method and practise it beforehand.

Scoring and evaluating the tool is then also vital. For a computerised tool, much of this may be done by the program, but again an understanding of the output from the tool is important: e.g. does it mean that further assessment is needed or that specific support procedures need to be applied? Again, the output from a computerised procedure will be determined by the theory that the authors of the tool subscribe to, so an understanding of this will help recognise from where recommendations have come. If this is not easy to determine, then be careful about using the tool. Similar statements can be made about methods that are not computerised. Such person-administered methods have the advantage that those giving the questionnaire/test/etc. can observe how the student performs the tasks, which can provide further information for full assessment purposes. A person-administered method can also allow the student to ask questions, whereas computerised tools rarely allow the range of verbal questions that a student with dyslexia might ask: e.g. a written response to 'frequently asked questions' may not be much use to a student with a major difficulty with reading. However, person-administered methods often require procedures for interpreting outcomes to be followed carefully by the administrator. This will require some understanding of the method – and again practice at scoring/interpreting. For example, a questionnaire may involve a scale that requires scoring, but the scoring may require a specific set of procedures. Again, an example may help. In the Smythe and Everatt checklist, most items indicate a level of difficulty so that higher score means great likelihood of difficulty. However, one item refers to a compensation strategy ('How easy is it to think of unusual (creative) solutions?') and indicating that this is easy to do would be more indicative of dyslexia. Hence, in order to total this item with the rest, it needs to be scored in the opposite direction. The same is true of many self-report scales and is often used to avoid respondents simply indicating the same answer throughout a questionnaire. This reverse coding of an item, though, is essential to produce a total score appropriate to make conclusions. Scoring an item the wrong way will lead to major problems with interpretation.

Such scoring procedures will also require the assessor to understand some basic maths. Adding up scores on a questionnaire scale is an obvious example following on from the above. However, more stand-ardised measures will require a little more sophistication in interpreta-tion and background understanding. A standardised measure of a skill is often the most exact of assessment tools – and most procedures that specify dyslexia will include such measures. Such standardised measures will have been developed to relate the score produced by the individual taking a test with an expected level of performance. The latter are often based on scores produced by a large number of individuals and are often referred to as the 'norms' for the test. In many standardised tests, norms are used to produce tables of converted scores: for example, a child score on a reading measure may be converted via a table to a reading age. The reading age will be based on the average score produced by children of a specific age: for example, on the test, the average score for eight year olds might be 20 – hence, if we give the test to a child and find that they score 20, and we look this score up on the reading age table, then we would find that this child most likely has a reading age of eight years. If the child were ten years old and had attended school regularly, then we are likely to interpret this difference as indicative of a difficulty in the acquisition of reading. Hence, such measures can be very useful in determining a deficit in a skill that is theoretically tied to dyslexia. In contrast to a checklist, this conclusion about a level of skill may be more accurate/reliable in terms of its identification of dyslexia.

Calculations of averages in such test tables will have likely been based on various statistical calculations. Statistics is an area of mathematics that relates scores of a sample with best estimates of scores of a population. For example, the reading test cannot measure all eight year olds (the population), so it will have based the average on a sample of eight year olds – this may be 100 eight year olds or 1000, but this is still a sample of eight year olds – it can never be the full population. However, we do want to state with some level of certainty that the average is close to what we would expect of the population of eight year olds – if it were limited to only the sample, then the test would be worthless. Therefore, we need to understand a little about statistics to understand the rationale behind such standardised measures. So, for example, an average in statistical terms is called a mean: and, typically, you calculate a mean in the same way as an average – add up all the scores and divide by the number of scores. There are other ways of calculating means in statistics, but this is likely to be the way a test has done it. Hence, interpretation of a mean in a table can be considered as talking about averages.

There are more complex ways of interpreting scores, however, and these are likely to occur in standardised measures as well. For example, if measuring a language skill, such as phonological awareness, it may not be that useful to talk about phonological age, but it may be useful to have some standard against which to compare an individual score against: a standard score, for example. Similarly, measures of intelligence often refer to scores around a value of 100 – an average intelligence quotient. When encountering such measures, an understanding of a second term, a standard deviation, will also be useful. A standard deviation is basically a statistical calculation of how spread out a set of scores is: basically, the standard difference between each score and the mean. The bigger the standard deviation, the more spread out the scores are. Hence, a mean tells us the middle or central point of a distribution of scores and the standard deviation tells us how spread out around the mean score they are. If these represent the expected distribution of reading scores, then they can tell us a great deal about an individual's ability compared to that population: the potential severity of a difficulty, for example. In order to use this idea, though, we need to assume that the population of scores on a test follows a specific distribution, called the normal distribution. This indicates that most people will fall around the middle point in a distribution: most people will be average readers, for example. If we take the reading analogy further, we would then expect very few people to be very good readers, and maybe very few people to be very poor readers. This will follow something similar to a normal distribution of scores, and, given that this is the case, we can make predictions about the sort of numbers of people who will produce scores within a particular range of scores. So, given that reading does follow a normal distribution, about 70 per cent of people will score between one standard deviation below and one standard deviation above the mean. This also means that about 15 per cent of people will score below one standard deviation from the mean and about 2.5 per cent of people will produce a score below two standard deviations from the mean. We can use standard deviations from the mean to interpret how weak a score is compared to a population: in this example, how much an individual is struggling with reading compared to what we would expect of the population of readers. Someone with a score below two standard deviations from the mean is a very poor reader compared to the population. If this individual is a seven year old and the population relates to seven year olds, then we can conclude that the individual is a very poor reader compared to the expected ability levels of seven year old readers.

Means and standard deviations (or the norms of a test) are also useful because standard (or standardised) scores that many measures use are also based on the number of standard deviations that an individual's score is from the average. These are sometimes referred to as z-scores. A z-score is simply the number of standard deviations away from a mean. Therefore, the mean has a z-score of zero, and scores below the mean are referred to in minus figures: two standard deviations below the mean has a z-score of minus two. These are particularly useful when interpreting test scores, because as long as certain assumptions about a skill are correct, they can allow us not only to refer to an individual's score in terms that we can compare with a population, but they also allow comparison across measures with different ranges of scores. For example, a reading test that produces scores between 0 and 40 and be compared with an IQ measure that produces standardised scores around 100. As long as we have a reasonable estimate of the mean and standard deviation, we can compare both in terms of these values. IQ norms are now often based on a mean of 100 and a standard deviation of 15 (it used to be 16, but most use 15 now as this is easier to calculate and interpret). Therefore, someone who scores 85 is one standard deviation below the mean. If the reading test has a mean of 20 and a standard deviation of five, then someone who scores 15 on the reading measure is also one standard deviation below the mean. In terms of z-scores, they score minus one on both measures. In the days of discrepancy methods for assessing dyslexia, this individual's reading level would be commensurate (equal to) their IQ. However, another individual with the same reading score, but an average IQ of 100, would have an IQ z-score of zero and a reading z-score of minus one, suggesting a discrepancy between these two scores. Calculations of z-scores are not only useful for discrepancy methods of assessing dyslexia, they can also be used to contrast any group of measures. We can see how useful these z-scores are in the Figures 4.1 to 4.4 (see the next section of this part).

However, note that the calculations of the standard scores above are based on the assumption of a normal distribution and, although this assumption may be correct for many skills, there are alternative ways of determining the level of difficulty presented by an individual which may be better when a normal distribution is unlikely. For example, one of the useful features of the normal distribution is that it can be used to relate scores on an assessment measure to proportions (or percentage) of a population: we can say that less than 2.5 per cent of a population will produce a score equal to a z-score of minus two. Equally, we can report findings from a test in terms of percentages below a certain score. Often referred to as centiles, these allow an assessor to indicate how many individuals are likely to produce a specific score, or less, on an assessment measure – and many assessment tools will include tables for centiles. If calculated based on percentages from a sample, these centiles should be less influenced by problems related to a non-normal distribution. Also, they can often convey meaning more simply than z-scores – a statement about being in the bottom 5 per cent of a population may be better understood by the individual being assessed than a load of scores and statistical terms. Although, z-scores should not be ignored, they can make comparison across measures easier (see the following sections of this part of the book) and, given that the assumptions about distributions are correct, they can allow us to calculate values such as confidence intervals, which can help with estimates of the likelihood of measurement error leading to problems with interpretation of an individual score, so they are still useful in many instances.

Indeed, all scores are subject to measurement error; i.e. rarely will a measure be a totally accurate assessment of an underlying skill. Better measures are subject to less measurement error – estimates of reliability are usually presented for tests to provide evidence that they are less subject to error: a higher reliability score suggests that the test is less subject to measurement error. However, error is also partly a feature of human behaviour as well as the accuracy of the measurement. Few human behaviours, even highly practised ones, are produced in exactly the same way on any two occasions. We all have good days when we do well in a test – and, equally, we all have bad days when we do poorly. If we could measure the skill many times over several different days with a good test, then the scores produced by an individual will range around a central point that is likely to be the individual's level of ability on the skill. In assessments, we rarely get the chance to measure a skill over good days and bad, though, so we are reliant on the reliability of the test to give us a reasonably accurate measure of performance on the day of assessment and the judgement of the assessor to make an evaluation based on the evidence. This should not be based on simply one test score – for example, in Figures 4.1–4.4, we will consider patterns of performance across measures of similar skills – and a good assessment protocol will consider the history of the potential problem as well as attempt to assess the problem on a specific occasion. Overall, making an informed decision based on the evidence, and using this informed decision to determine appropriate support strategies, is the most important aspect of assessment. Assessment should be for a purpose, and the most useful purpose in the case of dyslexia is to find ways to support learning. In the following section we will discuss some assessment procedures that were performed with specific purposes in mind. One of the purposes was to determine the best way to support learning by identifying areas of difficulties, but also by considering skills that may lead to compensatory strategies and consequences of learning experiences that can lead to challenges for intervention procedures.

Comparisons of the performance of dyslexic against norms

Consistent with the framework presented in this book, the following assessment procedures were used to show potential differences between those with a prior assessment of dyslexia and the norms of the test.

Where available, the norms were based on the means and standard deviations reported in test manuals. Such norms would have been derived from very large samples of learners that may have included students with dyslexia, but, given the size of the sample, the proportion of dyslexics in the sample would be expected to be indicative of the general population. Where such large-sample norms were not available for a measure, they were derived from a large number of individuals for whom there was no history of dyslexia-related learning problems. Three graphs are presented to represent the scores for early primary aged students (around six years of age – Figure 4.1), late primary aged students (around 11 to 12 years of age – Figure 4.2) and adults (18 years of age and older – Figure 4.3) – the data were collected in the UK. The graphs represent z-scores on the vertical axis. As indicated above, these allow us to determine the relative difficulties experienced by the students with dyslexia in each task and thus provide a profile of average performance of individuals with dyslexia over the measures. In each graph, the zero horizontal line is the norm mean (i.e. the expected level of performance for students at the age/school level of the dyslexics) and each lighter line is half a norm standard deviation away from the mean. The squares indicate the average performance of the students with dyslexia – between 70 and 100 students with dyslexia completed each task, representing a relatively large number of students and a reasonable estimate of average performance. Dotted-lines between the squares are simply to help

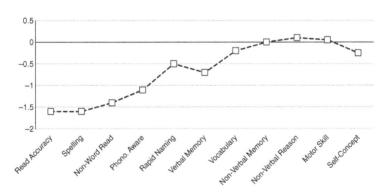

FIGURE 4.1 Performance of early primary school UK students with dyslexia

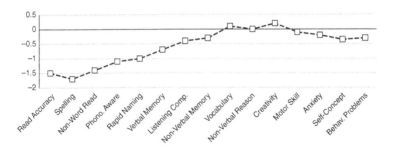

FIGURE 4.2 Performance of late primary school UK students with dyslexia

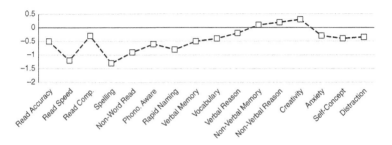

FIGURE 4.3 Performance of adult UK students with dyslexia

observe the pattern of performance across the measures. The measures are presented at the bottom of each graph and are in order from literacy based on the left, through more language and non-verbal skills in the middle, to more self-concept and behavioural factors on the right.

Given that dyslexia is defined as a difficulty with learning to read and write, measures of literacy would be a key part of an assessment protocol. In the present work, for the two children groups, literacy was assessed by measures of both word reading and spelling, based on the framework view that word-level literacy is the main area of deficit related to dyslexia. However, for older cohorts, assessment of reading comprehension and reading fluency (which would include speed of reading) would also be worthwhile, and this is represented in the data for the adult cohorts. Measures of reading and spelling were also appropriate for the age groups targeted in the three figures: easier, more familiar and earlier learnt, words for the youngest group, but words or text more appropriate for older and adult readers with the older groups. This variation in difficulty levels is consistent with general assessment practices and based on the assumption that dyslexia is related to difficulties with learning – it does not mean that learning does not happen. Therefore, materials need to be appropriate for the age group targeted and the specific measure of reading/spelling used will vary depending on the target age group. In the present case, the reading measure for the youngest cohort involved the child attempting to read aloud 100 individual unrelated words printed on a sheet of paper and divided into ten sections of increasing difficulty. The division based on word difficulty provides the opportunity to include a stop-rule in the procedures such that if none of a group of ten were read correctly, then the test could be stopped under the assumption that harder words would also not be read correctly. The reading scores for the older children comprised a combination of two measures; a single word reading measure similar to that given to the younger children, and a sentence reading measure that assessed reading connected text. In both cases, the child read the words out loud and the number of reading errors was noted. For the adults, the measure required the reading of passages of meaningful text out loud, with the number of words read correctly providing a measure of reading accuracy, the number of words read correctly per minute giving a measure of reading speed and the number of questions about the passages answered correctly giving a measure of reading comprehension. In contrast, the spelling measure assessed the ability to spell individual words within each age cohort. The procedure involved orally presenting a series of individual words of increasing difficulty. These same words were then verbally presented in the context of a sentence and, lastly, individually presented again. Instructions emphasised that the single (repeated) words were to be written, not the sentences. Such measures of reading and spelling skills include the Adult Reading Test (the second edition is Brooks, Everatt & Fidler, 2016), Helen Arkell Spelling Test (which can be accessed at www.arkellcentre.org.uk/bookshop/), Neale Analysis of Reading Ability (Neale, 1999), Schonell word reading measure (Schonell, 1950), the Wide Range Achievement Test spelling measure (Jastak & Wilkinson, 1984), Woodcock-Johnson reading measures (the fourth edition is Schrank, Mather & McGrew, 2014).

The framework proposed in this book argues that dyslexia is due to a phonological processing deficit, which impacts on the decoding of unfamiliar or unknown words. To assess the latter, a measure of non-word reading was included. This required the individual being assessed to read out loud non-words which can be pronounced using a knowledge of basic grapheme–phoneme relationships, but which have no meaning and therefore are unlikely to have been seen before: akin to the first time that a child would have seen a word (see Rack et al., 1992). The verbal assessment of phonological processing included measures of awareness, storage and rapid access in order to show the range of performance on such measures, and due to the evidence that different aspects of phonological processing have been found to be relatively independent predictors of literacy level (Everatt et al., 2004; Wagner & Torgesen, 1987). The phonological awareness tasks were all verbally presented and required mainly verbal or pointing responses from the student. Such tasks required the ability to: (i) identify sounds, as in indicating which of the following has a different initial sound 'coat seat calm' or indicate how many sounds in 'fox' (the latter being a more complex task for older individuals); (ii) delete sounds, such as 'Say rainbow without /bow/' or 'Say tall without /t/' (relatively easy syllable or phonemic segmentation) versus 'Say flag without /f/' (a more complex division of the initial sounds for older learners); (iii) manipulate sounds, as in reversing the initial sounds of two words, 'King John', to produce 'Jing Kon' (again more for older/adult students). To measure verbal/phonological memory, a Digit Span procedure from the Wechsler Intelligence Scale for Children (WISC; Wechsler, 1992) was used (repeating increasing lengths of verbally presented digits in the same order until repetition could not be maintained) along with a non-word repetition task (repeating verbally presented items such as 'splob' or 'randbil') in which the length (number of spoken syllables) of the verbal stimulus increased until repetition was not possible. Finally, rapid naming, or efficient access to verbal/phonological labels was assessed by asking the student to name line drawings or pictures of familiar objects (e.g. a desk or pen) as quickly as possible in an array of four or five objects repeated six or seven times – numbers were increased for older students. A colour naming task was also used, with blocks of colour (blue, green, red, yellow) to be named as quickly as possible. The time taken to name all items in the arrays was calculated and any errors in naming led to a one second penalty on the time. Practice prior to the tasks ensured that the students could name the objects/colours. Such phonological tasks were derived from the Comprehensive Test of Phonological Processing (the second edition is Wagner, Torgesen, Rashotte & Pearson, 2013), Dyslexia Screening Test (Fawcett & Nicolson, 1996), Phonological Assessment Battery (Frederickson, Frith & Reason, 1997), Preschool and Primary Inventory of Phonological Awareness (Dodd, Crosbie, MacIntosh, Teitzel & Ozanne, 2000), Working Memory Test Battery for Children (Pickering & Gathercole, 2001) – see also resources provided by Gillon at www.canterbury.ac.nz/education/research/phonological-awareness-resources/.

Given the framework perspective that dyslexia is related to language skills, and the potential consequences on word knowledge that can be associated with dyslexia if early intervention has not been implemented (Stanovich, 1986), assessments of listening comprehension, vocabulary and verbal reasoning were also undertaken. All groups completed a receptive vocabulary measure: either the British Picture Vocabulary Scale (third edition is Dunn et al., 2009). In such tasks, the individual was required to select from a set of options the picture that represented a verbal label spoken by the assessor, with correct answers being based on those accepted in the test manual. For the older children, a listening comprehension task was also used (based on Wechsler Individual Achievement Test, Wechsler, 2005). This required the child to listen to short passages and answer questions about each passage. Passages and questions were verbally presented and the child responded verbally. For the adult cohort, a verbal reasoning task was used (based on Wechsler Adult Intelligence Scale, Wechsler, 2008) which required individuals to recognise how two words were alike and choose a third semantically related word from a list.

Non-verbal measures were also included to assess areas where dyslexics should not experience major difficulties – again, based on the framework used in this book. A visual-spatial short-term memory task (based on the Corsi blocks task; see Smythe, 2002 – see also Pickering & Gathercole, 2001) used nine identical black squares arranged randomly on card. The assessor pointed to a specified sequence of squares and then asked the student to repeat the pointing movements in the same order – the number of pointing movements increased until accurate repetition could not be maintained. This task therefore provided a visual–spatial alternative of the verbal memory assessment outlined above. A non-verbal reasoning task was included which required students to work with visual patterns and, therefore, did not involve a large amount of verbal ability, except in terms of following the instructions. Raven's Coloured Progressive Matrices (Raven, 1976), or the advanced version for adults, were used. This test involved sets of abstract patterns (shapes, colours) that formed incomplete sequences. The task was to complete the sequence by working out the sequence in the pattern and choosing a correct option from a set of options provided.

Motor performance was assessed by a bead threading task based on that used in the Dyslexia Screening Test (Fawcett & Nicolson, 1996) and a hand-movement repetition task (see Smythe, 2002). The former task required the children to thread beads on to a piece of string as quickly as possible, with the number of beads that the child could thread in 30 seconds being recorded. The hand-movement task involved the assessor making a series of movements in the air in front of the student which they then repeated in the same order – the number of movements increased until accurate repetition could not be maintained.

A creativity task was also included for the older cohorts, based on Everatt, Steffert and Smythe (1999). This task assessed non-verbal creativity by asking the student to draw as many objects as possible from a series of shapes presented on a sheet of paper. The score achieved was the number of novel items produced. A second task asked the student to think of novel uses for things (such as a pile of tin cans); again the number of novel uses referred to was used as the measure. In both cases, novel here refers to non-repetition of an object or use.

Self-concept was assessed by a self-report questionnaire completed by the students (see Part 6 on self-concept in this book), as was the anxiety scale (see Culture Free Self Esteem Inventory, Battle, 1982; Coopersmith Self Esteem Inventory, Coopersmith, 1967; State-Trait Anxiety Inventory for Children, Spieleberger, 1973). Behavioural problems were also assessed via questionnaire, this time completed by the teachers of the children in the study and which answered a series of statements about the children they were teaching that were part of the study – the older cohort of students were assessed on this scale. Statements were taken from those used in Goodman's Strengths and Difficulties Questionnaire (Goodman, 1997) and focused on conduct and hyperactivity: behaviours that can be described as negative, such as oppositional defiance, and those that focused more on impulsive behaviours, the inability to concentrate and susceptibility to distraction. Responses were scored based on manual instructions and, for present purposes, were combined for ease of presentation in the graphs: a higher score indicated more reported difficulties. In contrast, a measure of interference was included with the adult students instead of a measure of behavioural problems. This assessed the potential for distraction experienced by the student. This was based on the Stroop incongruous colour-word task (Stroop, 1935) and an incongruous coloured object task (see discussion of such tasks in Everatt, McCorquodale et al., 1999). Levels of interference have been found to be related to attention deficits (Lovoie and Charlebois, 1994; Lufi, Cohen and Parishplass, 1990). In each task, an array of colours was presented and the task was to rapidly name the colours. In the incongruent word condition, the colours were presented in the form of incongruous colour-words (e.g. the word green presented in red, blue or yellow). In the incongruent object condition, the colours were presented in the form of colour-associated objects (e.g. the sun was coloured red, green or blue). The level of colour naming interference produced by the word or object was assessed against a baseline condition in which the same colours were presented as blocks of colour (without words or objects).

Typical assessment procedures were followed. Individuals were given the tasks individually in a quiet room away from distractions. Each test session lasted no longer than 30 minutes. The test taken was based on the pace of the individual student as determined by an experienced assessor who was trained on each test prior to the assessment procedure – if the student was showing signs of stress, which may lead to errors in the assessment, the test was stopped and returned to at a later point. Procedures were explained prior to the task and examples given. Practise trials were also included to ensure understanding of the task. Help was provided in the practise trials but not in the test trials.

Overall, the pattern of difficulties presented in the graphs was consistent with the framework proposed in this book. As expected, those with dyslexia performed poorly on measures of reading and spelling. However, note the differences with age here. Whereas both primary school age cohorts showed relatedly poor performance on reading accuracy and spelling, the adults showed fewer problems with reading accuracy, but maintained difficulties in spelling. The main feature of the adult students' reading profile was one of poor levels of speed reading. These findings are consistent with the view that some aspect of literacy may develop incompletely (possibly reading speed and spelling) whereas others develop with great difficulty, since there are still clear weaknesses in reading accuracy across the primary school data. For all groups tested, though, there are also weaknesses in the phonological areas assessed, consistent with this being the main area of difficulty associated with the literacy weaknesses. In contrast, there are fewer difficulties in non-verbal visual–spatial and motor areas, as well as in areas of reasoning and creativity. When literacy is not vital for the development or assessment of a skill, then there is no reason why a student with dyslexia cannot perform as well as their peers. Measures of word knowledge, and assessments of self-concept and emotional/behavioural problems, also show the potential consequences, with weaknesses in each developing across the different cohorts. Although these are not as large as in the literacy and phonological areas, they are consistent with some individuals with dyslexia showing potential negative consequences of a lack of appropriate support. It should be noted that many of the dyslexic students in this work were (or had) received some level of educational support and hence the level of negative consequences may be larger amongst those who have not.

Differentiating dyslexia from other learning difficulties

The same sort of assessment measures can be used to distinguish those with dyslexia from those with other conditions that can influence educational outcomes. This can be seen in Figures 4.4 and 4.5). These data are based on those presented in Everatt et al. (2008), though further data have been included in these graphs and the interpretation is slightly different in this book compared to the previous paper. Note that these are selective comparisons, since we do not have the space to contrast a larger number of learning and behavioural difficulties. However, the sort of profiling procedures presented in this section can be used to separate most conditions given an understanding of the features of the condition and the right measures to assess those features. Again, what

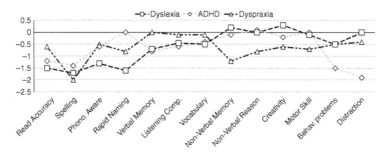

FIGURE 4.4 Comparisons of students with dyslexia, attention deficit hyperactivity disorder and dyspraxia

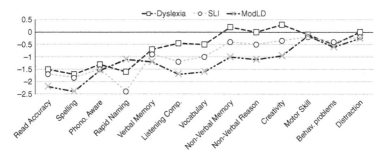

FIGURE 4.5 Comparisons of students with dyslexia, specific language impairments and moderate learning disabilities

measures to use in an assessment will depend on good practice and an understanding of the history of the difficulties: good practice may also require a change to the focus of an assessment if the initial interpretation of the area of difficulty appears wrong. No assessor can use all the measures necessary to identify all possible learning or behavioural difficulties on one assessment occasion – and extended testing on one occasion will lead to fatigue that will increase error. It is always necessary to use judgement and good practice to determine what to assess and how to evaluate the results of an assessment – and the purpose of the assessment always needs to be kept in mind (in the case of dyslexia, this is almost always to help determine ways to support the learning of the individual).

Each graph contrasts the performance of a reasonably large group of students with dyslexia against norms on the measures used: consistent with the above, the zero line is the average expected level of performance on the task, with lines above and below indicating points half a standard deviation away from the mean. In addition, Figure 4.4 includes students who have had an independent assessment of dyspraxia or ADHD, and Figure 4.5 includes students with an assessment of a specific language impairment (SLI) or a more general learning difficulty (often referred to as a moderate learning disability; ModLD in the graph). Those with SLIs are children who have had a history of difficulties with language processing – this would be more widespread than the focus on phonological weaknesses found in those with dyslexia and will impact on meaning as much as sounds. Those with a moderate learning disability would also show weaknesses in language processing, but are also likely to show poor scores on non-verbal measures as well, which will lead to generally low IQ scores: hence, any weaknesses in reading or writing are likely to be commensurate with their IQ. These two groups, therefore, will likely overlap with dyslexia in terms of language-related problems. In contrast, those with dyspraxia are likely to show problems with coordinating skills, and maybe fine or gross motor control, which may lead to overlaps with dyslexia in situations where motor skills are useful. Whereas those with ADHD are likely to show problems in learning due to a lack of attention and/or hyperactive and/or impulsive behaviours, which can lead to problem with task completion, issues of exclusion due to negative behaviours and a lack of ability to learn material that may lead to a lack of attention.

All data are from students at the end of primary school or beginning of secondary school in the UK: i.e. students aged from 10 to 13. Scores below the $z = 0$ line are indicative of weaknesses in a task compared to expected level of performance – and the more negative the z-score, the more evidence of difficulties. As can be seen in Figures 4.4 and 4.5, there was a great deal of overlap in the performance of the different groups across the measures. Of particular note was the data indicating that all five groups presented evidence of literacy difficulties compared to expected levels of ability. Although very few of the individual measures on their own showed a clear distinction between the norm for the measure and one of the five groups included in these graphs, the five groups may be differentiated based on the general profiles across all the measures. Hence, if the aim is to differentiate these different types of learning difficulties, then more than measures of literacy will be needed. Clearly, there is a need to avoid large amounts of testing, hence more experienced assessors will likely only use some tests when a problem is suspected.

Weaknesses in phonological measures were also as large for the SLI and ModLD groups as for those with dyslexia. These data were consistent with deficits in literacy (reading and spelling) and phonological processing (awareness, memory and rapid access) being related to a history of language impairments, suggesting that dyslexia may be regarded as a sub-group of children with language difficulties (Adams, 1990; Bishop & Snowling, 2004; Catts et al., 2002; Gillon, 2018; Snowling, 2000); although, children with specific language acquisition difficulties may also show problems in vocabulary, syntax and comprehension (Stackhouse & Wells, 1997). These findings suggest that the majority of students with these conditions may be best treated similarly in educational programmes designed to reduce literacy-related weaknesses due to phonological deficits. All three groups should benefit from this type of intervention.

However, the dyslexic, SLI and ModLD groups can be differentiated by measures of listening comprehension and vocabulary, as well as areas of visual–spatial processing or non-verbal ability. Although the dyslexics produced negative z-scores on both language tasks (listening comprehension and vocabulary), their performance on most of the non-verbal tasks was as good or slightly better than expected based on the norms (see also Jeffries & Everatt, 2004). These differences may provide potential for compensatory strategies in the areas of vocabulary and semantics, or non-verbal reasoning/creativity. Such compensatory strategies can be a source of strategy development for support procedures (see the intervention Part 5 of this book) or they may mask difficulties: finding alternative ways to complete a literacy task may hide difficulties with reading and spelling, for example. Hence, some assessment of potential areas of strength as well as areas of difficulty may be useful in certain assessment circumstances.

In contrast to the three groups above, the performance of the students with dyspraxia and those with ADHD was not consistently worse than the expected levels of performance on measures of phonological processing, despite evidence of problems with literacy. These findings indicate that additional difficulties can lead to poor literacy outcomes. Individuals with attention/behavioural problems have often been found to show deficits in literacy (see Barkley, 2006), although these may be less widespread than for other learning difficulties groups, particularly in non-comorbid cohorts (Ghelami, Sidhu, Jain & Tannock, 2004; Raberger & Wimmer, 2003). Similar, although individuals with Developmental Verbal Dyspraxia may show more consistent deficits in both literacy and phonological processing (e.g. Stackhouse & Snowling, 1992; Everatt & McNeill, 2014), the present data suggest that the majority of children with dyspraxia do not show consistent deficits across all areas of word literacy and phonological processing. Dyslexics and dyspraxics also differed in terms of their performance on measures of verbal versus visual–spatial measures: for example, those with dyspraxia showing more deficits in a spatial span task compared to dyslexics' more pronounced difficulties in the verbal memory task (see also Jeffries & Everatt, 2004). The dyspraxic students also produced the lowest average score on the motor task. This profile of weaknesses in visual–spatial and motor areas may be co-incidental with their poor performance in spelling. However, these data do suggest that dyslexia can be distinguished from dyspraxia and ADHD by considering weaknesses in literacy that correspond to weaknesses in a range of phonological processing tasks, which again may focus the type of intervention that would be best for these differing groups of learners.

Dyslexia across orthographies, languages and educational contexts

As the preceding pages have argued, the reading/spelling problems associated with dyslexia seem to be related to weaknesses in making links between aspects of the language (phonemes) and its written form (graphemes). However, as previously discussed, different languages/orthographies are associated with different ways of making these links between the spoken and written form. We have already considered this in terms of theories of dyslexia, but these potential differences may also need to be taken into account in assessment practices, particularly for those from multilingual backgrounds who may have learnt another language/ orthography in addition to the language of education. The issue is of particular relevance now, as multilingualism (i.e. those who have learnt to communicate to a reasonable extent in more than one language) has become more prevalent than monolingualism: there are more individuals who interact in two or more languages than individuals who can interact only in one (see Bhatia & Ritchie, 2013). A focus on English in this context is also relevant as the language has increasingly become an important international language (Crystal, 2003; Smith & Nelson, 2006), often for economic advancement. This has led to many students learning English as a second or additional language; and the same is also true of a number of other major languages around the world, such as Chinese. Furthermore, increasing numbers of peoples migrating between communities means that children speaking several languages is a common feature in education. Taking such backgrounds into account may be vital in educational and assessment contexts. The position argued in this book is that dyslexia will have a common causal factor across languages and writing systems (the phonological perspective discussed previously), but the way dyslexia manifests will be dependent on aspects of both language experience and orthography, and these potential differences in manifestation will need to be taken into account in assessment practices.

Work (both research and practice) targeting students speaking several languages is complicated by the lack of theoretical models explaining literacy development in an additional language (see Koda, 1994). Hence, whereas models of reading in a first language, and particularly in English, have provided the basis on which to predict poor reading levels among children, the same level of prediction has not been achieved for work in second or additional language reading. Obviously, if reading in a second/ additional language were identical to reading in a first language, then there will be no problem: models that predict first language reading comprehension weaknesses will be applicable to multi-language learners. However, differences in learning experiences across languages may mean that those underlying skills which have been found to predict reading in a first/only language do not develop in the same way for children from different language backgrounds. Additionally, skills may vary from predicted because a home/first language skill supports or interferes with a second language skill. Evidence for skills transfer across languages is controversial (see Antoniou, 2019; Bialystok, Majumder & Martin, 2003; Sadeghi & Everatt, 2015), but it does increase the potential difficulties of identifying a language-related difficulty since bilingual performance in assessments may not be represented by either first or second language norms. This may mean that different assessment procedures may be needed to assess those skills that are indicative of dyslexia in multilingual populations.

As discussed above, in order to compare the performance of an individual being assessed against their peers, standardised psychometric tests use norms obtained from a representative sample of individuals within the context in which the test is to be used. However, test norms are often obtained for a certain community and it is rare to find measures that have been standardised on a large number of different communities. As such, those conducting and evaluating assessments often have to use norms that are based on a population of learners that might be very different from the population that the person taking the assessment comes from. For example, a New Zealand assessor might utilise a test of reading that is normed on children in the United States. Although this may not seem too much of a problem, given that both contexts comprise primarily English first-language speakers, problems may be evident in responses that are cultural-specific – the assessor will need to be aware of such differences between answers accepted in the test manual versus those that are culturally acceptable. Malta is a good example since both Maltese and English are official languages. Although Maltese is the more widely spoken language, the lack of Maltese assessment tools means that English standardised tests have been typically used in assessments of dyslexia. When Grech (2011) investigated the performance of Maltese language dominant children on the Neale Analysis of Reading Ability (NARA; Neale, 1999), she found that the majority of these children would have reading comprehension scores approximately two years below what would be expected based on the test's norms. Given that the majority of these children were not struggling readers, these findings suggest that the English language data may not be appropriate for comparison with these Maltese children. In the context of Malta, experienced assessors are aware of this problem and take this into account in their conclusions. However, finding tools appropriate for the assessment context can be a problem for assessors. One way forward is to develop standardised measures for different language contexts (see examples in Sadeghi, Everatt & McNeill, 2014) and there is an emergent cross-language research literature that can provide the basis of a search for appropriate measures (see discussions in Everatt et al., 2013). Similarly, the growing use of international assessments to produce league tables of countries, such as the Progress in International Reading and Literacy Study (PIRLS – see www.iea.nl/pirls_2016.html), may provide the basis on which to search for a measure in another language.

Furthermore, given the view that dyslexia has the potential to manifest in different ways across languages/orthographies, different emphasis may need to be placed on different sub-components of the reading process. For example, for English assessments of reading, the accuracy of reading words may be a simple and reliable indicator of reading problems. However, in an orthography that is more transparent than English, speed (or rate) of reading might be a more important indicator of reading difficulties (see Everatt et al., 2002). Therefore, it is good practice for those conducting and interpreting assessments to understand the sub-components of the reading process and how the nature of the language/orthography used by the individual might influence the manifestations of reading problems in that individual. The simple division into word-level decoding processes and multi-word-level comprehension suggested at the beginning of this book can provide a basis on which to understand reading across language contexts (e.g. Florit & Cain, 2011). However, such differences may also influence other areas of assessment. Given that reading accuracy develops faster when learning a more transparent orthography, and that there is a reciprocal relationship between reading and phonological processing (improvements in reading can support the development of phonological skills as much as the other way round), then it is possible that phonological processing difficulties related to dyslexia will be less apparent in contexts where the child has learnt a more regular orthography. Also, if skills can transfer from one language/orthography to another, then improved phonological skills in a first language may support the development of making links between letters and sounds in a second. Although these possible links between language skills are yet to be fully understood, they do mean that further work is needed to inform assessment expectations.

Despite this, the link between phonological awareness/decoding and literacy has been found across many studies and languages (see Part 3 of this book). This potential commonality in skills across languages has the potential to be useful in assessment work. For example, Everatt et al. (2002) found that assessments of underlying phonological skills provided a distinction between individuals with dyslexia and second language learners, despite both groups showing equally poor literacy levels. However, as with assessments of first language students, a range of measures would be useful in order to identify areas of weakness – the assessment profile discussed above provides a basis on which to consider such a range. Overall, the cross-language studies and research on multilingual groups indicates that weaknesses in phonological skills, and decoding difficulties, often associated with dyslexia may be identifiable through appropriate assessment across a range of languages and additional language contexts (see also Everatt et al., 2010).

The ability to decode strings of letters (non-word, or pseudo-word, reading) has been a feature of many dyslexia assessment tools. However, experience with an orthography leads to better processing of the elements of the orthography. Hence, those with higher levels of experience (first language individuals) typically score higher than those with lower levels of experience (second/additional language individuals) on measures of non-word reading. Controlling for experience of an orthography may be necessary in an assessment process. An alternative that may be worth considering is that proposed by Elbro, Daugaard and Gellert (2012) in which individuals are given a set of orthographic patterns (letters) that they are unlikely to have experienced before and are asked to learn the sound associated with these new letters. The level of learning of these associations between letters and sounds is an indication of the level of phonological decoding skills possessed by the individual. Given that neither first nor second/additional language learners were likely to have experienced these new associations, the range of scores should be similar across both. Such a task may be a better assessment of decoding skills than a non-word reading task in the target language – although further research is necessary to determine expected levels of performance with such a test.

Given the potential usefulness of measures of phonological processing, accurate and reliable procedures for measuring phonological processing would be useful. However, again, the assessor will need to take account of their own background as well as the background of the individual they are assessing. If the assessor has an accent with which the individual being assessed is unfamiliar, then the accuracy and reliability of the responses in a phonological task may suffer. Hence, local dialects and pronunciations are factors that need to be taken into account when working within a multi-language context. Clearly, a native speaker would be a useful member of a special needs team working within a multilingual context; however, this may not be possible. Therefore, to avoid potential problems in the accuracy with which tasks are administered, computerised tools have been developed to allow assessments to be consistent and familiar in form. For example, Carson, Boustead and Gillon (2014) show how a well-designed computerised phonological awareness measure can be as predictive of phonological weaknesses as a person-administered version. This computer-based assessment has a local accent voice recorded and materials that require the child to make a touch-screen response. It can, therefore, be administered by an assessor with a completely different accent from that of the individual tested. As technology improves, varying accents in such tests may also be possible (see discussions of technology ideas in Smythe, 2010).

Studies of bilinguals versus monolinguals typically conclude that bilinguals know fewer words than their monolingual peers in the language common to the two groups (Bialystok, Luk, Peets & Yang, 2010). Therefore, when assessing children in their second or additional language, test scores that rely on vocabulary knowledge may not be as accurate as for first language speakers. This will impact on tests of vocabulary, say in a measure of IQ. Similarly, measures that include complex vocabulary in their instructions will also present problems. Assessments including measures of vocabulary and that use complex vocabulary should be avoided unless the aim of the assessment is to make evaluative conclusions about vocabulary. Obviously, assessments of language levels will often need to use materials that vary in vocabulary levels: increases in language complexity needed to assess the level of language performance often require the need to use less frequent vocabulary. A specific measure of vocabulary, though, may be useful to determine potential impacts of vocabulary levels on performance in other tasks. This may allow the assessor to use alternative measures or control for vocabulary in assessment conclusions.

Clearly, there is a need for further research in different languages/ orthographies to inform the development of appropriate literacy and literacy-related assessment procedures for use with children from multilingual backgrounds who may have dyslexia. An appreciation of language influences (including cross-language transfer effects) will lead to a better understanding of the child's performance in both language and literacy tests. If available (and practical), use of first language assessments may support an understanding of an underlying deficit (Everatt et al., 2010). Furthermore, good assessment of second language skills will be informative of problems in that second language and can form the basis of education support recommendations. Based on the perspective presented in this book and elsewhere, assessments will be influenced by the languages and orthographies experienced by the student. However, good assessment practices should still lead to appropriate support for those with dyslexia whether in their first or additional language.

5

INTERVENTION

Introduction

If dyslexia is considered as an educational problem, with difficulties that focus on the acquisition of literacy skills, then the main focus of the intervention should be educational, with a concentration on improving literacy skills. On the other hand, views that see dyslexia as more than a weakness in literacy acquisition may see intervention as requiring work in areas beyond those directly related to literacy, which may involve non-educational interventions. Clearly these differing perspectives will relate to many of the ideas that we have discussed so far about dyslexia and literacy ability, and can be categorised based on these perspectives. At one extreme, dyslexia could simply represent the lower end of a normal distribution of reading (and perhaps spelling) ability. Therefore, teaching methods will be based on the same general teaching methods that are appropriate for all children. These may need to be more intensive and may take longer to be effective, but teaching should be based on the usual 'best' methods used in schools. Hence, an effective way of teaching literacy to any child should be appropriate for the dyslexic too. In contrast, the opposite viewpoint would see dyslexics as representing a qualitatively different population of individuals, particularly in their ways of dealing with, and thinking about, reading and writing. According to this perspective, intervention methods may involve practices that differ greatly from those used with other children. Often this latter view will consider remediating the cause underlying dyslexia, and the intervention procedures may have little direct connection to the teaching of reading and writing. Under this model, a cure of the underlying problem will be implemented allowing normal levels of learning to follow. Such intervention may occur outside the school and should allow the normal teaching of reading and writing to follow. Oddly, the extreme positions of these opposing views would likely lead to the dyslexic following the same literacy teaching methods as their non-dyslexic peers: the first may require these literacy teaching methods to be more intensive, but they will be basically the same; the second requires additional remediation practices to be implemented, but once remediation has occurred, literacy teaching methods will again be the same.

Based on the framework for dyslexia presented in this book, there will need to be more of a middle ground considered. Given that dyslexia is a specific difficulty with learning to read and spell, the focus will have to be on literacy learning – and these are likely to be similar to teaching methods that are used to support all learners. However, the level of difficulty experienced by the individual as well as potential co-occurring difficulties and the consequences following feelings of failure to acquire a fundamental skill in education, will need to be taken into account. This is likely to require some special procedures to support learning that may be more specific to the needs of the individual student with dyslexia. Obviously, this range of potential issues will add to the complexity of teaching practices, but they are more likely consistent with practices implemented in school systems that aim to support students with learning difficulties. It is also likely to fit aspects of Response to Intervention procedures, which we will discuss later in this part. Hence, procedures will need to take into account the specific problems faced by a dyslexic individual, but they will still have a focus on the development of reading and writing skills, and acquisition of strategies that support literacy learning. The level of modifications may vary across individuals with dyslexia, and they may require special provisions in school (e.g. additional resources to support learning), but there is also likely to be commonalities with the teaching method used for the majority of learners, which means that learning can occur within a typical classroom environment as long as the modifications are considered carefully within that context.

A classification of intervention perspectives

Such differing perspectives on dyslexia mean that a range of different procedures has been argued as appropriate for use with dyslexic individuals; too many, in fact, to cover in this part of the book. However, we can classify them into five general standpoints – or put them into five different classrooms.

Class A. The first general idea is based on the possibility that dyslexia does not have a constitutional origin – it is due to less than optimal teaching methods. Therefore, the way to overcome the problems with reading and writing acquisition that we have assumed is dyslexia is to change the teaching methods for all children to the optimal method. This will then mean that dyslexics' literacy skills will improve and potentially be as good as their peers, since all will be given the best opportunity to learn. Basically, literacy learning difficulties are a function of poor teaching methods. This viewpoint may be best exemplified by the arguments of Solity for the use of a systematic phonics teaching programme in their Early Reading Research projects (e.g. Solity, Deavers, Kerfoot, Crane & Cannon, 2000). Obviously, changes in general education policies, and the professional development of teachers, will be vital to implement this general approach to improving teaching. This means that even if this is a potential solution, the arguments about its use or not for all learners become as much political as research/theory based. However, as we will discuss, there is a lot to be said for the sort of systematic phonics approach advocated. Whether this will be the solution for all those who would be considered to have dyslexia in the framework presented in this book is debatable, but the idea of using the best evidence-based teaching methods for all students is difficult to argue against.

Class B. A less stringent version of the above is to change the teaching methods used to the best evidence-based methods so as to improve the literacy skills of most children – this would be very close to the arguments presented in the previous paragraph. However, this may not be enough for all children and extra intervention procedures may be necessary for those with more extreme or persistent literacy acquisition problems. In terms of dyslexia, such extra intervention procedures would likely focus on the need to improve phonological processing. These interventions methods may move from group work to more intensive, possibly individualised instruction, in order to support those children with varying levels of specific deficits. This general idea is best exemplified by Response to Intervention methods (we will discuss these further below). The framework discussed in this book, focusing on specific deficits in literacy due to phonological processing weaknesses, but with additional challenges related to the potential consequences of learning difficulties and possible co-occurring difficulties, fits best within this general viewpoint. Hence, we will discuss this further below.

Class C. A third general idea is to change the teaching methods used with those with dyslexia, but base the changes on the range of methods that have been used to teach literacy to all children. The multisensory methods discussed below probably provide the clearest example of this position. Such methods can be, and often are, used with young learner. Also, consistent with the framework presented in this book, they are likely to focus on literacy learning. However, it may be seen as the main method for use with those with dyslexia, and the procedures are much more focused on the need to present information in varying forms for the dyslexic student. Hence, it may be seen as much more appropriate for the dyslexic's style of learning, whereas for the typical learner it may be used less frequently and less rigidly. These ideas may require the teacher to be specifically trained in dyslexia-support practices – there may be specific strategies that will be useful specifically for students with dyslexia. Furthermore, given that most education systems do not have the resources to train all teachers to be specialists in dyslexia, this often requires a specialist teacher to work with those with dyslexia. Given that this level of specific and specialist support can rarely occur in a classroom with the child's usual teacher, this type of intervention often requires the separation of the dyslexic student from the rest of their peers and into a special classroom, at least for classes aimed at literacy learning. This viewpoint is likely to overlap with the views in class B, in that many of the specific dyslexia methods may form part of more intensive interventions – say as part of tier 3 of a Response to Intervention model (see below).

Class D. A fourth way of thinking about interventions for those with dyslexia is to focus on the cause of the problems. This might lead to the use of a remediation method that has little to do with the teaching of literacy, but which will need to be used during literacy learning. These ideas are best exemplified by the use of a coloured overlay or tinted lenses during reading. These visual aids will have to be used during literacy lessons, but they do not change the teaching methods used in those lessons. For the education system, such methods have the advantage of requiring few (maybe no) additional resources. Often, the parents of the children with dyslexia, or the dyslexic adults themselves, may foot the costs of the visual aid. Also, apart from training to understand why a child may be wearing coloured glasses, such methods may require little extra professional development for teachers.

Class E. This has some features common with class D, in the use of a non-literacy-based remediation method to alleviate the learning problem. However, this may occur outside the literacy lesson and the normal methods of teaching literacy will be used with little change. This may be best exemplified by methods that have been argued to improve learning by remediating cerebellum deficits: those methods advocated by Dore (2006) are the most obvious case. The remediation of the deficits can take place outside school, say in a clinic for dyslexics. Once the problem is remediated, the normal teaching methods used in school will lead to improved literacy skills for the dyslexic individual. Additionally, assessment of remediation success need not be related to literacy either. If the motor skills related to cerebellum deficits have improved to 'normal' levels, then the problem is remediated and normal learning should follow. Hence, these procedures may have little or nothing to do with literacy learning or assessment at all.

The first three general procedures require a detailed understanding of how to teach literacy and how to change teaching to benefit all or some children. In addition to some understanding about how learning occurs, this relies on an understanding of much of the work that has already been covered in this book, particularly related to theories of skilled reading and literacy acquisition difficulties. Hence, the background covered in this book will form part of the subsequent discussions about different teaching/intervention methods. Similarly, discussions of specific dyslexia remediation procedures will assume some understanding of the theories of dyslexia discussed in previous parts of this book.

General learning viewpoints

Learning can be defined as the ability to store, recall and use facts, knowledge and skills. Rather than try to cover the many different views on how learning occurs (e.g. Pressley & McCormick, 1995; Woolfolk-Hoy, 2006), the present discussion will focus on some general psychological perspectives in order to provide a background to understand the differing viewpoints discussed in this part of the book. Many psychological theories of learning fall into a small number of broad camps: from behaviourist to cognitivist viewpoints, from more individualist to more social viewpoints. A behaviourist approach would argue for learning to be relatively passive, reactive and permanent, and would see a specific behaviour as an adaptive response to an individual's environment. Such behaviours can be practised, leading to a change of performance levels: i.e. a practised behaviour becomes more fluent and error-free. However, the behaviourist framework does not easily account for individual differences in learning – why, in the same context, different people learn at different rates and to different levels of competence. It also has problems with recognising that the purpose (enjoyment) of learning may affect practice/fluency in skill acquisition. The focus on the environmental conditions that lead to automatic learning can neglect specific abilities and variability across times within the individual. In contrast, cognitive theories argue for the importance of the individual's interaction with their environment. Learning occurs since the individual is goal-oriented and pays attention to what is being learnt. Information retention can occur either by rote learning, but can also involve an understanding of the concepts and processes involved in skills acquisition. This approach allows for cognitive strengths and weaknesses to impact on learning.

More combined approaches accept that both internal and environmental factors are important to the process of learning, and attempt to modify behaviour through changes to an individual's cognitions, acknowledging that learning typically occurs within a social framework and advocating that instruction is directed towards the demands of a changing environment (Bruner, 1986). Often, a more combined approach may lead to focusing on strategies for learning in different contexts. Torgesen (1982), for example, described three different kinds of interventions for children with learning difficulties, each of which utilises ideas from each of these approaches. The first concentrated on providing incentives for individuals to use abilities that they may not have been using. The second approach used orienting tasks to improve retention and therefore aid learning. The third involved teaching strategies that could be used with particular tasks or in specific contexts, as well as more general problem-solving strategies. A more cognitive approach may also focus on the idea of understanding how learning occurs, which may become a general or specific strategy for skill acquisition. For example, Deschler, Alley and Carlson's (1980) approach was to teach learning-disabled students meta-cognitive skills (to teach them how to learn), as opposed to teaching specific content areas.

Literacy teaching methods

Although there have been many methods used for the teaching of reading and writing, two general and somewhat opposing views have emerged in the literature. One argues for a focus on 'whole word' or 'look and say' methods, which treat words as whole units and does not advocate breaking words down into smaller, sound-related parts. The second is more consistent with many of the points discussed in this book and advocates for the use of some form of training of an awareness of the relationship between written forms (often individual letters or graphemes) and language sounds. Such methods are often subsumed under the term 'phonics'. These two ways of teaching reading have dominated the debate over how reading should be taught for some time (see discussions in Beech, 1985; Chall, 1967; Clark & Uhry, 1995; Smith, 1994). The phonics method is based on the idea that verbal language is a vital component in the acquisition of literacy skills. This position argues that to read text, we need to be able to translate the visual stimulus (the written word) into a verbal form, since the written word is a representation of the already, at least partially, acquired verbal language. Given that the learner will have an understanding of verbal language, written words need only to be translated into the verbal form for understanding to take place. This is basically the position that we have discussed throughout the book so far.

However, reading is more than a phonological/verbal skill. As we have discussed, most skilled readers show evidence of having developed a sight vocabulary. This may be particularly useful when reading words that do not fit with normal letter-sound translation rules, and most writing systems have irregularities of this sort. For example, 'have', 'yacht', 'pint', 'know', are all English words that are exceptions to the norm, yet all can be pronounced correctly out of context by an experienced English reader. Even more telling, homophones such as 'piece' and 'peace' or 'there' and 'their' sound alike, yet the meaning of these words can be deciphered by an experienced English reader even if those words are presented in isolation. If translating into a sound form was the only way of reading such words, then exception words may be mispronounced and the meaning of homophones would be impossible to determine out of context. Therefore, the development of a sight vocabulary is a necessary part of successful reading acquisition.

Given the argument in the preceding paragraph, it may be further argued that simply teaching sight vocabulary is all that is needed to make a skilled reader. Breaking words into bits is simply delaying the acquisition of a sight vocabulary. Teaching methods that focus on a recognition of whole words, rather than methods that may unreliably break down words, would lead to skilled readers. Methods such as 'look and say' focus on recognising a word by its whole, visual form, and would seem more appropriate to teach a sight vocabulary than methods that split the word into individual letters or groups of letters to sound them out. However, as we have seen in previous parts of this book, rejecting the importance of teaching an understanding of basic sound units within words, and the relationship of these sounds with basic written forms, goes against the wealth of evidence that shows a relationship between phonological skills and literacy level (see also Byrne & Fielding-Barnsley, 1993; Funnell & Stuart, 1995; Johnston & Watson, 2004; Torgesen, 2005). It seems unlikely that these data are all wrong. Rather, it seems likely that the two skills (literacy learning and phonological awareness) are reciprocally related in some fundamental way.

Even if the evidence for specific literacy–phonological relationships are rejected as an artefact of task performance (see Uppstad & Tønnessen, 2007), it seems to make sense practically to teach decoding skills to children as a strategy in the initial stages of reading development or as a tool for dealing with new words. Without such skills, how does a child attempt to read a word that they have not seen before? One possible solution that has been argued by the proponents of pure whole-word teaching methods is to encourage the child to use different information around the word to be read to derive the intended meaning of the author and hence the most likely meaning of an unfamiliar written item. Basically, the child is encouraged to guess at words based on context. This context may be the other words in a sentence that they do know. It may be pictures presented with the words, or a teacher's prompts that may provide evidence for the intended meaning. This view has been most clearly argued by Goodman in the 1970s who suggested that 'More simply stated, reading is a psycholinguistic guessing game. ... Efficient reading does not result from precise perception and identification of all elements, but from skill in selecting the fewest, most productive cues necessary' (Goodman 1970).

However, the use of semantic knowledge to guess at individual word meaning and pronunciation is a relatively sophisticated skill that requires a good level of verbal language to decipher meaning from context. Even in contexts where meaning can be derived from a sentence, this may be beyond most beginning readers. Often then, guesses will be based on non-textual information, such as a picture. But is diverting attention away from text really a good way to teach a child to read text? Additionally, semantic-based guesses are often inaccurate and, therefore, highly unreliable. To take an example that has been used to show how written context can support recognition of new words, what is the meaning of 'blen' in the sentence 'At dawn, the blen arose on the horizon and shone brightly'? Most adult readers would take a guess at 'blen' being another word for the sun. However, to determine this meaning, there are a lot of complex words that need to be deciphered first – and a good level of verbal knowledge will be required to make this guess. Additionally, to read 'blen' aloud, the whole-word learner will be dependent on an experienced reader to pronounce the word for them; a strategy that takes much of the independence out of acquisition. Furthermore, this is a fairly unusual sentence context. Most sentence are not so constraining in their meaning. They are more like 'The cat ran after the ...', which could be completed with a large number of individual words, such as 'rat/mouse/bird/boy/ball'; even if some are more likely than others.

Guessing based on context, therefore, is a strategy that may be more associated with poorer reading skills (see Perfetti & Roth, 1981) or less developed reading skills (e.g. Stanovich, West & Feeman, 1981) than expert reading. Indeed, those with dyslexia show more evidence of a sentence context supporting word processing compared to their non-dyslexic peers (Nation & Snowling, 1998). As we have discussed before, this is more likely a compensatory strategy – that a student with dyslexia is using context to support poor word processing. It is unlikely to be a feature of skilled word processing.

In contrast, using letter–sound (or grapheme–phoneme) correspondences provides a more accurate and reliable strategy for decoding unfamiliar words in most literacy contexts. Although there is a number of words that are inconsistent in terms of their relationship between letters and sounds, the number of these can be reduced considerably by an understanding of orthographic rules and word origins (see Joshi et al., 2008). This may be a fairly sophisticated level of understanding, but apart from high frequency exception words, many of these 'problematic' words will only be experienced when the individual is older (e.g. words such as 'psychology' – and the word 'yacht' need not be a typical word for young learners). Hence, although a sight vocabulary is necessary, so is an appreciation of the alphabetic principle which can support the understanding of the link between written text and verbal language, and provide a strategy for the independent development of a large sight vocabulary. Therefore, the most appropriate teaching methods would seem to be those that develop skills in grapheme–phoneme translation, as well as providing a basis for building a sight vocabulary, which would include an understanding of meaning as well as pronunciation.

Such a combined approach to teaching reading and spelling can be found in the work of Hatcher, Hulme and Ellis (1994). These researchers divided six and seven year old UK children showing difficulties in the acquisition of literacy into four groups. One group (call them group A) received no additional literacy tuition as part of the research study. The other three groups did received additional lessons on reading, but these varied in terms of the focus on the additional tuition. One of these groups (call them group B) experienced mainly verbal tasks (games) that focused on improving phonological awareness: the ability to identify and manipulate sounds within words. These included tasks in which the child had to identify words that rhymed, indicate the number of sounds in a word and change sounds in a word – many of the phonological processing skills that we have discussed in previous parts of this book. Another group (group C) read stories and manipulated words within text to see how this changed the meaning of the text. A final group (group D) experienced a mixture of the type of tasks/games used with the other two groups: i.e. both phonological and reading based. For this final group, the link between phonological aspects of words and their written form, as well as their meaning, would likely be clearer than for group B, and the alphabetic/phonological units within written words would be made clearer than for group C. The same amount of extra tuition was given to all three groups. However, group D showed the largest gains in single word reading and spelling and text reading.

Phonological awareness training

Consistent with the above, the most comprehensive data related to teaching literacy to those with literacy difficulties, included those diagnosed with dyslexia, has been found for the benefits of phonological training methods, particularly if performed early in the literacy learning process and linked clearly to reading (Gillon, 2018). Data from such studies typically show the similar effects to those reported by Hatcher et al. (1994): i.e. simply teaching phonological awareness as a separate skill from literacy is not as effective as when the links between phonology and literacy are made clear. The key point here is to use the phonological training strategies as part of literacy learning rather than as a separate skill taught independently of reading and spelling. This is so that the phonological skills developed are used in reading and spelling. After all, if a child is struggling with phonological processing, why would they use such a skill in reading unless they explicitly experience the benefits of using this skill when reading? From the child's perspective, teaching phonological awareness outside reading simply gives the child a skill to perform phonological tasks better.

Clearly, the dominant phonological deficit hypothesis is compatible with the benefits of phonological training on literacy ability. Put simply, given that dyslexia is related to the poor recognition of sounds within words and difficulties associating those sounds with written symbols, then an intervention that improves the ability to recognise sounds, and associate such sounds with letters, should lead to a reduction in dyslexia-related problems. However, how best to do this is still debatable. Advocates of a more synthetic approach to teaching argue for the importance of the relationship between basic sounds and letters. This will lead to focusing the intervention around phonemes, learning basic grapheme–phoneme correspondences, which can then be used to build up into words. The opposite approach is to consider how whole words possess common elements which can be used to break words down into smaller, phonological-based, units: words can be broken down into syllables and then syllables can be broken down into phonemes. Such approaches emphasise an analysis of the components of words; as such they are often referred to as analytic approaches (Uhry & Clark, 2005). The difference between the two approaches is the emphasis on building up words from basic units versus breaking down words into basic units. Although many phonics-based teaching methods will cover both, there is still an ongoing debate about which is the best starting point from which to develop an understanding of the alphabetic principle (Johnston & Watson, 2004; Solity, 2000).

Further subtle differences of viewpoint relate to how phonological processing is supposed to develop. Children can often recognise that spoken words have a certain number of syllables or that two words rhyme before they can identify a phoneme. If an awareness of syllables or rhymes (or sometimes referred to as rimes within the field) is important as part of the development of a phonological system, then strategies to support an awareness of syllables or rhymes could be argued to be an important part of a phonological-based programme. However, those who see the alphabetic principle as the vital component in developing literacy may see teaching syllable- or rhyme-level analysis as a distraction from the important process of teaching the relationship between phonemes and graphemes (see Bryant, 1998; Goswami & Bryant, 1990; Muter et al., 1998). Again, many phonological-based approaches include a mixture of strategies, but it may be that optimal learning will be found by a focus on one of the two approaches, or that the different approaches may need to be varied for different individuals based on their learning experiences.

In addition to the differences in emphasis of different phonological-based programmes, further arguments against these intervention procedures are that they can be resource-heavy, particularly in staff/student time, and that there is evidence that not all dyslexics benefit from intervention methods that focus purely on phonics training. For example, Torgesen and colleagues (see review in Torgesen, 2005) concluded from a series of relatively large studies in the USA that phonological-based literacy remediation needs to be long and intensive; this analysis suggested that 150 hours of one-to-one tuition might be needed to bring a poor reader up to average ability levels. This level of one-on-one support is rarely available in typical education systems. In addition, even with such intensive intervention, between 5 and 25 per cent of children with poor literacy skills did not show reliable gains in literacy. Interestingly, one of the main factors that predicts successful intervention is how early it occurs. Basically, the earlier the intervention, the better the chance of a positive outcome. In contrast, the later intervention is left, the harder it is for the same method to show the same level of gains. Therefore, educational interventions that are based on teaching the relationship between graphemes and phonemes should be implemented as early as possible during literacy learning to show maximum gains; and a synthetic approach seems best designed for such an early start.

However, the initial level of phonological ability of the child may influence successful outcome too. Although there is also some evidence that those with generally low levels of ability show poor intervention outcome (Wise, Ring & Olson, 1999), investigations of individual differences among intervention participants suggests that those with severe and specific deficits in phonological skills are the hardest to remediate with phonological interventions (Lundberg, 1988; Torgesen & Davis, 1996). For example, Lundberg (1988) discusses findings indicating that children in the lowest quartile on phonological awareness tasks did not show a great deal of benefit from a phonological training approach. Similarly, even though the eight-week phonological training programme used in a study by Torgesen, Morgan and Davis (1992) was effective with the majority of children, still some 30 per cent of the sample of at-risk kindergartners failed to show reliable gains in phonological awareness skills. Such intractable phonological skills are likely to lead to more problems for phonics-based intervention methods. This suggests that the more severe the phonological deficit, the harder it is to remediate, requiring more intensive and longer-term support procedures.

As we have discussed before, a final issue for the phonological deficit viewpoint, and hence potentially for phonological or phonics-based interventions, is the differences in the relationship between spoken language and written form that can be found across orthographies. However, as we have mentioned already, studies have indicated that early phonological training, together with suitable linkage to early orthography and literacy experience, improves word literacy and reduces the likelihood of literacy difficulties across a range of orthographies (see previous section on the phonological deficit viewpoints). Data also argue for methods that are appropriate for monolingual English children with dyslexia to be effective for bilingual and young English second language learners. As with first language English children, interventions that focus on phonological awareness, and that link this directly to word processing and text reading, are the most effective at improving literacy levels for the majority of children (e.g. D'Angiulli, Siegel & Maggi, 2005; Lipa & Siegel, 2007). However, second language data also argue that children who are not using English as much as a monolingual speaker may show some additional difficulties with understanding words (i.e. vocabulary acquisition). Therefore, interventions that pair phonological strategies with the development of vocabulary should be particularly useful for those individuals who may not be using English as much as others due to the regular use and acquisition of another language.

Response to intervention

Although the majority of evidence supports the view that a phonological-based intervention/teaching strategy will work for most children, alternative approaches may be more effective with some children, particularly if there is a delay in implementing the intervention or the individual has severe phonological weaknesses. A procedure for identifying who will benefit from these alternatives, therefore, would be valuable. One way to do this is to monitor progress in the intervention and vary the teaching strategy if the expected improvements are not occurring. For example, Response to Intervention procedures typically use smaller scale, group-based interventions for the majority of those with poor literacy progress and then focus more intensive remediation processes on those who are not showing improvements with the group-based work (see discussions in Bradley, Danielson & Doolittle, 2005; Burns, Appleton & Stehouwer, 2005; Fuchs, Mock, Morgan & Young, 2003; Justice, 2006; Vaughn & Fuchs, 2003). Thus, children who are showing poor scores on literacy measures (most likely within the first year or two of formal education) will be given special help within the school, most likely by a school teacher trained in using the less intensive intervention procedures. This will form part of normal school practices, and most likely will focus on basic phonological-related training procedures to attempt to improve early literacy, or word-level decoding, skills. Improvements during this intervention should then be monitored. If, after an appropriate time period (which is variable across different Response to Intervention methods), improvements have not been made, or fall below a designated threshold, then further interventions will be implemented, potentially under special educational provisions that are likely to be tailored to individual need. The idea is that the majority of children with weak literacy skills will benefit from the first level of intervention to such a degree that they do not require the more intensive intervention provided by the special provisions. The latter more resource heavy and longer interventions (as suggested by the work of Torgesen, 2005) can then be focused on those who require them, and may involve further phonological training or additional individualised support. This process can also provide an argument against those who argue that current literacy-focused interventions are too costly and time-inefficient as it has the potential to reduce the number of children requiring more intensive special education (Burns et al., 2005).

As suggested above, there is a large number of Response to Intervention methods, most of them developed within English language contexts. Most have been developed for early literacy learning contexts, though there are those that are targeted at older learners and which aim to support mathematics learning. Hence, Response to Intervention might be better looked upon as a framework for intervention methods, rather than a specific method based on a specific theory of dyslexia. Indeed, it started as a way of identifying those with dyslexia, or developmental literacy learning difficulties, by separating those with a neurological cause of their reading difficulties (dyslexia) from those who were just experiencing 'bad' teaching (Vellutino et al., 1996). The idea is that getting teachers to teach reading based on 'evidence-based' 'best practice' should solve the problem for those who are struggling simply because of 'bad' teaching: with good teaching, the majority of these children will reach appropriate curriculum levels. However, if you have a congenital or developmental disability, then simply changing the teaching to 'best practice' may not work. It is likely you will need extra support that is individualised to your needs. Hence, in its original (research) form, Response to Intervention was a way to identify 'true' dyslexics from those with a more teaching environment cause of their problems (see Vellutino et al., 1996). However, this focus has changed to a framework of monitoring and varying teaching/intervention methods to support the learning of all children – and hence it is often designed for early teaching and intervention.

A typical framework would require an initial teaching strategy that is based on the best, evidence-based teaching methods for every child in a class – often referred to as tier 1. The aim of tier 1 is for most children (e.g. 80 per cent or more of students) in a class to reach pre-subscribed levels based on the monitoring process. The levels would be related to set curriculum levels or some level of development or acquisition in a target skill or skills, which would be set at the start of the process and measured via the monitoring process. Monitoring should normally start as early as possible and be regular enough to determine when intervention should take place. Normally, the monitoring process should be within the first year of school, and there would be several points of monitoring over this first year to assess progress and determine intervention as early as possible. Therefore, the first key to success is good assessment and teaching of all children in year one of school.

The second phase (tier 2) is targeted at the rest of the learners (for example, about 20 per cent) who do not reach the pre-subscribed levels based on the monitoring process. These children will be given appropriate group-based intervention within the classroom. This again should be evidence-based, best practice. It may be provided by the classroom teacher or teacher support staff, and will be fairly intensive. There may be some flexibility in the procedures due to the group-based work, but it will be targeted enough to make sure that most of the 20 per cent of children catch up with the rest of the class in a relatively short period of time – hopefully within a school term or so. The success of this intensive group-base intervention will be determined by the majority of the children who were struggling reaching the pre-subscribed levels based on the monitoring process. Often a figure of less than 5 per cent of the students not reaching the expected levels is quoted as a target figure after the tier 2 intervention work. Although views vary as to the proportion of students with dyslexia, a figure of around 5 per cent with a more severe form of dyslexia, with about another 5 to 10 per cent with difficulties that are less severe would fit with this sort of framework. Those children with the more severe difficulties would then go through further, tier 3, intervention procedures. These are likely to involve more individual assessment and support, possibly by specialist educators or groups external to the school, and depending on the needs of the student, and such specialist interventions would be best occurring within the first year or two of school for best results – again based on the view that the earlier the intervention, the more likely the results will be positive. Although the individualised intervention phase is often described in terms of a one-off plan, ongoing monitoring of progress is needed and this may lead to variations in the education plan over time for the child. Therefore, the overall Response to Intervention model is for three tiers, but the individual methods used to monitor progress and intervene at the various tiers vary across different users/designers.

One of the advantages of a tiered approach to intervention is in terms of the reduced costs that come from a relatively small number of students needing the one most expensive type of support which is the focus of tier 3. Most should meet the pre-subscribed levels of the monitoring process through tier 1, and most in tier 2 should reach these levels through the more cost-effective group-based intensive short-term in-school support. But, obviously, this only works if tier 1 teaching and the tier 2 intervention are up to the job. Many of the specific Response to Intervention methods have developed from the phonological viewpoint, which means that the tiers of teaching and intervention will be based on the sort of methods discussed in previous sections of this part of the book, and the monitoring procedures will be focused around literacy and phonological levels. This may not be surprising, given the level of evidence for these sorts of assessment and intervention methods, and the emphasis on evidence-based practice in the Response to Intervention framework. Indeed, whichever version of Response to Intervention is used, the success of the method relies on reliable initial literacy assessment and intervention monitoring tools, as well as teachers trained in using these tools and identifying those who are not showing appropriate levels of success with the intervention. Hence, it is still not a cheap option in terms of teacher training and school resources, but it has shown good levels of effectiveness. Some have criticised many of the methods for being too phonologically based and ignoring other areas of strength and weakness that can support individual intervention identification (Fiorello, Hale & Snyder, 2006). This has led to speculation as to whether a two-level intervention process is any better than a one-off assessment followed by a targeted intervention (though see arguments in Vellutino, Scanlon, Small & Fanuele, 2006). However, this is a useful framework for implementing best practice and monitoring progress in order to determine educational plans.

Assessment–intervention profiling

The alternative one-off assessment followed by intervention process typically involves profiling the abilities of the individual to identify the best method, or series of methods, for use with an individual child. This will often involve the assessment of specific strengths and weaknesses related to educational achievement and general cognitive functioning, which will then lead to a determination of the best intervention for the individual. Such an assessment–intervention interaction model is most likely to lead to an individual education plan being devised for the child and may involve a series of different educational procedures to improve learning and educational outcome. In many ways, this may be similar to tier 3 of the Response to Intervention framework. However, with the right set of assessments and interventions, it may not be necessary to put children through small scale, group-based interventions as in the Response to Intervention framework. Rather, we go straight for the best method for the individual learner. The potential problem with this is to make the assessments cost-effective, which may require methods that can be used by general classroom teachers.

Specifically targeting the individual's cognitive strengths and weaknesses for teaching purposes is not a new approach and has often been associated with sub-typing views of dyslexia. For example, Myklebust and Johnson (1962) argued for two sub-types of dyslexia, one involving visual perceptual deficits, which would require something akin to a synthetic phonics intervention approach, and a second sub-type involving auditory processing deficits and requiring a whole-word, more visual approach to teaching. However, this view suffers from the same problems that afflict most sub-typing theories (such as sub-type overlap and unreliable sub-type identification), particularly those that argue for a visual deficit sub-type (see Everatt, 1999). There is also a lack of supporting evidence for the effectiveness of targeting teaching based on modality preference: i.e. whether visual processing is preferred over processing auditory material. For example, Robinson (1972) found the use of modality preference as an indicator of the best way to teach reading to be ineffective, even when the children included in the intervention practice showed clear differences in modality strengths. The meta-analytic study of Kavale and Forness (1987) also concluded that there was little evidence for a benefit of teaching more visual methods (e.g. look-and-say) to children with a visual preference versus phonological methods (phonics) to children with an auditory preference.

Despite negative evidence for an association between visual/auditory modality and teaching method, the assessment for intervention approach is still favoured by a large number of educationalist/assessors in the field of dyslexia; although the exact form of the approach varies. For example, Brooks and Weeks (1999) argued that profiles of strengths and weaknesses, derived from cognitive- and curriculum-based assessment procedures, and which go beyond simply verbal–visual dichotomies, can inform the best method of teaching spelling to children (see also Fiorello et al., 2006). Gaskins and Baron (1986) stressed the need for students to become aware of their particular learning characteristics and to be part of the process of developing appropriate strategies to support their own learning. This approach may suggest that these types of methods would be better seen as a way to support the individual becoming aware of how to learn something, and hence provide a basis on which to support self-regulation of learning. However, at present, the lack of evidence for these differing methods argues for caution before one is used routinely for large numbers of students.

One of the more popular ways of attempting to identify the best teaching method for a particular child is based on the idea of learning style (Entwistle, 1981; Riding & Cheema, 1991; Schmeck, 1988). The idea is to identify the learning style and then vary teaching so that the learning style is the focus – consistent with the above cases, a visual learning style will lead to materials and concepts being presented visually as much as possible, whereas a more motor style might involve a great deal of movement in the teaching method. Learning styles are proposed as general, and relatively stable, cognitive/affective characteristics of the learner and again go beyond a simple modality-based (or multisensory) viewpoint. Often procedures related to assessing learning styles have the advantage of being relatively easy for the teacher to follow and perform, making them appropriate for classroom practice (see examples in Given & Reid, 1999). However, the learning styles viewpoint suffers from the large number of differing perspectives on the type of styles found within children. There is also a lack of reliable evidence for their identification and usefulness for determining teaching procedures. Similarly, despite the large number of theoretical viewpoints that argue for the need to correspond intervention with assessment, there have been relatively few intervention studies that have considered teaching and learning methods in conjunction with an examination of the cognitive profile of the individual undergoing intervention. Of those that have, the majority has concentrated on single cases (e.g. Brooks, 1995; Broom & Doctor, 1995) and, therefore, suffer from the level of generality provided. Hence, although identification of difficulties (and possibly compensatory strengths) is useful to determine an education plan, these will likely need to be fairly wide-ranging and costly in order to determine intervention (see assessment measures discussed in Part 4). Therefore, in order to convince stakeholders of the cost-effectiveness of procedures, such wide-ranging assessments for intervention practices may need to be used only when necessary. The Response to Intervention framework, in which potentially expensive full assessments are only performed at the point when less costly group-based interventions have not worked, may be more persuasive in such circumstances. Alternatively, if identification of learning style is difficult or costly, then it might be possible to present information in ways that cover a range of styles that might support learning without the need for costly assessment procedures. For some practitioners, this is one of the advantages of multisensory learning techniques.

Multisensory learning

Given worries related to phonological training outlined above, interventions specifically developed for those with dyslexia have typically recommended more than the phonological remediation tactic. This has been particularly the case when older learners are the target of the intervention (see discussions in Brooks & Weeks, 1999). For example, positive results with older learners have been found following literacy teaching methods that have focused on visual or more whole-word/look-and-say methods. This can be explained from the same causal position as the phonological training interventions, though with a different outcome decision: i.e. dyslexics will have problems converting letters into sounds due to the phonological deficits, but should have fewer problems if we teach words as if they were exception words, and use the visual features of words to support the memory of those words and build an orthographic lexicon (or sight vocabulary). Similarly, intervention programmes that aim to train fluency in word identification have also been found to improve exception word reading among children with literacy learning difficulties, particularly those with specific naming deficits (Lovett, Steinbach & Frijters, 2000). Similar arguments can be provided for methods that focus on more semantic strategies, which may involve the use of pictures to support understanding, or the use of rhymes/songs or mnemonic strategies to support memory (McFadden, 1998; Scruggs & Mastropieri, 1990). As with the whole-word/look-and-say, or more visual analysis, methods, the idea here is to support learning through strategies that focus on the abilities of the child and circumnavigate the areas of deficit. Additional strategies may involve motor movements or the kinaesthetic senses to support recall: for example, using letter shapes that can be touched by the child, or getting the child to use exaggerated hand movements when writing a letter or word to help the child remember the shape of the letter and the spelling of the word. Alternatively, they might involve getting the child to think about the shape and movement of the mouth when pronouncing words or producing letter sounds. Combining all these sorts of strategies into one method leads to what are often referred to as 'multisensory learning'. These will include aspects of looking at words to improve visual memory, saying words to support verbal memory and using other sensory systems (motor based) to provide a range of stored representations of words.

Multisensory learning methods are some of the most popular ways of teaching literacy to children with learning difficulties, such as dyslexia. The idea of using different senses to overcome reading disabilities has been around since the work of Orton in the 1920s/1930s (see Part 2 on the history of dyslexia in this book). This long-standing history has led to a range of highly influential teaching programmes that are used widely in organisations established for the purpose of educating children with dyslexia – Orton–Gillingham, or OG, practitioners can be found in many parts of the world. The basic idea behind these methods is to involve most senses (seeing, hearing, feeling through touch, sensing movements of muscles) in the child's experience with letters and words. Auditory, visual and kinaesthetic senses are involved since information presented to more than one sense will be retained better than information presented to a single sense. Hence, the child will see a written word, hear the teacher say the word and may even feel the word if it is written in felt or raised letters. As such, aspects of the different phonological, visual and motor theories of dyslexia discussed in previous parts of this book will be incorporated in the multisensory methodology, which may be consistent with some views of dyslexia as multifaceted (see Connor, 1994). Such approaches often also include a consideration of factors such as emotional well-being and family support, but may recognise that one of the potential benefits of multisensory procedures is that they target lots of areas so that something will sink in. Hence, rather than focusing on one modality to support learning, all are incorporated so that learning can take place no matter what the child's learning preference or area of weakness.

One example of a multisensory method is Simultaneous Oral Spelling, which is a technique for teaching spelling that has been around, and further developed, since its first use in the 1930s by Stillman (see Montgomery, 1997, for a review of such techniques for teaching spellings). This type of technique includes a range of experiences/interaction with a word spelling; for example (i) the teacher writes the word while saying each letter name as it is written; (ii) the child writes the word and says each letter (name or sound) as it is written; (iii) the child says the whole word and checks against correct written form; (iv) the child traces over word or word is presented so that it can be touched/felt (e.g. word is written on sand paper). Although there are variations across different methods (see Gillingham & Stillman, 1956, and contrast with Combley, 2001 – see also discussions in Clark & Uhry, 1995), the basic format of multiple ways to interact with a word spelling are the common feature. And for many practitioners, these methods can be incredibly useful.

Oddly, despite the long history behind such multisensory methods, and their clear influence on teaching approaches used within the learning disabilities field, there is a surprising lack of formal, independent research evidence for their efficacy – independent here means evidence presented by others than those who have developed the teaching practice. Furthermore, there is a lack of a developed underlying theory for why such methods might be useful specifically for those with dyslexia. Although it is not impossible that dyslexia may be caused by multiple underlying problems (e.g. phonological, visual or motor), the 'something might work' explanation for a multisensory approach is not very scientific. However, many practitioners feel that they are useful for students with dyslexia and there are data supporting the effectiveness of at least some of the methods incorporated into multisensory learning strategies (for example, see Hulme, 1981; Joshi, Dahlgren & Boulware-Gooden, 2002; Thomson, 1988): Bryant and Bradley (1985) have advocated the use of multisensory methods with children and Guyer and Sabatino (1998) have argued for the effectiveness of multisensory methods with adult students with learning disabilities.

Several possible reasons for their usefulness could be proposed though, without needing to conclude that dyslexia must have multiple causes. One is the active interaction with learning that these methods emphasise, as well as the level of enjoyment that they can give to young learners. Another positive feature of such methods is that they allow repetition of a skill, or learning of associations between language and writing, but avoid problems that can occur when simply copying a task. A simple copying strategy might lead to problems such as off-task behaviours to alleviate boredom, or inattention due to lack of interest. For example, Everatt, Al-Sharhan, Al-Azmi, Al-Menaye and Elbeheri (2011) report data that a multisensory method for teaching spellings reduced off-task behaviour compared to a simple copying method, even though both methods involved the same number of times that a word spelling was produced.

Working memory or meta-cognitive methods

One of the explanations for the usefulness of multisensory methods is that they allow the accessing a range of senses and, therefore, provide a basis on which to store information in different forms. As we have discussed before, passive memory stores may also be influenced by working memory. This working system may provide the basis on how information is stored, how it is connected with other information (e.g. visual and phonological information) and how the stored information is used in task completion (resolving ambiguity in text comprehension). Also, as we have discussed before, this active mechanism is limited in how much it can do, particularly in terms of how much it can store for short periods of time (theories about short-term memory are consistent with these ideas about capacity limitations). If those with dyslexia are limited in short-term memory or working memory, then strategies to eliminate these limitations may improve learning.

One possible way to do this is to attempt to train rote rehearsal ability. This would involve students practising recalling series of digits, for example, over an extended period of time. For most of us, roughly seven digits can be recalled by simply rehearsing them – repeating them over and over to ourselves. After hundreds of hours of training, the number that an individual can remember over short periods of time can be increased (e.g. Ericsson, Chase & Faloon, 1980). This may reduce capacity limitations. However, one problem with this simple rehearsal learning strategy is that it is usually task specific – learning to recall digits may have little effect on recalling sets of letters, for example (see also Klingberg, 2010). Additionally, rote rehearsal is not necessarily a good way to support learning – after all, learning to read is not a simple rote learning process, unless you use rote learning to recall whole-words, and we have already discussed the evidence that more skilled reading acquisition is related to phonological-based decoding strategies than whole-word guessing strategies.

Alternative working memory training methods have looked at another possible function related to working memory, that of holding information in short-term memory for a period of time while performing another task. This may be particularly useful in making inferences about text. For example, in the phrase 'Paul went to the bank', the last word could refer to a river bank or a money bank. If the next sentence states 'He needed a loan', then we can now infer the intended meaning of 'bank'. Working memory may support this sort of processing by storing words that are ambiguous until the processing of further information provides a way of deciphering the intended meaning. Similarly, working memory may play a part in deciphering text by searching long-term stores for possible explanations of material. In the example of the 'butler did it' sentence that we considered in the first part of this book, working memory may play a part in searing memory for past examples of such phrases or by focusing processing on ideas related to past reading of crime novels. Either way, information may need to be stored for short periods while such disambiguation processes are performed. Consistent with this, complex working memory tasks often require storing of information while processing other information (see original ideas in Daneman & Carpenter, 1980). This is a more complex task than simply retaining information for short periods of time and may be important in supporting text processing and hence literacy learning.

More complex working memory training programmes, therefore, often include elements of practising storing information while processing. For example, a computerised task might include deciding if objects (a picture of a house, a horse, a car and a cow) are pictured the right-way-up or up-side-down. One of two keys on the computer might be pressed to indicate if the house is the right-way-up or up-side-down – and the same would be for the horse, car and cow pictures. Then after a number of these simple decisions (four in this example), a prompt requires the objects to be recalled in order. If the prompt is the pictures presented on the computer, then the task is to click on them in order: house, horse, car, cow, in that order. The number of objects to be recalled in order will then increase over the period of training, with increases being determined by the proportion of correct trials: if the trainee gets four items correct most of the time, then it will increase to five – if they get only a small number of trials correct with five items, then it will reduce to four. This training programme might continue until a set level of performance is reached, which is argued to be consistent with the underlying working memory processes performing such skills more effectively.

Consistent with the findings for the more simple rote rehearsal training tasks, such complete working memory training methods do lead to improvements in the tasks trained. However, a more important finding is that this trained skill can then be used in tasks related to educational achievement. Again, this is the key problem for working memory training ideas. There is still major debate about whether long periods of practice on the sort of tasks included in working memory training procedures can lead to improvements in skills such as reading and writing. Some have shown transfer of skills across different tasks, including to reading (Loosli, Buschkuehl, Perrig & Jaeggi, 2012), but others have not (Banales, Kohnen & McArthur, 2015); and the precise reason for these differences are still unknown (see the review by Schwaighofer, Fischer & Buhner, 2015), meaning that the methods are still controversial (see Sala & Gobet, 2017). Furthermore, some of the original work focused on children with attentional problems (ADHD; see Klingberg et al., 2005) rather than dyslexia, so again it may be that although some see working memory as a factor in dyslexia, the research evidence is still inconclusive.

Training in actively working with information may also relate to theories about meta-cognitive processing. Meta-cognitive training often revolves around the idea of getting the learner to actively think about how to learn something. Although this goes against some of the ideas of the working memory training approach (i.e. the passive enhancement of brain-based functioning: see Klingberg, 2010), relationships between the executive functioning aspects of working memory and meta-cognition might be expected. After all, one of the supposed functions of the executive system is goal direction, and meta-cognition will include processes of planning (see Leather, Hogh, Seiss & Everatt, 2011). Hence, some working memory training methods may lead to teaching the learner how to perform a task, rather than increasing the amount of information that can be processed efficiently. Furthermore, meta-cognitive strategies, in which students are taught how to think about performing a task, can support learning, particularly reading comprehension (e.g. McNamara, O'Reilly, Rowe, Boonthum & Ozuru, 2007; Thiede, Anderson & Therriault, 2003).

Determining the meaning of text and integrating new information across a text may be akin to the strategies used when actively questioning text during reading or when summarising the text. Study skills strategies may involve highlighting key sections of text and effective note taking, each of which could be described as a form of meta-cognitive process and an individual is taught (or learns) to perform such strategies well. As discussed before, text may be better internalised/integrated when the reader is already thinking about the subject concerned or they are familiar with the subject to some extent. Meta-cognitive strategies, such as preparing for reading by reviewing the text, thinking about the subject area and recalling pre-existing knowledge may lead to easier integration of new information into an internal mental framework. Readers taught to actively engage with a text, to review their pre-existing knowledge and to learn how to understand the structure of the texts, should be better readers. Similarly, training in monitoring text reading should also improve text comprehension. And study skills training can be as useful for adults with dyslexia as any group of students (e.g. Miles, Gilroy & Du Pre, 2007). Consistent with this, Fidler and Everatt (2012) found that meta-cognitive strategies improved the reading comprehension performance of adult students with dyslexia greater than getting the computer to read the same text for them. This sort of active engagement with text was more time-consuming than using text-to-speech computer programs, but led to better understanding and retention. This is not to argue that technology resources are not useful for those with dyslexia: tools such as text-to-speech and voice-activated software, spell-checkers and graphic organiser, are all worth considering, as is the advantage of typing rather than handwriting (see Brunswick, 2011; Smythe, 2010). Rather, the point here is that training in how to interact actively with text can be a useful strategy for those with dyslexia, and it may be particularly useful for those who are studying in adult education contexts.

Visual- and motor-related interventions

As discussed previously in this book, Orton considered that reading disabilities were due to the inappropriate dominance of the right brain hemisphere in visual word recognition tasks, which led to mirror images of the word being processed. Although this view seemed to explain some of the most noticeable features of dyslexia, such as reversal errors, it is incompatible with current understanding of the functioning of the hemispheres and does not fully explain the sort of errors produced by dyslexics (i.e. reversal errors are not mirror images). Despite this, Orton's views were influential in suggesting that reading disabilities might be due to laterality dominance problems and/or visual-related processing deficits. The brain dominance ideas have been retained in the theories of Geschwind and others (Geschwind, 1982), whereas the visual processing deficit viewpoint has been the main alternative to the phonological theories as a causal explanation of dyslexia. One viewpoint that combines both aspects, and leads to a potentially simple and cheap intervention procedure, is the eye dominance theory proposed by Stein and colleagues (see Stein, Riddell & Fowler, 1987, 1989).

Stein and colleagues found that when ocular dominance was measured under conditions in which the eyes were made to converge or diverge, most reading-able subjects showed dominance in one eye across trials, whereas reading disabled children showed alternating dominance between the left and right eye. This, Stein et al. (1989) argued, is related to an inability to converge or diverge the eyes (one aspect of eye movement control), which can lead to the individual potentially 'seeing double'. In an intervention study, a group of reading disabled children were given spectacles with a single lens covered with opaque tape. These were to be worn during reading. After a six month period of wearing these glasses, half of the children showed improvement both in vergence control and in reading; in contrast to a control group of children with reading problems who were not given the spectacles and did not improve in either vergence control or reading ability. In explaining these findings, Stein et al. (1989) argued that the poor readers had an inappropriately functioning right hemisphere leading to responses analogous to a left sided unilateral neglect (a condition associated with attentional difficulties – see Posner, Walker, Friedrick & Rafal, 1984). In order to explain why not all individuals responded to treatment, Stein et al. argued that there are individuals with underlying phonological or linguistic problems, which lead to reading problems, in addition to those with the identified visual deficits (see also Stein, 2001). Visual deficits related to eye movement control weakness have also been linked with the magnocellular pathway deficit hypothesis (Stein & Walsh, 1997), since the movements of the eyes may be controlled primarily by areas of the brain (such as the superior colliculus and the posterior parietal cortex) which receive input from the magnocellular pathway. As such, Stein and Walsh (1997) suggested that impaired magnocellular pathway functioning might destabilise binocular fixation. However, the dominant eye argument is controversial and has not been consistently found in the literature: see Goulandris et al. (1998) and Lennerstrand, Ygge and Jacobsson (1993) for contradictory findings. Also Cornelissen, Munro, Fowler and Stein (1993) found that the magnitude of vergence errors made by a group of reading-able students were as large as those found amongst dyslexics. Furthermore, Everatt, Bradshaw and Hibbard (1999) used a task comprising the identification of images in random dot stereograms that required successive and precise convergence/divergence movements and found poor vergence control to be rare amongst adult dyslexics. Hence, although eye dominance ideas may provide a simple solution, the evidence to support them is poor.

Another area of visual processing where magnocellular pathway deficits may play a vital role is in the processing of depth information. Despite the evidence suggesting that few dyslexics show deficits in this area (Everatt, Bradshaw & Hibbard, 1999), problems with processing depth have been associated with Scotopic Sensitivity Syndrome (Cotton & Evans, 1990), which has itself been considered as a feature of dyslexia, and led to the use of visual filters to improve reading amongst dyslexics (Irlen, 1991). Research has suggested that visual filters (coloured lenses that are worn, or coloured overlays that are placed over the page, when reading) may be effective for alleviating (at least some) reading difficulties (see Wilkins, 2005 for a review). However, despite the research and practitioner evidence, the rationale for the use of such visual filters lacks specification and is often contradictory. For example, there may be a requirement for a precise colour specification when prescribing and producing lenses, since a specific colour may be the cause of the problem. However, this would also suggest the need to changes lenses when moving between lighting conditions, such as between an inside area lit by a normal lightbulb and an outside area lit by the sun, since this will change the perceived colour of the same object. The diagnosis of Scotopic Sensitivity Syndrome is itself controversial (see Lopez, Yolton, Kohl, Smith & Sexerud, 1994) and it is unclear what mechanism is responsible for the hypothesised sensitivity that is the foundation of the syndrome and intervention procedure. Additionally, the typical intervention practice of allowing dyslexics to choose the filter that they feel improves their reading is open to placebo effects. Indeed, in one study that attempted to control potential placebo effects (Wilkins et al., 1994) there was a lack of reliable improvements in reading amongst the individuals provided with correct filters compared to a placebo filter condition. However, dramatic improvements have been claimed for this treatment and it is a pity that this is one of the weakest visual-based areas in terms of research and theory.

Interestingly, magnocellular pathway functioning may provide a theoretical framework for the use of coloured filters. For example, Breitmeyer and Williams (1990) present evidence that magnocellular pathway activity may be inhibited by red compared to white or green backgrounds. Also, in studies comparing red versus blue visual filters, or text presented on red versus blue screens, Lovegrove and Williams (1993) found that reading disabled students showed reduced performance in red conditions and better performance with blue. Similarly, in a study looking at the effectiveness of tinted glasses, Maclachlan, Yale and Wilkins (1993) found that those dyslexics who continued to wear tinted glasses appeared to prefer blue hues. These findings are consistent with the view that red decreases magnocellular pathway functioning, making things worse than they already are, while blue enhances magnocellular pathway activity, potentially alleviating deficits. Although these findings are appealing, they are not in accord with the current practice of allowing dyslexics to choose the coloured filter that best suits them. Under such self-selecting procedures, dyslexics sometimes select filters at the red end of the spectrum, even though this should reduce their reading ability.

Another intervention procedure that has developed from this school of thought is that related to the use of food supplements that contain appropriate levels of complex (long chain or polyunsaturated) fatty acids (see Stordy & Nicholl, 2000, for a review of this intervention procedure). The use of such supplements has been argued to improve visual processing, particularly hand–eye coordination, motion perception and the processing of low contrast visual stimuli (i.e. those areas of visual processing often associated with magnocellular pathway functioning). Supplementation is argued to be important due to the lack of these fatty acids in the modern diet and their hypothesised importance in the rapid transmission of ions across cell membranes. A lack of rapid transmission of ions may slow down processing, leading to many of the features associated with speed of processing deficits found in some children with learning difficulties. However, the deficits in fatty acid uptake described also argue for dyslexics showing the physical features of such a deficiency. These include skin and hair problems that are not typically associated with dyslexic individuals. Therefore this particular intervention procedure has yet to be shown to be appropriate for use with dyslexic individuals (see also the evidence reported by Voight et al., 2002, for a lack of efficacy of such supplementation procedures for children with behavioural difficulties).

As we have discussed before, other theories that have considered speed of processing deficits have focused on auditory (perceptual-based) processes (Tallal, Miller, Jenkins & Merzenich, 1997). The origins of this perspective can be found in work in which children with speech and language difficulties were found to be poor at discriminating sounds separated by short (millisecond) gaps. These findings located the children's problems in the area of processing rapidly changing temporal information and led to a remediation programme in which the child is trained to identify sounds rapidly (see Tallal, 2000). In this remediation, speech sounds are played to the child at a much slower speed than normally experienced. In addition, certain features in the sounds are enhanced to make them clearer to the child. The child is then trained to distinguish different auditory forms that include these changes until they reach normal accuracy levels in an identification test. When this happens, the speech forms are varied to be closer to normal and training continues until competence is reached again. This process continues until the sounds played to the children are in their normal form and training leads to normal levels of accuracy. This intervention procedure was concluded not only to improve speech processing, but also general language understanding and literacy levels. Hence, following intervention, the child can resume normal classroom practices and should learn in the typical way of all children. Although this seems a potentially valuable contribution to intervention techniques, as we have mentioned previously, the primary deficit associated with the auditory temporal processing theory has been difficult to replicate, particularly with children with specific reading difficulties (see Marshall et al., 2001; Mody et al., 1997). These findings indicate that not all children with word-level literacy problems (i.e. dyslexics) show temporal processing deficits, and such deficits are not predictive of the level of literacy problems presented by the child. As such, the intervention is a questionable technique for dyslexic children even if it is found to help children with certain types of language problems.

Despite the problems with the auditory temporal processing deficit viewpoint, such views are consistent with findings for deficits in the processing of rapidly changing visual information that have been used to argue for a transient or magnocellular deficit (e.g. Lovegrove, 1996). These commonalities have led theorists such as Stein (2001) to combine visual and auditory temporal processing deficits within the same theoretical framework. The argument is that this common/related deficit might lead to visual and/or auditory deficits and, thereby, explain the variations in difficulties evident in the visual and phonological literature described above (though see Marshall et al., 2001). Similarly, the framework may combine with perspectives that have proposed timing and/or automaticity deficits related to the activity of the cerebellum and, hence, explain a range of deficits found in the performance of dyslexic children (Fawcett & Nicolson, 2001). However, as Heath, Hogben and Clark (1999) have argued, such auditory processing deficits cannot be the unitary cause of phonological and language deficits in disabled readers. Although auditory problems may lead to language and, hence, phonological deficits, the latter occur independently of hearing difficulties: for example, the inability to translate a letter into a corresponding sound can occur without auditory processing deficits (see discussion in Snowling, 2000). In addition, some of the findings for the automaticity deficits described by Nicolson and Fawcett (1996) do not involve rapidly changing stimuli or responses that seem to involve systems similar in functioning to the magnocellular system (e.g. it is difficult to see why a bead threading task would involve a magnocellular-type system).

The motor deficits identified by Nicolson and Fawcett (1996) have instead been associated with a different intervention method. This focuses on training motor movements to develop interactions between and processes within different brain areas. In the case of the Nicolson and Fawcett work, the brain area of focus has been the cerebellum (Fawcett & Nicolson, 2001), which has been related to an intervention method proposed by Dore (2006) and originally referred to as DDAT (since it focuses on Dyslexia, Dyspraxia and Attention-deficit Treatment). In a study of the DDAT procedures by Reynolds et al. (2003), improvements in the motor movement as well as literacy skills were identified. However, this particular study has been controversial in terms of its design and conclusions (see commentaries after the Reynolds et al. (2003) paper) and despite a follow-up study, many researchers have argued that the study is too poorly designed to be able to make appropriate conclusions about the intervention's effectiveness (see Rack, Snowling, Hulme & Gibbs, 2007).

The DDAT methods seem to revolve around various motor training tasks: balancing, catching and movement activities. And such motor training methods have been around for some time (see discussions in Everatt, McNamara, Groeger & Bradshaw, 1999; Goddard, 1996). As with the previous temporal processing interventions, it has the attractive feature that the remediation is independent of school teaching; meaning that it will not disrupt conventional teaching processes. The child is remediated so that they can benefit from normal teaching methods with the rest of the class. The main problem with such motor-based interventions is that it is difficult to see how they relate to reading difficulties and spelling problems that are not due to poor hand-movement control. Some of the original intervention methods focused primarily on training gross motor movement control, such as crawling or remaining steady on a moving surface, or stimulating basic reflexive movements (McPhillips et al., 2000), and although there have been studies suggesting possible advantages from such methods, much of the evidence for such remediation techniques has been questionable, equivocal or negative (see Cratty, 1996). Hence, although such intervention procedures are used by practitioners, there are major weaknesses with both the theories and research evidence associated with these interventions.

Conclusion

The current evidence suggests that intervention methods that target literacy are the most likely to reduce the difficulties associated with dyslexia as conceptualised in this book. This would be best achieved through teaching methods or early intervention strategies (i.e. near the start of literacy learning) that focused on training the link between graphemes and phonemes. For those with phonological deficits, training in recognising sounds within words would be important, but this still needs to be linked to reading for maximum effectiveness. Although this may be costly in terms of resources, the consequences of not supporting such key skills as reading and writing for educational success may outweigh these costs, and effective Response to Intervention methods may provide the basis on which to minimise costs. As discussed previously, problems with learning to read are related to poor educational achievement, negative emotions, poor self-concept and behavioural problems (e.g. Everatt, Almurtaji, Al-Sharhan & Elbeheri, 2017; Prochnow, Tunmer & Chapman, 2013), which will influence general well-being (see McBride & Siegel, 1997). In the USA, the National Institutes of Health (NIH) have argued that dyslexia and related language learning disabilities are a major challenge to public health and societal welfare, and a meta-analysis of more than 80 studies worldwide concluded that intervention prior to experiencing the stigma of failure in school results in social and economic benefits (Beddington et al., 2008). An understanding of the processes that go into reading (and writing), as well as an understanding of skills assessment procedures should also provide a basis on which to make sure teaching and intervention methods are as effective as possible, as early as possible.

However, many practitioners in the field of dyslexia consider the need for a range of intervention methods. Although the main recommendation that comes from much of the work presented in this book is that an intervention implemented for the dyslexic should target literacy (i.e. the methods should be embedded in an understanding of the processes in literacy), there are still situations where further work/strategies may be needed and these may move beyond a focus on literacy learning itself. An obvious example may be cases where a student with dyslexia has a comorbid problem – it may be useful to deal with literacy learning and the additional difficulties as part of a whole-person approach to learning. However, this goes slightly beyond the remit of this book on dyslexia, and there is not a great deal of research that can help specify combination approaches to support procedures. A range of strategies, though, may also be important when working with older dyslexics, since many intervention methods may not be as effective for older individuals. An older learner who has experienced years of difficulties in learning, and failure in literacy classes, may need additional support, including a focus on success and re-engagement in learning, which we will cover in the final part of this book. The older learner's attempts to maintain self-esteem may also lead to the need for additional strategies. Strategies such as negating the importance of education, or distracting the class with off-task behaviours, may need to be dealt with for learning to occur with any intervention method. For example, we have discussed the idea that one of the most useful aspects of multisensory instructional methods is that they provide interesting ways to involve repetition of learning and, therefore, might reduce problems of boredom or fatigue that can counteract acquisition. However, additional strategies may be needed to reduce negative behaviours: for example, in previous research we have combined the teaching of relatively difficult spellings with methods aimed at self-regulating behaviour and relaxation techniques to reduce hyperactivity (see Everatt et al., 2011), and such targeted combined methods seem to be better at reducing off-task behaviours as well as improving spelling performance in students with a history of dyslexia-related difficulties. We will continue this discussion in the final part of this book, where we discuss how feelings and thoughts about the self may impact on literacy learning and intervention practices. This will provide a detailed example of why these multi-method approaches may need to be considered and how they might be conceptualised.

6
SELF-CONCEPT AND DYSLEXIA

Introduction

As we have discussed before, the difficulties that children with dyslexia experience in terms of their reading and writing and the consequences of those difficulties on academic achievement can be wide-ranging. There is growing acknowledgement of underlying factors within the wider educational context that influence academic outcomes. Emotional response to learning and appropriate behaviour during learning are two factors that are often identified as playing a key role in the academic achievement of students. However, the psychosocial development of the individual in terms of their sense of self can also influence the engagement of individuals in teaching and learning sequences, which in turn can influence not only academic achievement but also subsequent psychosocial development. In this part of the book, we will focus on three constructs of psychosocial development; self-esteem and self-concept, self-efficacy, and resilience. Notions around self-esteem and self-concept are often emphasised within educational contexts and low self-esteem is commonly associated with individuals with dyslexia. Self-efficacy has been identified as an influential variable in educational achievement, and dyslexia can be viewed as a risk factor for an individual in terms of academic achievement and wider development, making resilience an influential construct to explore.

Defining self-esteem

Self-esteem has become inextricably linked to one's everyday life (Harter, 2012). The multiple manifestations of self-esteem that have emerged in different fields, such as education and medicine, influence conceptions of self-esteem, meaning that understanding self-esteem is complex and that conceptualisation varies. Early conceptualisations of self-esteem were used to explain the impetus driving an individual's behaviour across contexts and was known as global self-esteem (Byrne, 1984). Later conceptualisations of self-esteem, however, moved away from the behavioural perspective to focus more on the role of affect (emotion) and cognition in the development of self-esteem (Rosenberg, Schoenbach, Schooler & Rosenberg, 1995). Key to self-esteem are the perceptions that one holds of oneself, which are derived from one's attitudes, emotions and knowledge (Byrne, 1984). The perceptions that one holds of oneself develop via the evaluations that an individual makes between two different aspects of one's self (Humphrey, 2004; Robins, Hendin & Trzesniewski, 2001). The first aspect includes the current perceptions that an individual holds regarding themselves. The second aspect includes the ideal self; the aspirations regarding how an individual would like to be. Perceptions develop as an individual experiences and interprets their social world. The social underpinning of self-esteem means that interactions are influential to self-esteem (via an individual's evaluations) but also that evaluations made within social interactions lead to individual differences within the development of self-esteem.

While current perceptions and the ideal self are important to understanding self-esteem, the value that an individual places on an outcome of an experience, such as assessment outcomes or feedback from social interactions, is also influential. The perceptions that an individual holds about themselves can be positive or negative, but the influence of those perceptions on self-esteem is dependent upon the value that the individual has placed on the outcome (Park & Crocker, 2013). This may be one reason why there is variability in research relating to the association between self-esteem and dyslexia, as well as the existence and importance of individual differences in the development and structure of self-esteem. Early research led self-esteem to be viewed as a singular domain of global self-esteem. According to Morris Rosenberg (1979), a global construct of self-esteem comprised specific domains of self-esteem that reflected the differential value that individuals placed on outcomes. Early research supported the global construct by finding large correlations between global self-esteem and constituent domains (Marsh & O'Mara, 2008). Thus, a global structure of self-esteem was viewed as being representative of its internal domains. However, later research (Marsh, Craven & Debus, 1998; Marsh & Craven, 2006) argued that findings supporting a global construct were due to research methodology, which was dominated by statistical analyses and the use of measures that aligned to a global perspective. Advanced statistical analysis, including structural equation modelling, by Marsh and colleagues found lower correlations within the internal structure of self-esteem. They argued that this variance meant that a global construct of self-esteem was insufficient to explain its constituent domains (Marsh & O'Mara, 2008) and that a multi-dimensional model was fundamental to understanding self-esteem (Marsh & Martin, 2011).

A multi-dimensional model of self-esteem

A multi-dimensional model of self-esteem posits that the internal structure of self-esteem comprises multiple domains, such as academic, physical, social and emotional. There are also sub-domains within domains, for example, reading and mathematics are sub-domains of the academic domain. Within a multi-dimensional model, the global component is usually referred to as self-esteem, while domains and sub-domains are often referred to as self-concept. For consistency the remainder of this part of the book refers to self-esteem for the global component and self-concept when addressing the domains and sub-domains. The model acknowledges the role of global self-esteem, but also recognises that an individual can hold different attitudes about different aspects of their self (Rosenberg et al., 1995). The multi-dimensional model of self-esteem posits that global self-esteem sits at the apex, with differentiation into specific domains and sub-domains of self-concept. See Figure 6.1.

One key debate in the use of the multi-dimensional model of self-esteem has been whether development occurs in a top-down trajectory

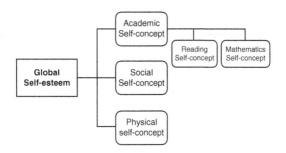

FIGURE 6.1 A simple model of self-esteem

from global self-esteem into domains and sub-domains or in a bottom-up trajectory from sub-domains and domains to a global domain. Much of this debate was due to different views around the age at which children can differentiate between experiences with specificity. Shavelson, Hubner and Stanton (1976) argued that the ability of young children to differentiate between experiences was precluded by a lack of cognitive understanding that only developed over time via experiences. This supported a top-down trajectory for the development of self-esteem. However, they did recognise the situational specificity of self-esteem, which supported the notion that young children are able to make evaluative judgements within different contexts. This has important implications because it suggested that the development of domains and sub-domains of self-concept may occur at an early age and variation is likely to exist between these domains.

The multi-dimensional model of self-esteem in children in Grades 1 to 3 has been more recently demonstrated in research (Ehm, Lindberg & Hasselhorn, 2014). There may, however, be differences in relation to the influence of age on increased differentiation (Marsh, 1989). Like Shavelson and colleagues, Harter (2006) argued that children lacked cognitive ability in terms of being able to integrate different aspects of themselves. As such, Harter viewed that global self-esteem did not develop until late childhood, when cognition became more influential, thus, supporting the development of self-esteem from a bottom-up trajectory. The influence of gender on self-esteem was also used to support a bottom-up trajectory because few gender differences have been found in studies involving younger students (Badayai & Ismail, 2012) but have been found to emerge during adolescence within domains and sub-domains (Kling, Shibley Hyde, Showers & Buswell, 1999).

One final way to view the development of self-esteem is that the relationships between domains and sub-domains are reciprocal in nature, thus, incorporating both top-down and bottom-up effects. As mentioned, a hierarchical nature of self-esteem is arguable due to findings that associations between domains of self-concept were weak, at times close to zero (Marsh & Craven, 2006). Furthermore, associations that would support a hierarchical structure demonstrated variations with age. For example, Marsh and Shavelson (1985) found that between pre- and late adolescence the hierarchical structure had all but disappeared, while finding support for the multi-dimensional nature of self-esteem. Marsh et al. (1998) found support for a model that included a specific academic domain in a sample of children ranging from kindergarten to Grade 2, although they did note that children discriminated differently from older children, which lent support for a developmental model of self-esteem.

Academic self-concept and education

Self-esteem has often been associated with the educational environment. However, to gain an understanding of self-esteem and dyslexia within an educational context, it is important to focus on academic self-concept, rather than global self-esteem. A focus on global self-esteem may result in a distorted view of self-esteem due to the variability that has been identified between domains of self-esteem (Marsh & O'Mara, 2008). Research has found clear support for the principle of matching specificity in gaining a clear understanding of self-esteem within the educational context. Byrne (1984) and Marsh and Craven (2006) found that academic outcomes were more closely correlated to the associated academic domain (i.e. reading or mathematics) of self-concept rather than non-academic sub-domains and global self-esteem. A multi-dimensional model of self-esteem allows researchers to examine and develop greater understandings about self-esteem in individuals with learning difficulties, which includes dyslexia (Cosden, Elliott, Noble & Kelemen, 1999). This is especially important given that research tends to suggest that students with learning difficulties hold lower levels of self-concept in comparison to students without learning difficulties.

Variation exists in terms of how academic self-concept is conceptualised. This variation appears to be related to the context in which academic self-concept is viewed. According to Marsh and Craven (1997), academic self-concept develops within the wider school context. Others view academic self-concept as developing within a narrower academic domain (Trautwein, Lüdtke, Köller & Baumert, 2006). According to Chapman and Tunmer (2003) academic self-concept is closely associated with the perceptions of one's self in relation to learning tasks. This supports a skills development model that posits that academic self-concept develops consequentially to academic achievement (outcomes of learning tasks). In contrast, the self-enhancement model posits that academic self-concept is a contributing factor to academic achievement (Guay, Ratelle, Roy & Litalien, 2010). While early research (Calsyn & Kenny, 1977) supported the skills development model, support currently lends towards a reciprocal association between academic self-concept and achievement (Marsh & Craven, 2006).

Declines in self-esteem in children have been noted to occur around seven to eight years of age (Chapman, 1988). This is thought to occur as expectations around one's abilities and achievement move from being idealistic to realistic in nature, as children become more cognisant of their actual abilities (Chapman, 1988). Within education, this is often in response to feedback and achievement criteria (Chapman, 1988). Children with learning difficulties, however, have often been found to hold lower levels of academic concept in comparison to their typically performing peers (Chapman, 1988). Children who have severe learning difficulties or who experience difficulties in multiple areas of learning may experience declines that are greater and more negative. These declines are largely attributed to compounding experiences of failure within the learning environment which influence the evaluations that children make about themselves. The accumulation of failure can also go beyond decreases in academic self-concept to have spinoff effects in other areas, such as in developing peer relationships (Chapman, 1988).

There is evidence to suggest that declines in academic self-concept may occur earlier than traditionally thought, in students who experience difficulties in their literacy development. Casserly (2013) examined the socio-emotional effects of students with dyslexia who attended special reading classes in Ireland. She found that 86 per cent of parents perceived adverse changes to their child's behaviour at the commencement of formal literacy education between the ages of six and seven. Chapman, Tunmer and Prochnow (2000) found that negative attitudes could emerge in children as early as six to eight weeks following the beginning of formal education at five years of age. Anderson and Meier-Hedde (2011) found that the introduction of phonemes (sounds) and graphemes (letters) and subsequent lower levels of achievement to be key to declines in self-concept. Thus, the variation that has been identified in research in relation to declines in self-concept in young children may be associated to literacy instruction rather than the commencement of formal schooling.

The relationship that exists between academic achievement and academic self-concept also means that as one reciprocates with the other, there may be additional decreases to both academic achievement and academic self-concept. This can be illustrated via expectancy-value theory, which hypothesises that prior experiences of failure within the learning environment and feedback influences academic self-concept, as well as future achievement via its influence on factors, such as task choice and effort investment (Trautwein et al., 2006). Students may also be more likely to demonstrate behaviours that reinforce existing expectations. As such, experiences of failure for students with dyslexia may result in students acting in ways that reinforce their negative experiences (Burden & Burdett, 2005).

However, research has also identified that the association between academic self-concept and academic achievement can be influenced by variables that contribute to explaining the association between academic self-concept and academic achievement. In her study of students with dyslexia and self-esteem, Casserly (2013) found that the type of educational environment in which a student was situated could positively or negatively influence the association between academic achievement and self-esteem. Retrospective research of first year university graduate students with dyslexia by Gibson and Kendall (2010) found that multiple factors influenced self-esteem in educational settings. These factors included educational placement (i.e. streamed or ability classes), promotion or restriction of course choice, the use of reductive texts or learning material, teaching styles, teacher attitudes towards learners and peer relationships. In particular, Gibson and Kendall found that the influence of negative experiences on respondents was variable and did not always lead to low self-concept or low academic achievement. Evidence of low self-esteem was also not evident in a study carried out by Burden and Burdett (2005). Their research included males with dyslexia between 11 and 16 years of age who attended a residential school for boys with dyslexia. They found that students viewed themselves positively, held positive attitudes towards their learning and viewed themselves as capable in their learning. However, it is plausible that variables within the school environment were influential to the positive perceptions held by students. This is because fundamental to the school's philosophy was notions of excellence, high achievement and personal responsibility for success and failure. Overall these findings highlight the idea that the influence of dyslexia on students' developing self-concept is variable and that aforementioned factors that include placement, as well as teachers and peers, can influence the development of self-concept and academic achievement for these students.

Another influential variable in the association between academic self-concept and academic achievement is the value that a student with dyslexia places on academic achievement. Research by Humphrey, Charlton and Newton (2004), which included high and low achieving Year 7 students, found significant differences between the groups in terms of the value placed on academic competence. Low achieving students attributed greater value to academic competence than high achieving students; however, academic competence was significantly more likely to negatively contribute to the development of self-concept for low achieving students, in comparison to higher achieving students. Humphrey et al. (2004) suggested that academic competence was likely to be a negative source due to experiences of failure for low achieving students.

While the sample in the research by Humphrey et al. (2004) allocated a high value on academic competence, a turning point may occur for a low achieving student; whereby, experiences of failure lead an individual to devalue academic competence. Devaluation appears to occur as an individual re-organises their evaluations of experiences within specific domains and sub-domains to protect their self-concept. According to Robinson and Tayler (1991) students can respond to low levels of academic achievement by placing value on non-academic pursuits that are potentially rewarding but which is counter to the academic context and, therefore, academic achievement. In a similar vein but without the counter-culture, Harter (1993) argues that students may seek to maintain self-concept by reducing the value placed on specific domains in order to protect themselves against threats to academic achievement and increasing investment in non-academic areas where rewards are more likely, such as physical ability or social relationships. It is less clear when these turning points or self-protection strategies are enacted. As aforementioned, Humphries and colleagues found that academic competence held significant importance to their sample of low achieving Year 7 (Grade 6) students. In contrast, Alves-Martins, Peixoto, Gouveia-Pereira, Amaral and Pedro (2002) reported that low achieving students in Grades 7 to 9 placed less value on scholastic competence than high achieving students. Alves-Martins et al. (2002) found that students in Grade 7 placed greater value on academic competence than students in Grades 8 and 9 and that differences in self-concept scores between high and low achievers had disappeared by the higher grades. This suggests that self-protection strategies may be enacted as students enter adolescence; however, according to Humphrey et al. (2004), it may also be related to entry into secondary-level education.

Self-efficacy

Self-efficacy has a comparatively shorter existence within the research literature than self-esteem/self-concept. One reason for this is that human behaviour and thus behavioural change has historically been viewed as being affected by performance outcomes, underpinned by biological or environmental forces, as seen in operant and classical conditioning theories (Bandura, 1977; Pajares & Schunk, 2001). However, Bandura argued that behavioural change was mediated by cognitive mechanisms, thus, giving rise to the importance of self-processes in the self-regulation of behaviour and the role of self-perceptions in controlling and achieving outcomes (Pajares & Schunk, 2001). Self-efficacy is defined as an individual's judgement of their performance capabilities within a specific task (Bandura, 1997; Bong & Skaalvik, 2003; Zimmerman, 2000).

Self-efficacy is not concerned about what skills and abilities an individual holds but rather judgements of capabilities around the execution of specific courses of action or tasks (Zimmerman, 2000). Self-esteem and self-efficacy have often been treated synonymously, usually under the guise of global self-esteem (Bong & Skaalvik, 2003). While self-esteem and self-efficacy are associated, the strength of the relationship between the two appears to be influenced by the activity and the value attributed to the activity by the individual. According to Bandura (1997), an individual is more likely to attribute value to developing one's abilities within activities that foster their self-esteem. Thus, he notes that a higher association between self-esteem and self-efficacy is likely to be found in activities that individuals attribute higher value to. Given that individuals function differently within contexts and situations and have differences in their capabilities, individual differences are also inherent in self-efficacy.

Self-efficacy develops through four primary sources; enactive mastery experiences, vicarious learning, verbal persuasion and physiological or psychological feedback (Bandura, 1997). Of the four sources the most influential is enactive mastery experiences because these experiences provide the most realistic evidence of what is required for an individual to succeed (Bandura, 1997). Successful experiences promote the development of self-efficacy, with unsuccessful experiences undermining development. Undermining is more likely to occur if self-efficacious beliefs are not firmly established; however, difficult experiences are also instrumental in developing self-efficacy. This is because effort, which includes perseverance, contributes to the development of resilient self-efficacy (Bandura, 1997). Difficult experiences also enable individuals to fine-tune their existing capabilities, allowing them to control events and achieve success, although this requires the synthesis of cognitive, behavioural and self-regulation capabilities. Not all experiences provide mastery information for individuals. Non-enactive experiences are those that do not reveal information that would contribute to developing self-efficacy (Bandura, 1997). However, these experiences still have the capacity to influence developing self-efficacy. This is because non-enactive and enactive experiences can result in contradictory outcomes, the interpretation of which can be integrated into new self-efficacy beliefs that influence subsequent experiences (Bandura, 1997). Thus, Bandura viewed self-efficacy as both the product and construct of experiences, which suggests that the development of self-efficacy is reciprocal in nature.

Activities do not always provide information that enable evaluations of capabilities to occur, which means that vicarious experiences can also be influential. Vicarious experiences provide an individual with models of success, which are then used to evaluate their capabilities (Bandura, 1997), even in the absence of one's own performance (Oettingen, 1995). Vicarious learning can extend beyond external models to include self-modelling and internal modelling where one's self-efficacy beliefs are influenced by their observations of their own accomplishments (Bandura, 1997). In some cases vicarious learning can supersede enactive experiences because modelling can alter one's perceptions of confidence, which is then applied to experiences (Bandura, 1997). Both the strength of the model (for social comparison) and the task at hand appear to influence the effect of the vicarious experiences on an individual's self-efficacy beliefs. Individuals tend to use models as referents when alignment exists between the tasks being completed. Greater alignment between the individual and model also results in a greater influence on self-efficacy beliefs (Bandura, 1997; Braaksma, Rijlaarsdam & Van den Bergh, 2002). Modelling is more influential if the individuals' understanding of their capabilities is less fixed or if, over time, experiences result in variable success and failure for the individual.

Verbal persuasion most commonly occurs for individuals via evaluative feedback around skill and effort (Bandura, 1997). The influence of verbal persuasion is associated with its effect on an individual's effort and perseverance within a task. The effectiveness of verbal persuasion is associated with the degree of realism identified within the statements given (Bandura, 1997; Chan & Lam, 2008). While the effect of persuasive statements is often short-lived, they can also negatively affect self-efficacy beliefs if they influence beliefs to an unrealistic level. This, in turn, results in failure for the individual, while discrediting the persuader. Persuasive statements can also be indirect, often conveying notions of negative social comparisons. With regard to the fourth source of self-efficacy, adverse and non-adverse physiological and psychological states act as indicators of self-efficacy for individuals. Expectations of success are more likely if an individual does not experience an adverse state of arousal, which can be seen as a sign of inefficacy (Bandura, 1997).

Self-efficacy and education

Given that self-efficacy beliefs influence one's task choice, engagement, effort expended and perseverance, it is not surprising that self-efficacy has been implicated in educational contexts. Self-efficacy is an influential factor in academic achievement, both directly and indirectly via its mediating effect on such variables as motivation (Lee & Jonson-Reid, 2016; Pajares & Schunk, 2001). An early meta-analysis by Multon, Brown and Lent (1991) found that the association between self-efficacy and academic outcomes was lower for elementary (primary) school children in comparison to high school and college students. The meta-analysis highlighted that the effect size was positive and stronger for context-specific variables in comparison to standardised measures (Pajares & Schunk, 2001). This is likely why research has tended to reflect a multi-dimensional construct of self-efficacy, including at domain level (i.e. academic, emotional and social) and sub-domain level (i.e. reading, writing and mathematics). See Figure 6.2.

Academic self-efficacy and beyond in education

Academic self-efficacy refers to the evaluation that an individual makes regarding their ability to achieve success within specific academic tasks (Bong & Skaalvik, 2003). While research relating to self-efficacy has grown given its association to academic achievement, debate exists regarding how they are associated. This debate appears to relate to the variables that mediate the association between academic self-efficacy

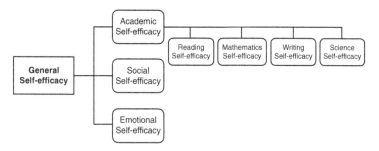

FIGURE 6.2 A simple model of self-efficacy

and academic achievement. According to Bandura (1997), Pajares (1996) and Zimmerman (2000) the association between academic self-efficacy and academic achievement is mediated by mechanisms such as motivation and self-regulation. However, others, such as Linnenbrink and Pintrich (2003) contend that the association is mediated by behavioural, motivational and cognitive engagement. Mediating variables may be influenced by developmental trajectories. Lee and Jonson-Reid (2016) found that motivational engagement, which can be influenced by external factors, was more influential than behavioural engagement in a sample of third grade students. Cognitive abilities may also be less influential in mediating the association between academic self-efficacy and academic achievement in young children because these abilities are lesser developed.

While research literature has supported the association between self-efficacy and academic achievement in older children, adolescents and young adults (Lee & Jonson-Reid, 2016), this association is less clear in younger children. One reason for the debate centres on the age at which children are developmentally capable of making decisions about their capabilities that are objective (Lee & Jonson-Reid, 2016). Recent research (Lee & Jonson-Reid, 2016; Liew, McTigue, Barrois & Hughes, 2008; Wilson & Trainin, 2007) has found that young children are able to differentiate between sub-domains of self-efficacy that included reading, writing and spelling, as well as identifying an association between literacy achievement and self-efficacy. Furthermore, not only was differentiation possible as young as Grade 1, but levels of self-efficacy differed between sub-domains. Wilson and Trainin (2007) found that reading self-efficacy held the lowest rating, while differences between spelling and writing self-efficacy were statistically significant. They suggested that this finding reflected a social-interactionist model whereby increasingly realistic self-efficacy beliefs were being developed in these students, due to teacher feedback and social comparisons within learning tasks. This was most likely to have occurred in reading because this is where students received the most feedback and engaged in social comparison, usually within a group setting that is formed using ability criteria.

Such findings have important implications for education because of how influential self-efficacy is future learning, through the tasks that students choose to engage in, the effort students expend during activities, as well as the perseverance students demonstrate during difficult tasks, which in turn influence academic achievement. Wilson and Trainin (2007) also found that higher ratings in these sub-domains were associated with higher levels of achievement. These associations appear not to be restricted to given grade levels. Research by Liew et al. (2008) identified associations between academic self-efficacy and reading and maths scores at Time 1 (Year 1) and Time 2 (one year later). Academic self-efficacy at Time 2 was also positively correlated with Time 3 scores on reading and maths, after controlling for age, gender, IQ, ethnicity and socioeconomic status. This supports the notion that self-efficacy may be generalised across domains (Bandura, 1997). Findings around generalisation were also identified in older students. In a study of Grade 4 and 5 students in Sweden, Jungert, Hesser and Träff (2014) found an association between mathematics self-efficacy and English self-efficacy. They suggested that generalisations across domains and sub-domains may be influenced by levels of achievement. However, it could also be argued that factors within the educational context are also influential, for example, the presence of literacy within the mathematical domain, as well as scenarios such as ability or mixed ability grouping.

Resilience

The concept of resilience first emerged within the area of psychopathology when researchers found that children who experienced a variety of negative circumstances, which put them at risk for maladaptation, demonstrated positive adjustment that continued into adulthood (Luthar & Cicchetti, 2000; Masten et al., 1999). Subsequent research focused on individuals who demonstrated resilient qualities while being at-risk for maladaptation. These qualities, which included temperament, self-esteem and self-efficacy led to resilience being viewed as a trait-like construct (Fletcher & Sarkar, 2013). These personal qualities were deemed to be protective because they were present in individuals relatively unaffected by higher levels of risk, although this tended to lead to differential treatment for individuals, both at the familial and community level (Boyden & Mann, 2005). An important issue, however, was that these traits were evident beyond individuals experiencing risk and did not presuppose individuals to adversity (Luthar, Cicchetti & Becker, 2000). The trait-like construct also failed to recognise the role that contextual and temporal factors played in affecting the severity of adversity experienced by individuals.

A second way that resilience can be conceptualised is as a process, which develops in an individual over time that enables the individual to cope with or overcome significant adversity (Cummings, Davies & Campbell, 2002; Ofiesh & Mather, 2012; Schoon, 2006; Werner, 2000). This conceptualisation recognises resilience as a multi-faceted construct that is underpinned by two key characteristics; the exposure to risk or adversity by an individual, and the experience of positive adaptation by an individual experiencing adversity (Fletcher & Sarkar, 2013). It also recognises the temporal and contextual factors that influence risk and adaptation (Fletcher & Sarkar, 2013) and that factors interact differentially to affect adaptation and, as such, the development of resilience (Rutter, 1987).

Debate exists around what constitutes risk or adversity. Luthar and Cicchetti (2000) view risk as comprising negative experiences, which are related to difficulties in individual adjustment. Underpinning this perspective is the relationship between adversity and the adjustment difficulties, which Luthar and Cicchetti (2000) determined by applying statistical significance. This meant that determining adversity was threshold-dependent (Luthar & Cicchetti, 2000). However, threshold-dependency fails to acknowledge the influence of factors, and individual differences, on outcomes of adaptation or maladaptation (Denston, 2016). Others, such as Davis, Luecken and Lemery-Chalfant (2009) view that risk is part of everyday life and that positive adaptation can be viewed in stressors that are experienced on a daily basis, which may also be chronic in nature. Disagreement tends to lie in whether the mechanisms that foster adaptation are the same for common daily stressors (similar to the argument around traits) given that exposure to daily stressors does not presuppose maladaptation by an individual (Fletcher & Sarkar, 2013).

Notions around adaptation are also debated within the research literature on resilience. Adaptation is primarily viewed as either meeting development tasks or levels of competence; however, operationalising adaptation must account for the risk factor at hand and the context in which it is occurring (Luthar, Lyman & Crossman, 2014). Boyden and Mann (2005) also argue that one must account for the individual themselves and their agentic nature, which is situated at any given point in time within a social and cultural context. Social and cultural contexts are very influential because contexts hold their own perceptions relating to both adaptation and risk and this can influence the situations that individuals can be exposed to. Thus, risk and adaptability can be different for individuals, which suggests that understanding resilience in individuals is highly complex and should be viewed through multiple lenses. Conceptions around adaptability are also affected by whether it is viewed as occurring within a single domain related to the area of risk, for example, within the area of literacy for individuals with dyslexia, or whether adaptability is viewed more widely across domains. According to Luthar et al. (2014) adaptation within a single domain is not indicative of overall functioning, while Vanderbilt-Adriance and Shaw (2008) noted that identifying positives outcomes was more probable if adaptability was restricted to a single domain. While a narrow focus may be advantageous to determining situational adaptability, it fails to identify or understand how factors can interact to affect how an individual functions overall.

Resilience and education

The focus on resilience within education has increased over the last three decades. According to Brooks (2006) this is partly due to difficulties around implementing policies involving resilience in other, non-school, contexts, such as the family and communities. Doll and Lyon (1998) argued that the focus of resilience in education has resulted in faddism with the emergence of programmes that are often non-substantiated by research. The educational context is where differences in the notion of adaptation are applicable. One can view the educational context as where the focus of risk could be placed on the development of competencies within learning, social or personal development (Doll & Lyon, 1998), however, the educational context is one where risk becomes exceedingly complex as multiple risk factors can present themselves within this context, including poverty, abuse, employment and mental health issues. As Doll and Lyon (1998) noted, these risk factors often fall outside the control of the child and can result in an accumulation of risk for the individual. Risk factors also exist within the educational context. The emergence of these risk factors may be due to the importance placed on educational achievement, which is typically viewed as fundamental to a child becoming a functional and therefore contributing member of society. Researchers, such as Forrest-Bank and Jenson (2015) found that school variables were associated with positive adaptation, over familial or community variables. Furthermore, their research also found that adaptability within the educational context during childhood has latent effects during adulthood, thus, suggesting that facilitating resilience in students is of critical importance.

There is no doubt that success in literacy is viewed as being of fundamental importance to education. Children with learning difficulties, which include dyslexia, have been of interest to researchers because learning difficulties can be viewed as a risk factor for maladaptation both in childhood and in adulthood. In addition, learning difficulties are viewed as being chronic, and often unrelenting, in nature. Difficulties in literacy development not only poses risk for adaptation within the literacy area but also within the wider learning context, due to the plethora of activities that involve literacy skills within other curriculum areas that can result in failure for the student. Research into learning difficulties has also identified spinoff effects, such as in task engagement, behavioural and/or emotional difficulties, and peer relationships that extend beyond the learning difficulty, meaning that children with learning difficulties may be at greater risk for maladaptation.

Developing resilience may also be affected by the type of learning difficulty and the severity of the learning difficulty being experienced by the individual (Ofiesh & Mather, 2012). Ofiesh and Mather (2012) state that specificity in relation to the learning difficulty is important because it provides a descriptor for treatment while also conveying the notion that the difficulty is specific in nature, rather than being global. While this perspective emphasises specificity that is advantageous for intervention purposes, it is also arguable that it is fundamental to understand how the learning difficulty influences overall functioning in order to understand the development of resilience in students with learning difficulties, including dyslexia. Literature suggests that developing skills, such as problem-solving, time management and relationships skills are influential to the development of resilience (Condly, 2006). Ofiesh and Mather (2012) observed that resilience in a student with learning difficulties emerged via an increase in independence, even though the student required long-term support for their academic learning. This suggests that focusing solely on academic competence, usually through achievement, may not reflect the development of resilience and that combined approaches that include specificity in terms of the difficulty alongside underlying skills, abilities and understandings is integral to the development of resilience. This may be even more important in the educational context because of the multiplicity of risk factors that can exist for an individual, which can increase over time, and which can influence one's ability to adapt. Condly (2006) further noted that the development of skills, such as those aforementioned, required modification over time. This suggests that factors that ameliorate risk and foster adaptability may not be static, and as an individual develops or experiences changes within their temporal, contextual, social, cultural context, some alteration may be required due to differences in interactions.

Overall

Research has found that children with dyslexia, and other learning difficulties, often hold lower levels of perceptions of themselves and their ability to execute tasks or actions. Resilience research has often viewed dyslexia and other learning difficulties as being chronic and unrelenting in nature, meaning that these children may be at risk for maladaptation. However, multiple factors, such as individual differences and temporal, situational and contextual factors, influence the development of self-esteem, self-efficacy and resilience, which can positively or negatively affect outcomes for an individual. The emergence of multi-dimensional models of self-esteem and self-efficacy recognises the existence of domains and subdomains, which has enabled greater understandings around the role of education in the development of these specific constructs to occur.

Research has identified associations between academic achievement and academic self-concept and academic self-efficacy, respectively. While these associations have been the focus of research in samples of older children, adolescents and young adults, there has been notably less research examining these associations in younger children. This appears to be based on arguments around whether younger children are developmentally capable of making required judgements related to their self-perceptions. However, recent research is clear; young children are able to make judgements related to their self-perceptions; furthermore, these children are able to make these judgements within specific contexts. Understanding psychosocial development in young children is crucial. Research has found that declines in self-esteem in children with dyslexia and learning difficulties can occur at a young age and these declines may be greater for children who experience multiple difficulties or more severe difficulties. While research often relates these declines to the commencement of formal education, the declines may also be related to aspects of literacy instruction. Turning points, which have been identified in later childhood, are also indicative of the chronic nature of dyslexia as a risk factor for future adaptation. Turning points occur as children re-organise the value placed on specific sub-domains, such as academic self-concept, as a result of outcomes experienced within the educational setting. While it is debated whether turning points act to counter the academic context for older children, resilience research has noted the latent effect of adaptability during childhood, on adulthood. Overall, having an understanding of self-esteem, self-efficacy and resilience in children with dyslexia, and other learning difficulties, is fundamental to supporting these children; furthermore, given the young age that declines in psychosocial development may occur, this understanding should extend across childhood.

Concluding views on improving literacy and self-concept

As discussed, difficulties with reading will impact on all areas of a curriculum where reading is the key to independent learning, and experiences of failure can lead to poor self-concept. Such consequences will not be experienced by all, but the chance of them occurring is likely to increase as the learner gets older, which may lead to increasing negative feelings about education and disengagement from learning. Given improvements in achievement, changes in self-concept would be expected to follow if those achievements were related to the self and important to the individual in some way (Denston, 2016; Everatt et al., 2017; Fidler & Everatt, 2012). If gains are short-lived, or perceived as external to the individual, or considered unimportant, then there is likely to be little effect on self-concept. Furthermore, strategies that build on strengths have been found to have positive effects on educational achievement in older children with dyslexia when trying to remediate areas of weakness have been less effective (see Weeks, Brooks & Everatt, 2002). If using what the child can do increases achievement for some period of time, thus improving re-engagement in learning, then further intervention targeting areas of weakness may also be more likely to be effective. Similarly, self-concept may be related to self-regulation, and self-regulation strategies can reduce negative behaviours that interfere with learning (Everatt et al., 2011). Combining these ideas in methods that are motivating and focus on key skills necessary for literacy success would be useful.

Research in New Zealand organised by the authors (funded by a Better Start & Cure Kids grant) has been looking at ways to support literacy learning in children aged eight to ten years who have struggled with reading/writing, while at the same time increasing self-concept, and reducing negative consequences. Assessments of literacy, self-concept and behaviour, at several points over the course of the study, and both before and after intervention, provided the data on which to determine effectiveness. The work was based on much of the research we have discussed in this book showing the benefits of targeted interventions for children with dyslexia. The intervention concentrated on developing strategies for reading and spelling that made use of skills that should lead to success in word decoding/processing. There was also a focus on language processes that included the development of vocabulary and phonological and morphological awareness, as well as an emphasis on the orthographic features related to these language concepts. As discussed previously, the development of phonological awareness has been identified as a key contributor to learning to read. However, the development of vocabulary and morphological awareness should also be beneficial. Vocabulary enhancement should be particularly useful for those with lower levels of reading practice/experience, given the potential impacts on word knowledge, but there were also a number of students with English as an additional language in the study, and these would also benefit from vocabulary support. A focus on morphology should also support spelling development, as we have discussed previously in this book.

Therefore, a feature of the intervention was the aim to support word reading/decoding through an awareness of the link between written letters (graphemes) and their corresponding language sounds (phonemes): i.e. explicitly linking this phonological awareness to word decoding and spelling tasks (Carson, Gillon & Boustead, 2013; Hatcher et al., 2006). Support for the development of vocabulary was also based on research that has shown evidence for the development of word learning and oral language development (e.g. Bowyer-Crane et al., 2008). Text reading strategies (Hatcher et al., 2006), and morphological awareness development strategies (Denston et al., 2018), were used to focus on meaning in text, as well as recognise commonalities in suffixes in order to determine consistencies in meaning and spelling patterns. Chronological-age appropriate texts were practised to support vocabulary development but also in order to increase motivation to read and understand (see also Elbeheri, Reid & Everatt, 2017). Although these may be above the reading age of the children, support was provided and strategies taught to maintain successful reading. Repeated reading practice of the texts that was appropriate for the student's age, background and interests, helped to maintain motivation, and aimed at improving fluency of text reading.

The results have provided evidence for the positive impact of the intervention on literacy. At the point when half of the students had experienced the intervention and the other half were about to undergo the intervention (a delayed intervention control group), the intervention group showed specific gains in most literacy areas compared to the waiting-control group. These differences disappeared once the waiting-control group had also experienced the same intervention. This evidence suggests that this relatively short-term intervention led to specific gains in morphological awareness, word reading and spelling, vocabulary development and reading comprehension. Smaller effects were found for non-word reading and phonological awareness suggesting the need for further support in these areas where the students were struggling, but consistent with previous findings that targeting areas of difficulty may need to follow the point when experience of success has occurred. There was also evidence of changes in measures of self-concept, self-efficacy, resilience and internalising (emotional feelings) and externalising (negative behaviours) problems. However, these latter effects developed over the course of a school year, rather than immediately after the intervention, suggesting a need for the strategies developed to be used outside the intervention and for a reasonable period of time to impact on self-concept and resilience. As such, these teaching strategies for older learners with evidence of dyslexia-related problems showed positive benefits in literacy and aspects of self-concept and resilient self-efficacy. Clearly, further work is needed here, but the findings show the potential link between the two and how appropriate support targeted at literacy can influence more than reading outcomes.

In conclusion, as our understanding of literacy learning problems and dyslexia increases, so we should get closer to identifying the best method, or set of methods, to support the learning of the individual. There may well be one method that can be used for all or most individuals with dyslexia, together with some multi-method approaches, that takes account of the consequences of dyslexia, and possible comorbidity. Clearly an understanding of language and the processes that go into reading (and writing) is vital, but work on both the difficulties encountered by those with dyslexia, as well as the compensatory strategies that they might use and the consequences of poor educational experiences is as equally important. As suggested in this book, assessment protocols that inform methods for supporting learning may need to take these factors into account. In addition, monitoring of progress will also be necessary, since all assessment measures are subject to error – no one-off assessment can ever be perfect for all circumstances. Response to Intervention methods that argue for monitoring as well as best practice in teaching are a good way to consider this. Such frameworks often encompass phonological awareness training linked to reading that are clearly useful as an intervention method, though an understanding of morphology (and word origins) can also support learning (possibly more so spelling than reading), and the development of vocabulary and strategies to support word processing and text understanding will also impact on acquisition, particularly for those from multilingual backgrounds.

In terms of practice, an understanding of skills assessment procedures should inform assessment protocols and the interpretation of assessment results. The present framework also suggests the need to understand, as best as possible, the background to the potential problems (interviews with the individual, and with parents and teachers, would be useful, though some questionnaires can be used as part of this). Assessment of reading and writing is vital – for younger learners, this will need to focus on early skills (familiarity with text, decoding skills, word reading accuracy, for example), but for older learners, it may need to focus on text reading, and consider a range of skills, such as accuracy, rate and comprehension as part of understanding the skills and strategies available to the individual. Assessment of phonological processing skills is vital, based on the current framework – such language skills are the most likely underlying area of difficulty, and they will provide a focus for intervention strategies. However, measures of additional language skills may be worthwhile to determine other areas of difficulties that can also influence literacy and inform intervention – these will also be useful for situations where the individual may be from a multilingual background. Brief assessments of non-verbal skills can also provide ideas for intervention, particularly for older learners, and it may be necessary to assess consequences on behaviour and self-concept, for example, to support strategies for re-engagement in learning.

Similarly, a range of intervention methods should also provide a basis on which to make sure teaching and learning are as effective as possible, and that identification of difficulties and appropriate support occurs as early as possible. A range of intervention methods will provide options for situations where additional challenges may be evident, possibly due to a co-occurring condition or consequences of poor experience. This will also provide options for short-term group-based intervention and more individually focused support. However, given the framework presented in this book, all should still be based on good teaching practice since the focus of the intervention should be to support learning: all should be well-informed, structured to build on skills and provide opportunities for success, monitor performance for signs of problems, they should be explicit and show how skills learnt can be generalised and applied, and they should be interesting and as motivational as possible. Therefore, although there are still some things that we do not fully understand, and no doubt further research work and theoretical development will likely lead to further improvements in practice, there is a lot that we do know about dyslexia and related learning difficulties. An understanding of this should lead to informed practice that better supports learning. We hope that this book provides a basis for that understanding as well as ideas for further work.

REFERENCES

Abu-Rabia, S. (2002). Reading in a root-based-morphology language: The case of Arabic. *Journal of Research in Reading, 25*, 299–309.

Abu-Rabia, S., Share, D. & Mansour, M. (2003). Word recognition and basic cognitive processes among reading disabled and normal readers in the Arabic language. *Reading and Writing, 16*, 423–440.

Abu-Rabia, S. & Taha, H. (2004). Reading and spelling error analysis of native Arabic dyslexic readers. *Reading and Writing: An Interdisciplinary Journal, 17*, 651–689.

Adams, J.W., Snowling, M.J., Nehhessy, S.M. & Kind, P. (1999). Problems of behaviour, reading and arithmetic. *British Journal of Educational Psychology, 69*, 571–585.

Adams, M.J. (1990). *Beginning to read*. Cambridge, MA: MIT Press.

Adler-Grinberg, D. & Stark, L. (1978). Eye movements, scan paths, and dyslexia. *American Journal of Optometry and Physiological Optics, 55*, 557–570.

Alves-Martins, M., Peixoto, F., Gouveia-Pereira, M., Amaral, V. & Pedro, I. (2002). Self-esteem and academic achievement among adolescents. *Educational Psychology, 22*(1), 51–62.

Anderson, P.L. & Meier-Hedde, R. (2011). Cross-case analysis and reflections. In P.L. Anderson & R. Meier-Hedde (Eds.), *International case studies of dyslexia* (pp. 283–306). New York: Routledge.

Antoniou, M. (2019). The advantages of bilingualism debate. *Annual Review of Linguistics, 5*, 395–415.

Arnbak, E. & Elbro, C. (2000). The effects of morphological awareness training on the reading and spelling skills of young dyslexics. *Scandinavian Journal of Educational Research, 44*, 229–251.

Badayai, A.R.A. & Ismail, A.H. (2012). *Life-span trajectory of self-esteem development: A myth or reality.* Spoken paper presented at the 2nd Southeast Asia Psychology Conference, Kota Kinabalu, Sabah, Malaysia.

Baddeley, A.D. (1986). *Working memory.* New York: Oxford University Press.

Baddeley, A.D. (1996). Exploring the central executive. *Quarterly Journal of Experimental Psychology, 49A*, 5–28.

Baddeley, A.D. (2000). The episodic buffer: A new component of working memory? *Trends in Cognitive Science, 4*(11), 417–423.

Baddeley, A.D. (2003). Working memory and language: An overview. *Journal of Communication Disorders, 36*(3), 189–208.

Baddeley, A.D. & Hitch, G.J. (1974). Working memory. In G.H. Bower (Ed.), *The psychology of learning and motivation* (pp. 47–89). London: Academic Press.

Baluch, B. & Besner, D. (1991). Visual word recognition: Evidence for strategic control of lexical and nonlexical routines in oral reading. *Journal of Experimental Psychology: Learning, Memory, and Cognition, 17*, 644–652.

Banales, E., Kohnen, S. & McArthur, G. (2015). Can verbal working memory training improve reading? *Cognitive Neuropsychology, 32*(3–4), 104–132.

Bandura, A. (1977). Self-efficacy: Toward a unifying theory of behavioral change. *Psychological Review, 84*(2), 191.

Bandura, A. (1997). *Self-efficacy: The exercise of control.* New York: W.H. Freeman and Company.

Barker, T., Torgesen, J. & Wagner, R. (1992). The role of orthographic processing skills on five different reading tasks. *Reading Research Quarterly, 27*, 334–345.

Barkley, R.A. (2006). *Attention deficit hyperactivity disorder.* New York: Guilford.

Barry, C. & Bastiani, P. (1997). Lexical priming of nonword spelling in the regular orthography of Italian. *Reading and Writing, 9*, 499–517.

Battle, J. (1982). *Culture-free self-esteem inventories* (2nd ed.). Texas: Pro-Ed.

Beaton, A., McDougall, S. & Singleton, C. (Eds.). (1997). Dyslexia in literate adults. *Journal of Research in Reading, 20*(1).

Beddington, J., Cooper, G., Field, J., Goswami, U., Huppert, F., Jenkins, R., Jones, H., Kirkwood, T., Shakian, B. & Thomas, S. (2008). The mental wealth of nations. *Nature, 455*(7216), 1057–1060.

Beech, J.R. (1985). *Learning to read: A cognitive approach to reading and poor reading.* London: Croom Helm.

Ben-Dror, I., Bentin, S. & Frost, R. (1995). Semantic, phonologic, and morphologic skills in reading disabled and normal children: Evidence from perception and production of spoken Hebrew. *Reading Research Quarterly, 30*, 876–893.

Bentin, S. & Frost, R. (1995). Morphological factors in visual word identification in Hebrew. In L.B. Feldman (Ed.), *Morphological aspects of language processing* (pp. 271–292). Hillsdale, NJ: Lawrence Erlbaum Associates.

Bentin, S. & Leshem, H. (1993). On the interaction of phonologic awareness and reading acquisition: It's a two-way street. *Annals of Dyslexia, 43*, 125–148.

Ben-Yehuda, G., Sackett, E., Malchi-Ginzberg, L. & Ahissar, M. (2001). Impaired temporal contrast sensitivity in dyslexics is specific to retain-and-compare paradigms. *Brain, 124*, 1381–1395.

Berlin, R. (1887). *Eine besondere art der Wortblindheit (dyslexie)*. Wiesbaden: J.F. Bergmann.

Berninger, V.W., Vaughan, K., Abbott, R.D., Begay, K., Coleman, K.B., Curtin, G., Hawkins, J.M. & Graham, S. (2002). Teaching spelling and composition alone and together: Implications for the simple view of writing. *Journal of Educational Psychology, 94*, 291–304.

Bhatia, T.K. & Ritchie, W.C. (Eds.). (2013). *The handbook of bilingualism and multilingualism* (2nd ed.). Chichester, UK: Wiley-Blackwell.

Bialystok, E., Luk, G., Peets, K.F. & Yang, S. (2010). Receptive vocabulary differences in monolingual and bilingual children. *Bilingualism: Language and Cognition, 13*, 525–531.

Bialystok, E., Majumder, S. & Martin, M.M. (2003). Developing phonological awareness: Is there a bilingual advantage? *Applied Psycholinguistics, 24*(1), 27–44.

Bishop, D.V.M. & Leonard, L.B. (Eds.). (2000). *Speech and language impairments in children: Causes, characteristics, intervention and outcome*. Philadelphia: Psychology Press.

Bishop, D.V.M. & Snowling, M.J. (2004). Developmental dyslexia and specific language impairment: Same or different. *Psychological Bulletin, 130*, 858–886.

Bong, M. & Skaalvik, E.M. (2003). Academic self-concept and self-efficacy: How different are they really? *Educational Psychology Review, 15*(1), 1–40.

Boudelaa, S. & Marslen-Wilson, W.D. (2005). Discontinuous morphology in time: Incremental masked priming in Arabic. *Language and Cognitive Processes, 20*, 207–260.

Bourassa, D.C., Treiman, R. & Kessler, B. (2006). Use of morphology in spelling by children with dyslexia and typically developing children. *Memory & Cognition, 34*, 703–714.

Bowers, P.G. & Ishaik, G. (2003). RAN's contribution to understanding reading disabilities. In H.L. Swanson, K.R. Harris & S. Graham (Eds.), *Handbook of learning disabilities* (pp. 140–157). New York: Guilford Press.

Bowers, P.N., Kirby, J.R. & Deacon, S.H. (2010). The effects of morphological instruction on literacy skills: A systematic review of the literature. *Review of Educational Research, 80*(2), 144–179.

Bowyer-Crane, C., Snowling, M., Duff, F., Carroll, J., Fieldsend, E., Miles, J., Goetz, K. & Hulme, C. (2008). Improving early language and literacy skills: Differential aspects of an oral language versus a phonology with reading intervention. *Journal of Child Psychology and Psychiatry, 49*, 422–432.

Boyden, J. & Mann, G. (2005). Children's risk, resilience, and coping in extreme situations. In M. Ungar (Ed.), *Handbook for working with children and youth: Pathways to resilience across cultures and contexts* (pp. 3–26). London: Sage Publications.

Braaksma, M. A., Rijlaarsdam, G. & Van den Bergh, H. (2002). Observational learning and the effects of model–observer similarity. *Journal of Educational Psychology, 94*(2), 405–415.

Bradley, R., Danielson, L. & Doolittle, J. (2005). Response to intervention. *Journal of Learning Disabilities, 38*, 485–486.

Breitmeyer, B.G. (1993). Sustained (P) and transient (M) channels in vision: A review and implications for reading. In D.M. Willows, R.S. Kruk & E. Corcos (Eds.), *Visual processes in reading and reading disabilities* (pp. 95–100). Hillsdale, NJ: Erlbaum.

Breitmeyer, B.G. & Williams, M.C. (1990). Effects of isoluminant-background color on metacontrast and stroboscopic motion: Interactions between sustained and transient channels. *Vision Research, 30*, 1069–1075.

British Psychological Society. (1999). *Dyslexia, literacy and psychological assessment*. Report of a Working Party of the Division of Educational and Child Psychology of the British Psychological Society. Leicester: British Psychological Society.

Brooks, J.E. (2006). Strengthening resilience in children and youths: Maximizing opportunities through the schools. *Children and Schools, 28*(2), 69–76.

Brooks, P.L. (1995). The effectiveness of various teaching strategies in teaching spelling to a student with severe learning difficulties. *Educational and Child Psychology, 12*, 80–88.

Brooks, P., Everatt, J. & Fidler, R. (2016). *Adult reading test* (2nd ed.). Hayling Island, UK: ART.

Brooks, P. & Weeks, S. (1999). *Individual styles in learning to spell: Improving spelling in children with literacy difficulties and all children in mainstream schools*. London: DfEE.

Broom, Y.M. & Doctor, E.A. (1995). Developmental phonological dyslexia: A case study of the efficacy of a remediation programme. *Cognitive Neuropsychology, 12*, 725–766.

Bruck, M. (1993). Word recognition and component phonological processing skills of adults with childhood diagnosis of dyslexia. *Developmental Review, 13*, 258–268.

Bruck, M., Genesse, F. & Caravolas, M. (1997). A cross-linguistic study of early literacy acquisition. In B. Blachman (Ed.), *Foundations of reading acquisition and dyslexia* (pp. 145–162). London: LEA.

Bruner, J.S. (1986). *Actual minds, possible worlds.* London: Harvard University Press.

Brunswick, N. (Ed.). (2011). *Supporting dyslexic adults in higher education and the workplace.* Chichester, UK: Wiley-Blackwell.

Bryant, P. (1998). Sensitivity to onset and rhyme does predict young children's reading: A comment on Muter, Hulme, Snowling and Taylor (1997). *Journal of Experimental Child Psychology, 71*, 29–37.

Bryant, P. & Bradley, L. (1985). *Children's reading problems.* Oxford, UK: Blackwell.

Bryant, P., Nunes, T. & Bindman, M. (1998). Awareness of language in children who have reading difficulties: Historical comparisons in a longitudinal study. *Journal of Child Psychology and Psychiatry, 39*, 501–510.

Burden, R. & Burdett, J. (2005). Factors associated with successful learning in pupils with dyslexia: A motivational analysis. *British Journal of Special Education, 32*(2), 100–104.

Burns, M.K., Appleton, J.J. & Stehouwer, J.D. (2005). Meta-analytic review of response-to-intervention research: Examining field-based and research-implemented models. *Journal of Psychoeducational Assessment, 23*, 381–394.

Byrne, B.M. (1984). The general/academic self-concept nomological network: A review of construct validation research. *Review of Educational Research, 54*(3), 427–456.

Byrne, B. & Fielding-Barnsley, R. (1993). Evaluation of a program to teach phonemic awareness to young children: A 1-year follow-up. *Journal of Educational Psychology, 85*(1), 104–111.

Cain, K. (2010). *Reading development and difficulties.* Chichester, UK: BPS Blackwell.

Cain, K., Lemmon, K. & Oakhill, J. (2004). Individual differences in the inference of word meanings from context: The influence of reading comprehension, vocabulary knowledge, and memory capacity. *Journal of Educational Psychology, 96*(4), 671–681.

Cain, K. & Oakhill, J. (Eds.). (2007). *Children's comprehension problems in oral and written language.* New York: Guilford Press.

Calsyn, R.J. & Kenny, D.A. (1977). Self-concept of ability and perceived evaluation of others: Cause or effect of academic achievement? *Journal of Educational Psychology, 69*(2), 136–145.

Carlise, J.F. (1987). The use of morphological knowledge in spelling derived forms by learning-disabled and normal students. *Annals of Dyslexia, 27*, 90–108.

Caron, C. & Rutter, M. (1991). Comorbidity in child psychopathology: Concepts, issues and research strategies. *Journal of Child Psychology and Psychiatry, 32*, 1063–1080.

Carson, K., Boustead, T. & Gillon, G. (2014). Predicting reading outcomes in the classroom using a computer-based phonological awareness screening and monitoring assessment. *International Journal of Speech-Language Pathology, 16*, 552–561.

Carson, K.L., Gillon, G.T. & Boustead, T.M. (2013). Classroom phonological awareness instruction and literacy outcomes in the first year of school. *Language, Speech & Hearing Services in Schools, 44*(2), 147–160.

Casalis, S., Cole, P. & Sopo, D. (2004). Morphological awareness in developmental dyslexia. *Annals of Dyslexia, 54*, 114–138.

Casserly, A.M. (2013). The socio-emotional needs of children with dyslexia in different educational settings in Ireland. *Journal of Research in Special Educational Needs, 13*(1), 79–91.

Catts, H.W. (1989). Defining dyslexia as a developmental language disorder. *Annals of Dyslexia, 39*, 50–64.

Catts, H.W. (1993). The relationship between speech–language impairments and reading disabilities. *Journal of Speech and Hearing Research, 36*, 948–958.

Catts, H.W. (2017). Early identification of reading disabilities. In K. Cain, D.L. Compton & R. Parrila (Eds.). *Theories of reading development (pp.* 311–332). Amsterdam: John Benjamins Publishing.

Catts, H.W., Fey, M.E., Tomblin, J.B. & Zhang, X. (2002). A longitudinal investigation of reading outcomes in children with language impairments. *Journal of Speech, Language and Hearing Research, 45*, 1142–1157.

Catts, H.W., Fey, M.E., Zhang, X. & Tomblin, J.B. (2001). Estimating risk for future reading difficulties in kindergarten children: A research based model and its clinical implications. *Language Speech and Hearing Services in Schools, 32*, 38–50.

Catts, H., Hogan, T. & Adlof, S. (2005). Developmental changes in reading and reading disabilities. In H. Catts & A. Kamhi (Eds.), *The connections between language and reading disabilities* (pp. 25–40). Mahwah, NJ: Lawrence Erlbaum Associates.

Catts, H., Kamhi, A. & Adlof, S. (2012). Defining and classifying reading disabilities. In A. Kamhi & H. Catts (Eds.), *Language and reading disabilities* (3rd ed., pp. 45–76). New Jersey, NJ: Pearson.

Chall, J. (1967). *Learning to read: The great debate.* New York: McGraw-Hill.

Chan, J.C.Y. & Lam, S.F. (2008). Effects of competition on students' self-efficacy in vicarious learning. *British Journal of Educational Psychology, 78*(1), 95.

Chapman, J.W. (1988). Learning disabled children's self-concepts. *Review of Educational Research, 58*(3), 347–371.

Chapman, J.W. & Tunmer, W.E. (2003). Reading difficulties, reading-related self-perceptions, and strategies for overcoming negative self-beliefs. *Reading & Writing Quarterly, 19*(1), 5–24.

Chapman, J.W., Tunmer, W.E. & Prochnow, J.E. (2000). Early reading-related skills and performance, reading self-concept, and the development of academic self-concept: A longitudinal study. *Journal of Educational Psychology, 92*(4), 703–708.

Chinn, S. (Ed.). (2015). *Routledge international handbook: Mathematics learning difficulties and dyscalculia.* Abingdon, UK: Routledge.

Clark, D.B. & Uhry, J.K. (1995). *Dyslexia: Theory and practice of remedial instruction.* Baltimore: York Press.

Clarke, P.J., Snowling, M.J., Truelove, E. & Hulme, C. (2010). Ameliorating children's reading-comprehension difficulties: A randomized controlled trial. *Psychological Science, 21*, 1106–1116.

Cline, T. & Shamsi, T. (2000). *Language needs or special needs? The assessment of learning difficulties in literacy among children learning English as an additional language: A literature review.* London: DfEE publications.

Coltheart, M., Rastle, K., Perry, C., Langdon, R. & Ziegler, J. (2001). DRC: A dual route cascaded model of visual word recognition and reading aloud. *Psychological Review, 108*, 204–256.

Coltheart, V. & Leahy, J. (1996). Procedures used by beginning and skilled readers to read unfamiliar letter strings. *Australian Journal of Psychology, 48*, 124–129.

Combley, M. (Ed.). (2001). *The Hickey multisensory language course* (3rd ed.). London: Whurr.

Condly, S.J. (2006). Resilience in children: A review of literature with implications for education. *Urban Education, 41*(3), 211–236.

Connor, M. (1994). Specific learning difficulty (dyslexia) and interventions. *Support for Learning, 9*, 114–119.

Coopersmith, S.A. (1967). *The antecedents of self-esteem.* San Francisco: W.H. Freeman.

Cornelissen, P., Munro, N., Fowler, S. & Stein, J. (1993). The stability of binocular fixation during reading in adults and children. *Developmental Medicine and Child Neurology, 35*, 777–787.

Cornoldi, C. & Oakhill, J. (Eds.). (1996). *Reading comprehension difficulties: Processes and intervention.* Mahwah, NJ: LEA.

Cosden, M., Elliott, K., Noble, S. & Kelemen, E. (1999). Self-understanding and self-esteem in children with learning disabilities. *Learning Disability Quarterly, 22*(4), 279–290.

Cotton, M.M. & Evans, K.M. (1990). An evaluation of the Irlen Lenses as a treatment for specific reading disorders. *Australian Journal of Psychology, 42*, 1–12.

Cowan, N. (2005). *Working memory capacity*. New York: Psychology Press.

Cratty, B.J. (1996). Coordination problems among learning disabled children. In B.J. Cratty & R.L. Goldman (Eds.), *Learning disabilities: Contemporary viewpoints* (pp. 141–185). Amsterdam: Harwood.

Critchley, M. (1970). *The dyslexic child*. London: Heinemann.

Cronin, V. & Carver, P. (1998). Phonological sensitivity, rapid naming, and beginning reading. *Applied Psycholinguistics, 19*, 447–461.

Crystal, D. (2003). *English as a global language* (2nd ed.). Cambridge, UK: Cambridge University Press.

Cummings, E.M., Davies, P.T. & Campbell, S.B. (2002). *Developmental psychopathology and family process: Theory, research, and clinical implications*. New York: Guilford Press.

Cunningham, A.E. (1990). Explicit versus implicit instruction in phonemic awareness. *Journal of Experimental Child Psychology, 50*, 429–444.

D'Angiulli, A., Siegel, L.S. & Maggi, S. (2005). Literacy instruction, SES, and word-reading achievement in English-language learners and children with English as a first language: A longitudinal study. *Learning Disabilities Research and Practice, 19*, 202–213.

Daneman, M. (1991). Working memory as a predictor of verbal fluency. *Journal of Psycholinguistic Research, 20*, 445–464.

Daneman, M. & Carpenter, P.A. (1980). Individual differences in working memory and reading. *Journal of Verbal Learning and Verbal Behavior, 19*, 450–466.

Davis, M.C., Luecken, L. & Lemery-Chalfant, K. (2009). Resilience in common life: Introduction to the special issue. *Journal of Personality, 77*(6), 1637–1644.

De Jong, P. & van der Leij, A. (1999). Specific contributions of phonological abilities to early reading acquisition: Results from a Dutch latent variable longitudinal study. *Journal of Educational Psychology, 91*, 450–476.

Dehaene, S., Cohen, L., Sigman, M. & Vinckier, F. (2005). The neural code for written words: A proposal. *Trends in Cognitive Sciences, 9*, 335–341.

Démonet, J.F., Taylor, M.J. & Chaix, Y. (2004). Developmental dyslexia. *Lancet, 363*, 1451–1460.

Denckla, M.B. & Rudel, R.G. (1976). Rapid automatized naming (RAN): Dyslexia differentiated from other learning disabilities. *Neuropsychologia, 14*, 471–479.

Denston, A. (2016). *Self-esteem and resilience in students with literacy learning difficulties within an educational context* (Doctorate, University of Canterbury, Christchurch, New Zealand).

Denston, A., Everatt, J., Parkhill, F. & Marriott, C. (2018). Morphology: Is it a means by which teachers can foster literacy development in older primary students with literacy learning difficulties? *Australian Journal of Language and Literacy, 41*(2), 94–102.

Deschler, D.D., Alley, G.R. & Carlson, S.C. (1980). Learning strategies: An approach to mainstream secondary students with learning disabilities. *Education Unlimited, 2*, 6–11.

Di Filippo, G., Brizzolara, D., Chilosi, A., De Luca, M., Judica, A., Pecini, C., Spinelli, D. & Zoccolotti, P. (2005). Rapid naming not cancellation speed or articulation rate, predicts reading in an orthographically regular language (Italian). *Child Neuropsychology, 11*, 349–361.

Dodd, B., Crosbie, S., MacIntosh, B., Teitzel, T. & Ozanne, A. (2000). *Primary and preschool battery of phonological awareness (PIPA)*. London: Psychological Corporation.

Doll, B. & Lyon, M.A. (1998). Risk and resilience: Implications for the delivery of educational and mental health services in schools. *School Psychology Review, 27*(3), 348.

Dore, W. (2006). *Dyslexia: The miracle cure*. London: John Blake Publishing Ltd.

Doyle, J. (2002). *Dyslexia: An introductory guide* (2nd ed.). London: Whurr.

Duncan, L., Seymour, P.H.K. & Hill, S. (1997). How important are rhyme and analogy in beginning reading? *Cognition, 63*, 171–208.

Dunn, L., Dunn, D., Sewell, J., Styles, B., Brzyska, B., Shamsan, Y. & Burge, B. (2009). *The British picture vocabulary scale* (3rd ed.). London: GL Education.

Eden, G.F., VanMeter, J.W., Rumsey, J.M., Maisog, J.M., Woods, R.P. & Zeffiro, T.A. (1996). Abnormal processing of visual motion in dyslexia revealed by functional brain imaging. *Nature, 382*, 66–69.

Ehm, J.-H., Lindberg, S. & Hasselhorn, M. (2014). Reading, writing, and math self-concept in elementary school children: Influence of dimensional comparison processes. *European Journal of Psychology of Education, 29*(2), 277–294.

Ehri, L.C. (1987). Learning to read and spell words. *Journal of Reading Behavior, 19*, 5–31.

Ehri, L.C. (1995). Phases of development in learning to read by sight. *Journal of Research in Reading, 18*, 116–125.

Elbeheri, G. & Everatt, J. (2007). Literacy ability and phonological processing skills amongst dyslexic and non-dyslexic speakers of Arabic. *Reading and Writing, 20*, 273–294.

Elbeheri, G. & Everatt, J. (2009). IQ and dyslexia: From research to practice. In G. Reid, G. Elbeheri, J. Everatt, D. Knight & J. Wearmouth (Eds.), *The Routledge companion to dyslexia* (pp. 22–32). Abingdon, UK: Routledge.

Elbeheri, G., Everatt, J., Mahfoudhi, A., Al-Diyar, M.A. & Taibah, N. (2011). Orthographic processing and reading comprehension among Arabic speaking mainstream and LD children. *Dyslexia, 17*, 123–142.

Elbeheri, G., Everatt, J., Reid, G. & Al-Mannai, H. (2006). Dyslexia assessment in Arabic. *Journal of Research in Special Educational Needs, 6*, 143–152.

Elbeheri, G., Reid, G. & Everatt, J. (2017). *Motivating children with specific learning difficulties*. Abingdon, UK: Routledge.

Elbro, C., Daugaard, H. & Gellert, A.S. (2012). Dyslexia in a second language? A dynamic test of reading acquisition may provide a fair answer. *Annals of Dyslexia, 62*, 172–185.

Elbro, C., Nielsen, I. & Petersen, D.K. (1994). Dyslexia in adults: Evidence for deficits in non-word reading and in the phonological representation of lexical items. *Annals of Dyslexia, 44*, 205–226.

Elbro, C., Rasmussen, I. & Spelling, B. (1996). Teaching reading to disabled readers with language disorders: A controlled evaluation of synthetic speech feedback. *Scandinavian Journal of Psychology, 37*, 140–155.

Elliott, J.G. & Grigorenko, E.L. (2014). *The dyslexia debate*. Cambridge, UK: Cambridge University Press.

Ellis, A.W. (1984). *Reading, writing and dyslexia*. London/Hove: LEA.

Ellis, A.W., McDougall, S.J.P. & Monk, A.F. (1996). Are dyslexics different? *Dyslexia, 2*, 31–58.

Entwistle, N. (1981). *Styles of learning and teaching*. Chichester, UK: Wiley.

Ericsson, K.A., Chase, W.G. & Faloon, S. (1980). Acquisition of a memory skill. *Science, 208*, 1181–1182.

Everatt, J. (1997). The abilities and disabilities associated with adult developmental dyslexia. *Journal of Research in Reading, 20*, 13–21.

Everatt, J. (Ed.). (1999). *Reading and dyslexia: Visual and attentional processes*. London: Routledge.

Everatt, J. (2002). Visual processes. In G. Reid & J. Wearmouth (Eds.), *Dyslexia and literacy: Theory and practice* (pp. 85–98). Chichester, UK: Wiley.

Everatt, J., Almurtaji, Y., Al-Sharhan, A. & Elbeheri, G. (2017). Relationships between emotion and educational achievement in Arabic children. *Asian Pacific Journal of Developmental Differences, 4*(1), 65–84.

Everatt, J., Al-Sharhan, A., Al-Azmi, Y., Al-Menaye, N. & Elbeheri, G. (2011). Behavioural/attentional problems and literacy learning difficulties in children from non-English language/cultural backgrounds. *Support for Learning, 26*(3), 127–133.

Everatt, J., Bradshaw, M.F. & Hibbard, P.B. (1999). Visual processing and dyslexia. *Perception, 28*, 243–254.

Everatt, J., McCorquodale, B., Smith, J., Culverwell, F., Wilks, A., Evans, D., Kay, M. & Baker, D. (1999). Associations between reading ability and visual processes. In J. Everatt (Ed.), *Reading and dyslexia: Visual and attentional processes* (pp. 1–39). London: Routledge.

Everatt, J., McNamara, S., Groeger, J.A. & Bradshaw, M.F. (1999). Motor aspects of dyslexia. In J. Everatt (Ed.), *Reading and dyslexia: Visual and attentional processes* (pp. 122–136). London: Routledge.

Everatt, J. & McNeill, B. (2014). Practical implications of research into dyspraxia. In A.J. Holliman (Ed.), *The Routledge international companion to educational psychology* (pp. 307–316). Abingdon, UK: Routledge.

Everatt, J., Ocampo, D., Veii, K., Nenopoulou, S., Smythe, I., Al-Mannai, H. & Elbeheri, G. (2010). Dyslexia in biscriptal readers. In N. Brunswick, S. McDougall & P. de Mornay Davies (Eds.), *Reading and dyslexia in different orthographies* (pp. 221–245). Hove, UK: Psychology Press.

Everatt, J., Sadeghi, A., Grech, L., Elshikh, M., Abdel-Sabour, S., AlMenaye, N., McNeill, B. & Elbeheri, G. (2013). Assessment of literacy difficulties in second language and bilingual learners. In D. Tsagari & G. Spanoudis (Eds.), *Assessing L2 students with learning and other disabilities* (pp. 27–43). Cambridge, UK: Cambridge Scholar Publishing.

Everatt, J., Smythe, I., Adams, E. & Ocampo, D. (2000). Dyslexia screening measures and bilingualism. *Dyslexia, 6*, 42–56.

Everatt, J., Smythe, I., Ocampo, D. & Gyarmathy, E. (2004). Issues in the assessment of literacy-related difficulties across language backgrounds. *Journal of Research in Reading, 27*, 141–151.

Everatt, J., Smythe, I., Ocampo, D. & Veii, K. (2002). Dyslexia assessment of the bi-scriptal reader. *Topics in Language Disorders, 22*, 32–45.

Everatt, J., Steffert, B. & Smythe, I. (1999). An eye for the unusual. *Dyslexia, 5*, 28–46.

Everatt, J., Warner, J., Miles, T.R. & Thomson, M.E. (1997). The incidence of Stroop interference in dyslexia. *Dyslexia, 3*, 222–228.

Everatt, J., Weeks, S. & Brooks, P. (2008). Profiles of strengths and weaknesses in dyslexia and other learning difficulties. *Dyslexia, 14*, 16–41.

Farrag, A.F., Khedr, E.M. & Abdel-Naser, W. (2002). Impaired parvocellular pathway in dyslexic children. *European Journal of Neurology, 9*, 359–363.

Fawcett, A. & Nicolson, R. (1994). *Dyslexia in children.* New York: Harvester-Wheatsheaf.

Fawcett, A.J. & Nicolson, R.I. (1996). *The dyslexia screening test manual.* London: Psychological Corporation.

Fawcett, A.J. & Nicolson, R.I. (2001). Dyslexia: The role of the cerebellum. In A. Fawcett (Ed.), *Dyslexia: Theory and good practice* (pp. 1–35). London: Whurr.

Felton, R.H., Naylor, C.E. & Wood, F.B. (1990). Neuropsychological profile of adult dyslexics. *Brain and Language, 39*, 485–497.

Ferrer, E., Shaywitz, B., Holahan, J., Marchione, K. & Shaywitz, S. (2010). Uncoupling of reading and IQ over time: Empirical evidence for a definition of dyslexia. *Psychological Science, 21*, 93–101.

Fidler, R. & Everatt, J. (2012). Reading comprehension in adult students with dyslexia: Areas of weakness and strategies for support. In N. Brunswick (Ed.), *Supporting dyslexic adults in higher education and the workplace* (pp. 91–100). Chichester, UK: Wiley-Blackwell.

Fiorello, C.A., Hale, J.B. & Snyder, L.E. (2006). Cognitive hypothesis testing and response to intervention for children with reading problems. *Psychology in the Schools, 43*, 835–853.

Fitch, R.H., Miller, S. & Tallal, P. (1997). Neurobiology of speech perception. *Annual Review of Neuroscience, 20*, 331–353.

Fletcher, D. & Sarkar, M. (2013). Psychological resilience: A review and critique of definitions, concepts, and theories. *European Psychologist, 18*(1), 12–23.

Florit, E. & Cain, K. (2011). The simple view of reading: Is it valid for different types of alphabetic orthographies? *Educational Psychology Review, 23*(4), 553–576.

Forrest-Bank, S.S. & Jenson, J.M. (2015). The relationship among childhood risk and protective factors, racial microaggression and ethnic identity, and academic self-efficacy and antisocial behavior in young adulthood. *Children and Youth Services Review, 50*, 64–74.

Frederickson, N. (1999). The ACID test – or is it? *Educational Psychology in Practice, 15*, 2–8.

Frederickson, N., Frith, U. & Reason, R. (1997). *Phonological assessment battery manual and test materials.* Windsor, UK: NFER-Nelson.

Frith, U. (1985). Beneath the surface of developmental dyslexia. In K. Patterson, J. Marshall & M. Coltheart (Eds.), *Surface dyslexia* (pp. 301–330). London: LEA.

Frith, U. (1999). Paradoxes in the definition of dyslexia. *Dyslexia, 5*, 192–214.

Frost, R. (2012). Towards a universal model of reading. *Behavioral and Brain Sciences, 35*(5), 263–279.

Frost, R., Foster, K.I. & Deutsch, A. (1997). What can be learned from the morphology of Hebrew? A masked-priming investigation of morphological representation. *Journal of Experimental Psychology: Learning, Memory, and Cognition, 23*, 829–856.

Fuchs, D., Mock, D., Morgan, P.L. & Young, C.L. (2003). Response-to-intervention: Definitions, evidence, and implications for the learning disabilities construct. *Learning Disabilities Research & Practice, 18*, 157–171.

Funnell, E. & Stuart, M. (1995). *Learning to read: Psychology in the classroom.* Oxford, UK: Blackwell.

Galaburda, A.M., Rosen, G.D. & Sherman, G.F. (1990). Individual variability in cortical organization: Its relationship to brain laterality and implications to function. *Neuropsychologia, 28*(6), 529–546.

Gaskins, I.W. & Baron, J. (1986). Teaching poor readers to cope with maladaptive cognitive styles: A training program. *Journal of Reading Disabilities, 18*, 390–394.

Gathercole, S.E. & Baddeley, A.D. (1993). *Working memory and language.* Hillsdale, NJ: Lawrence Erlbaum Associates.

Gathercole, S.E. & Pickering, S.J. (2001). Working memory deficits in children with special educational needs. *British Journal of Special Education, 28*, 89–97.

Gathercole, S.E.C., Willis, C.S., Emslie, H. & Baddeley, A.D. (1992). Phonological memory and vocabulary development during the early school years. *Developmental Psychology, 28,* 887–898.

Gersons-Wolfensberger, D. & Ruijssenaar, W. (1997). Definition and treatment of dyslexia: A report by the Committee on Dyslexia of the Health Council of the Netherlands. *Journal of Learning Disabilities, 30,* 209–213.

Geschwind, N. (1982). Why Orton was right. *Annals of Dyslexia, 32,* 12–30.

Geva, E. & Siegel, L. (2000). Orthographic factors in the concurrent development of basic reading skills in two languages. *Reading and Writing, 12,* 1–30.

Ghelami, K., Sidhu, R., Jain, U. & Tannock, R. (2004). Reading comprehension and reading related abilities in adolescents with reading disabilities and attention-deficit/hyperactivity disorder. *Dyslexia, 10,* 364–384.

Gibson, S. & Kendall, L. (2010). Stories from school: Dyslexia and learners' voices on factors impacting on achievement. *Support for Learning, 25*(4), 187–193.

Gillingham, A.M. & Stillman, B.U. (1956). *Remedial training for children with specific disability in reading, spelling and penmanship.* New York: Sachett & Wilhems.

Gillon, G.T. (2018). *Phonological awareness: From research to practice* (2nd ed.). New York: Guilford Press.

Given, B.K. & Reid, G. (1999). *Learning styles: A guide for teachers and parents.* St Annes-on-Sea, UK: Red Rose Publications.

Goddard, S. (1996). *A teacher's window into the child's mind.* Eugene, OR: Fern Ridge Press.

Gonzalez, J.E.J. & Santana, G.R. (2002). Identifying subtypes of reading disability in the Spanish language. *Spanish Journal of Psychology, 5,* 3–19.

Goodman, K.S. (1970). Reading: A psycholinguistic guessing game. In H. Singer & R.B. Ruddell (Eds), Theoretical models and processes in reading (pp. 259–271). Newark, DE: International Reading Association.

Goodman, R. (1997). The strengths and difficulties questionnaire: A research note. *Journal of Child Psychology and Psychiatry, 38,* 581–586.

Goswami, U. (1999). The relationship between phonological awareness and orthographic representation in different orthographies. In M. Harris & G. Hatano (Eds.), *Learning to read and write: A cross-linguistic perspective* (pp. 134–156). New York: Cambridge University Press.

Goswami, U. (2000). Phonological representations, reading development and dyslexia: Towards a cross-linguistic theoretical framework. *Dyslexia, 6,* 133–151.

Goswami, U. & Bryant, P. (1990). *Phonological skills and learning to read.* Hillsdale, NJ: Erlbaum.

Goswami, U., Thomson, J., Richardson, U., Stainthorp, R., Hughes, D. & Rosen, S. (2002). Amplitude envelope onsets and developmental dyslexia: A new hypothesis. *Proceedings of the National Academy of Sciences of the United States of America, 99*, 10911–10916.

Gough, P.B. & Tunmer, W.E. (1986). Decoding, reading, and reading disability. *Remedial and Special Education, 7*, 6–10.

Goulandris, N. & Snowling, M.J. (1991). Visual memory deficits: A plausible cause of developmental dyslexia? Evidence from a single case study. *Cognitive Neuropsychology, 8*, 127–154.

Goulandris, N., McIntyre, A., Snowling, M., Bethel, J.-M. & Lee, J.P. (1998). A comparison of dyslexic and normal readers using orthoptic assessment procedures. *Dyslexia, 4*, 30–48.

Grech, L. (2011). *Reading comprehension in Maltese-English bilinguals* (PhD thesis, University of Surrey, UK).

Guay, F., Ratelle, C.F., Roy, A. & Litalien, D. (2010). Academic self-concept, autonomous academic motivation, and academic achievement: Mediating and additive effects. *Learning and Individual Differences, 20*(6), 644–653.

Gupta, A. & Garg, A. (1996). Visuo-perceptual and phonological processing in dyslexic children. *Journal of Personality and Clinical Studies, 12*, 67–73.

Guyer, B.P. & Sabatino, D. (1998). The effectiveness of a multisensory alphabetic approach with college students who are learning disabled. *Journal of Learning Disabilities, 22*, 430–433.

Hammill, D.D. (2004). What we know about correlates of reading. *Exceptional Children, 70*, 453–468.

Hampshire, S. (1981). *Susan's story*. London: Sidgwick & Jackson.

Harris, M. & Giannouli, V. (1999). Learning to read and spell in Greek: The importance of letter knowledge and morphological awareness. In M. Harris & G. Hatano (Eds.), *Learning to read and write: A cross-linguistic perspective* (pp. 112–133). New York: Cambridge University Press.

Harter, S. (1993). Causes and consequences of low self-esteem in children and adolescents. In R.F. Baumeister (Ed.), *Self-esteem: The puzzle of low self-regard* (pp. 87–116). Boston: Springer.

Harter, S. (2006). The self. In N. Eisenberg (Ed.), *Handbook of child psychology* (6th ed., Vol. 3, pp. 505–570). Hoboken, NJ: John Wiley & Sons, Inc.

Harter, S. (2012). *Self-perception profile for children: Manual and questionnaires (Grades 3 to 8)*. Denver, CO: University of Denver.

Hatcher, P., Goetz, K., Snowling, M., Hulme, C., Gibbs, S. & Smith, G. (2006). Evidence for the effectiveness of the early literacy support programme. *British Journal of Educational Psychology, 76*(4), 351–367.

Hatcher, P., Hulme, C. & Ellis, A.W. (1994). Ameliorating early reading failure by integrating the teaching of reading and phonological skills. *Child Development, 65*, 41–57.

Heath, S.M., Hogben, J.H. & Clark, C.D. (1999). Auditory temporal processing in disabled readers with and without oral language delay. *Journal of Child Psychology and Psychiatry, 40*, 637–647.

Hinshelwood, J. (1917). *Congenital word-blindness.* London: H.K. Lewis.

Ho, C.S.-H. (1994). *A cross-cultural study of the precursors of reading* (DPhil thesis, University of Oxford, UK).

Ho, C.S.-H. & Bryant, P. (1997). Phonological skills are important in learning to read Chinese. *Developmental Psychology, 33*, 946–951.

Ho, C.S.-H., Chan, D., Tsang, S.-M. & Lee, S.-H. (2002). The cognitive profile and multiple-deficit hypothesis in Chinese developmental dyslexia. *Developmental Psychology, 38*, 543–553.

Hoien, T. (2002). Word recognition: The impact of phonological and orthographic components. In E. Hjelmquist & C. von Euler (Eds.), *Dyslexia & literacy* (pp. 54–68). London: Whurr Publishers.

Hoover, W.A. & Gough, P.B. (1990). The simple view of reading. *Reading and Writing, 2*, 127–160.

Howard, D. & Best, W. (1997). Impaired non-word reading with normal word reading: A case study. *Journal of Research in Reading, 20*, 55–65.

Huey, E.B. (1908). *The psychology and pedagogy of reading.* Cambridge, MA: MIT Press.

Hulme, C. (1981). *Reading retardation and multisensory teaching.* London: Routledge.

Hulme, C. & Mackenzie, S. (1992). *Working memory and severe learning difficulties.* Hove, UK: Lawrence Erlbaum Associates.

Hulme, C., Muter, V. & Snowling, M. (1998). Segmentation does predict early progress in learning to read better than rhyme: A reply to Bryant. *Journal of Experimental Child Psychology, 71*, 39–44.

Hulme, C. & Roodenrys, S. (1995). Verbal working memory development and its disorders. *Journal of Child Psychology and Psychiatry, 36*, 373–398.

Hultquist, A. (1997). Orthographic processing abilities of adolescents with dyslexia. *Annals of Dyslexia, 47*, 89–107.

Humphrey, N. (2004). The death of the feel-good factor? Self-esteem in the educational context. *School Psychology International, 25*(3), 347–360.

Humphrey, N., Charlton, J.P. & Newton, I. (2004). The developmental roots of disaffection? *Educational Psychology, 24*(5), 579–594.

Hutzler, F., Kronbichler, M., Jacobs, A.M. & Wimmer, H. (2006). Perhaps correlation but not causal: No effect of dyslexic readers' magnocellular system on their eye movements during reading. *Neuropsychologia, 44*, 637–648.

Ibrahim, R., Eviatar, Z. & Aharon-Peretz, J. (2002). The characteristics of Arabic orthography slow its processing. *Neuropsychology, 16*, 322–326.

Irlen, H. (1991). *Reading by the colors.* Garden City Park, NY: Avery Publishing Group.

Jastak, J. & Wilkinson, G. (1984). *Wide range achievement test revised*. Wilmington, DE: Jastak Associates.

Jeffries, S. & Everatt, J. (2004). Working memory: Its role in dyslexia and other learning difficulties. *Dyslexia, 10*, 196–214.

Joanisse, M.F., Manis, F.R., Keating, P. & Seidenberg, M.S. (2000). Language deficits in dyslexic children: Speech perception, phonology, and morphology. *Journal of Experimental Child Psychology, 77*, 30–60.

Johnston, R.S. & Watson, J.E. (2004). Accelerating the development of reading, spelling and phonemic awareness skills in initial readers. *Reading and Writing: An Interdisciplinary Journal, 17*, 327–357.

Jones, M.W., Snowling, M.J. & Moll, K. (2016). What automaticity deficit? Activation of lexical information by readers with dyslexia in a rapid automatized naming Stroop-switch task. *Journal of Experimental Psychology: Learning, Memory, and Cognition, 42*(3), 465–474.

Joshi, R.M., Dahlgren, M. & Boulware-Gooden, R. (2002). Teaching reading through multi-sensory approach in an inner city school. *Annals of Dyslexia, 53*, 235–251.

Joshi, R., Tao, S., Aaron, P.G. & Quiroz, B. (2012). Cognitive components of componential model of reading applied to different orthographies. *Journal of Learning Disabilities, 45*, 480–486.

Joshi, R.M., Treiman, R., Carreker, S. & Moats, L.C. (2008). How words cast their spell. *American Educator, 32*(4), 6–42.

Juel, C., Griffith, P.L. & Gough, P.B. (1986). Acquisition of literacy: A longitudinal study of children in first and second grade. *Journal of Educational Psychology, 78*, 243–255.

Jungert, T., Hesser, H. & Träff, U. (2014). Contrasting two models of academic self-efficacy: Domain-specific versus cross-domain: In children receiving and not receiving special instruction in mathematics. *Scandinavian Journal of Psychology, 55*(5), 440–447.

Justice, L. (2006). Evidence-based practice, response to intervention and the prevention of reading difficulties. *Language, Speech and Hearing Services in the Schools, 37*, 284–297.

Kamhi, A. & Catts, H. (Eds.). (2012). *Language and reading disabilities* (3rd ed.). New Jersey, NJ: Pearson.

Kaplan, B.J., Dewey, D.M., Crawford, S.G. & Wilson, B.N. (2001). The term comorbidity is of questionable value in reference to developmental disorders: Data and theory. *Journal of Learning Disabilities, 34*, 555–565.

Katz, L. & Frost, R. (1992). The reading process is different for different orthographies: The orthographic depth hypothesis. In R. Frost & L. Katz (Eds.), *Orthography, phonology, morphology and meaning* (pp. 67–84). Amsterdam: North-Holland.

Kaufman, A.S. (1994). *Intelligent testing with the WISC-III*. New York: Wiley.

Kavale, K.A. & Forness, S.R. (1987). Substance over style: Assessing the efficacy of modality testing and teaching. *Exceptional Children, 54*, 228–239.

Kennedy, A. (1987). Eye movements, reading skill and the spatial code. In J. Beech & A. Colley (Eds.), *Cognitive approaches to reading* (pp. 169–186). Chichester, UK: Wiley.

Kling, K.C., Shibley Hyde, J., Showers, C.J. & Buswell, B.N. (1999). Gender differences in self-esteem: A meta-analysis. *Psychological Bulletin, 125*(4), 470–500.

Klingberg, T. (2010). Training and plasticity of working memory. *Trends in Cognitive Sciences, 14*(7), 317–324.

Klingberg, T., Fernell, E., Olesen, P.J., Johnson, M., Gustafsson, P., Dahlström, K., Gillberg, C.G., Forssberg, H. & Westerberg, H. (2005). Computerized training of working memory in children with ADHD: A randomized, controlled trial. *Journal of the American Academy of Child and Adolescent Psychiatry, 44*, 177–186.

Koda, K. (1994). Second language reading research: Problems and possibilities. *Applied Psycholinguistics, 15*(1), 1–28.

Kussmaul, A. (1877). Diseases of the nervous system and disturbances of speech. In H. von Ziemssen (Ed.) *Cylopedia of the practice of medicine* (pp. 770–778). New York: William Wood.

Laasonen, M., Service, E. & Virsu, V. (2001). Temporal order and processing acuity of visual, auditory, and tactile perception in developmentally dyslexic young adults. *Cognitive, Affective & Behavioral Neuroscience, 1*, 394–410.

Landerl, K. (2001). Word recognition deficits in German: More evidence from a representative sample. *Dyslexia, 7*, 183–196.

Landerl, K., Wimmer, H. & Frith, U. (1997). The impact of orthographic consistency on dyslexia: A German-English comparison. *Cognition, 63*, 315–334.

Leather, C. (2018). *Explaining the relationship between aspects of metacognitive and cognitive function and the workplace success of dyslexic people* (PhD thesis, University of Surrey, UK).

Leather, C., Hogh, H., Seiss, E. & Everatt, J. (2011). Cognitive function and work success in adults with dyslexia. *Dyslexia, 17*(4), 327–338.

Lee, Y.S. & Jonson-Reid, M. (2016). The role of self-efficacy in reading achievement of young children in urban schools. *Child and Adolescent Social Work Journal, 33*(1), 79–89.

Lennerstrand, G., Ygge, J. & Jacobsson, C. (1993). Control of binocular eye movements in normals and dyslexics. *Annals of the New York Academy of Science, 682*, 231–239.

Liberman, I.Y., Shankweiler, D., Fischer, F.W. & Carter, B. (1974). Explicit syllable and phoneme segmentation in the young child. *Journal of Experimental Psychology, 18*, 201–222.

Liew, J., McTigue, E.M., Barrois, L. & Hughes, J.N. (2008). Adaptive and effortful control and academic self-efficacy beliefs on achievement: A longitudinal study of 1st through 3rd graders. *Early Childhood Research Quarterly, 23*(4), 515–526.

Linnenbrink, E.A. & Pintrich, P.R. (2003). The role of self-efficacy beliefs in student engagement and learning in the classroom. *Reading & Writing Quarterly, 19*(2), 119–137.

Lipa, O. & Siegel, L.S. (2007). The development of reading skills in children with English as a second language. *Scientific Studies of Reading, 11*, 105–131.

Lonigan, C.J., Burgess, S.R. & Schatschneider, C. (2018). Examining the simple view of reading with elementary school children: Still simple after all these years. *Remedial and Special Education, 39*, 260–273.

Lonigan, C. & Shanahan, T. (Eds). (2008). *Developing early literacy: Report of the National Early Literacy Panel. A scientific synthesis of early literacy development and implications for intervention.* Retrieved from www.nichd.nih.gov/sites/default/files/publications/pubs/documents/NELPReport09.pdf.

Loosli, S.V., Buschkuehl, M., Perrig, W.J. & Jaeggi, S.M. (2012). Working memory training improves reading processes in typically developing children. *Child Neuropsychology, 18*, 62–78.

Lopez, R., Yolton, R.L., Kohl, P., Smith, D.L. & Sexerud, M.H. (1994). Comparison of Irlen Soctopic Sensitivity Syndrome test results to academic and visual performance data. *Journal of the American Optometric Association, 65*, 705–713.

Lovegrove, W.J. (1996). Dyslexia and a transient/magnocellular pathway deficit: The current situation and future directions. *Australian Journal of Psychology, 48*, 167–171.

Lovegrove, W.J. & Williams, M.C. (1993). Visual temporal processing deficits in specific reading disability. In D.M. Willows, R.S. Kruk & E. Corcos (Eds.), *Visual processes in reading and reading disabilities* (pp. 311–329). Hillsdale, NJ: Erlbaum.

Lovett, M.W., Borden, S.L., DeLuca, T., Lacerenza, L., Benson, N.J. & Brackstone, D. (1994). Treating the core deficits of developmental dyslexia: I Evidence of transfer of learning after phonologically and strategy based reading training programs. *Developmental Psychology, 30*, 805–822.

Lovett, M.W., Steinbach, K.A. & Frijters, J.C. (2000). Remediating the core deficits of developmental reading disability: A double-deficit hypothesis. *Journal of Learning Disabilities, 33*, 334–358.

Lovoie, M.E. & Charlebois, P. (1994). The discriminant validity of the Stroop colour and word test: Towards a cost-effective strategy to distinguish subgroups of disruptive preadolescents. *Psychology in the Schools, 31*, 98–107.

Lufi, D., Cohen, A. & Parishplass, J. (1990). Identifying attention deficit hyperactivity disorder with the WISC-R and the Stroop color and word test. *Psychology in the Schools, 27*, 28–34.

Lukatela, K., Carello, C., Shankweiler, D. & Liberman, I.Y. (1995). Phonological awareness in illiterates: Observations from Serbo-Croatian. *Applied Psycholinguistics, 16*, 463–487.

Lundberg, I. (1988). Preschool prevention of reading failure: Does training in phonological awareness work? In R.L. Masland & M.W. Masland (Eds.), *Prevention of reading failure* (pp. 163–176). Parkton, MD: York Press.

Lundberg, I. (1989). Lack of phonological awareness: A critical factor in dyslexia. In C. von Euler, I. Lundberg & G. Lennerstrand (Eds.), *Brain and reading* (pp. 221–232). New York: Stockton.

Luthar, S.S. & Cicchetti, D. (2000). The construct of resilience: Implications for interventions and social policies. *Development and Psychopathology, 12*(4), 857–885.

Luthar, S.S., Cicchetti, D., & Becker, B. (2000). The construct of resilience: A critical evaluation and guidelines for future work. *Child Development, 71*(3), 543–562.

Luthar, S.S., Lyman, E.L. & Crossman, E.J. (2014). Resilience and positive psychology. In M. Lewis & K.D. Rudolph (Eds.), *Handbook of developmental psychopathology* (pp. 125–140). Boston: Springer.

McBride, H.A. & Siegel, L.S. (1997). Learning disabilities and adolescent suicide. *Journal of Learning Disabilities, 30*(6), 652–659.

McBride-Chang, C. & Ho, C.S.-K. (2000). Naming speed and phonological awareness in Chinese children: Relations to reading skills. *Journal of Psychology in Chinese Society, 1*, 93–108.

McBride-Chang, C., Wagner, R.K., Muse, A., Chow, B.W.Y. & Shu, H. (2005). The role of morphological awareness in children's vocabulary acquisition in English. *Applied Psycholinguistics, 26*, 415–435.

McFadden, T.U. (1998). The immediate effects of pictographic representation on children's narratives. *Child Language Teaching and Therapy, 14*, 51–67.

Maclachlan, A., Yale, S. & Wilkins, A.J. (1993). Open trials of precision ophthalmic tinting: One-year follow-up of 55 patients. *Ophthalmic and Physiological Optics, 13*, 175–178.

MacLeod, C.M. (1991). Half a century of research on the Stroop effect: An integrative review. *Psychological Bulletin, 109*, 163–203.

McLoughlin, D., Leather, C.A. & Stringer, P.E. (2002). *The adult dyslexic: Interventions and outcomes.* London: Whurr.

McNamara, D.S., O'Reilly, T., Rowe, M., Boonthum, C. & Levinstein, I. (2007). iSTART: A web-based tutor that teaches self-explanation and metacognitive reading strategies. In D.S. McNamara (Ed.), *Reading comprehension strategies: Theories, interventions, and technologies* (pp. 397–420). New York: Lawrence Erlbaum Associates.

McPhillips, M., Hepper, P.G. & Mulhern, G. (2000). Effects of replicating primary-reflex movements on specific reading difficulties in children: A randomised, double-blind, controlled trial. *Lancet, 355*, 537–541.

McPhillips, M. & Jordan-Black, J.-A. (2007). Primary reflex persistence in children with reading difficulties (dyslexia): A cross-sectional study. *Neuropsychologia, 45*(4), 748–754.

Mahfoudhi, A., Elbeheri, G., Al-Rashidi, M. & Everatt, J. (2010). The role of morphological awareness in reading comprehension among typical and learning disabled native Arabic speakers. *Journal of Learning Disabilities, 43*(6), 500–514.

Manis, F.R., Seidenberg, M.S., Doi, L.M., McBride-Chang, C. & Petersen, A. (1996). On the bases of two subtypes of developmental dyslexia. *Cognition, 58*, 157–195.

Mann, V. & Liberman, I.Y. (1984). Phonological awareness and verbal short-term memory: Can they presage early reading success? *Journal of Learning Disabilities, 17*, 592–599.

Marsh, G., Friedman, M., Welch, V. & Desberg, P. (1981). A cognitive-developmental theory of reading acquisition. In G.E. MacKinnon & T.G. Waller (Eds.), *Reading research: Advances in theory and practice* (Vol. 3, pp. 199–221). New York: Academic Press.

Marsh, H.W. (1989). Age and sex effects in multiple dimensions of self-concept: Preadolescence to early adulthood *Journal of Educational Psychology, 81*(3), 417–430.

Marsh, H.W. & Craven, R. (1997). Academic self-concept: Beyond the dustbowl. In G. D. Phye (Ed.), *Handbook of classroom assessment: Learning, achievement, and adjustment* (pp. 364–390). Orlando, FL: Academic Press.

Marsh, H.W. & Craven, R.G. (2006). Reciprocal effects of self-concept and performance from a multidimensional perspective: Beyond seductive pleasure and unidimensional perspectives. *Perspectives on Psychological Science, 1*(2), 133–163.

Marsh, H.W., Craven, R. & Debus, R. (1998). Structure, stability, and development of young children's self-concepts: A multicohort-multioccasion study. *Child Development, 69*(4), 1030–1053.

Marsh, H.W. & Martin, A.J. (2011). Academic self-concept and academic achievement: Relations and causal ordering. *British Journal of Educational Psychology, 81*(1), 59–77.

Marsh, H.W. & O'Mara, A. (2008). Reciprocal effects between academic self-concept, self-esteem, achievement, and attainment over seven adolescent years: Unidimensional and multidimensional perspectives of self-concept. *Personality and Social Psychology Bulletin, 34*(4), 542–552.

Marsh, H.W. & Shavelson, R. (1985). Self-concept: Its multifaceted, hierarchical structure. *Educational Psychologist, 20*(3), 107–123.

Marshall, C.M., Snowling, M.J. & Bailey, P.J. (2001). Rapid auditory processing and phonological ability in normal readers and readers with dyslexia.
Journal of Speech, Language, and Hearing Research, 44, 925–940.

Masten, A.S., Hubbard, J.J., Gest, S.D., Tellegen, A., Garmezy, N. & Ramirez,
M. (1999). Competence in the context of adversity: Pathways to resilience
and maladaptation from childhood to late adolescence. *Development and
Psychopathology, 11*(1), 143–169.

Mather, N. & Wendling, B.J. (2012). *Essentials of dyslexia assessment and intervention.* Hoboken, NJ: Wiley.

Mazi, M., Nenopoulou, S. & Everatt, J. (2004). Dyslexia in Greece. In I.
Smythe, J. Everatt & R. Salter (Eds.), *The international book of dyslexia, Part 2.*
London: Wiley.

Meyler, A. & Breznitz, Z. (2005). Visual, auditory and cross-modal processing
of linguistic and nonlinguistic temporal patterns among adult dyslexic
readers. *Dyslexia, 11*, 93–115.

Miles, T.R. (1993). *Dyslexia: The pattern of difficulties* (2nd ed.). London: Whurr.

Miles, T.R., Gilroy, D. & Du Pre, E.A. (2007). *Dyslexia at college.* London:
Routledge.

Miles, T.R. & Miles, E. (1999). *Dyslexia: A hundred years on* (2nd ed.). Bucking-
ham, UK: Open University Press.

Mody, M., Studdert-Kennedy, M. & Brady, S. (1997). Speech perception deficits in poor readers: Auditory processing or phonological coding? *Journal of
Experimental Child Psychology, 64*, 199–231.

Montgomery, D. (1997). *Spelling: Remedial strategies.* London: Cassell.

Morais, J., Cary, J., Alegria, J. & Bertelson, P. (1979). Does awareness of speech
as a consequence of phones arise spontaneously? *Cognition, 7*, 323–331.

Morton, J. (1979). Facilitation in word recognition: Experiments causing change
in the Logogen model. In P.A. Kolers, M. Wrolstad & H. Bouma (Eds.),
Processing of visual language (pp. 259–268). New York: Plenum Press.

Multon, K.D., Brown, S.D. & Lent, R.W. (1991). Relation of self-efficacy
beliefs to academic outcomes: A meta-analytic investigation. *Journal of Coun-
seling Psychology, 38*(1), 30.

Muter, V., Hulme, C., Snowling, M. & Taylor, S. (1998). Segmentation, not
rhyming predicts early progress in learning to read. *Journal of Experimental
Child Psychology, 71*, 3–27.

Myklebust, H.R. & Johnson, D.J. (1962). Dyslexia in children. *Exceptional Children, 29*, 14–25.

Nation, K. (2001). Reading and language in children: Exposing hidden deficits.
Psychologist, 14, 238–242.

Nation, K. & Snowling, M.J. (1998). Individual differences in contextual facilitation: Evidence from dyslexia and poor reading comprehension. *Child
Development, 69*, 996–1011.

Neale, M.D. (1999). *Neale analysis of reading ability*. Windsor, UK: NFER-Nelson.

Needle, J., Nicolson, R.I. & Fawcett, A.J. (2015). Motor sequence learning in dyslexia: Is consolidation the key? *Applied Psychology Bulletin, 273*(64), 5–15.

Newman, E.H., Tardif, T., Huang, J. & Shu, H. (2011). Phonemes matter: The role of phoneme-level awareness in emergent Chinese readers. *Journal of Experimental Child Psychology, 108*(2), 242–259.

Nicolson, R.J. & Fawcett, A. (1990). Automaticity: A framework for dyslexia research? *Cognition, 35*, 159–182.

Nicolson, R.I. & Fawcett, A.J. (1996). *Dyslexia early screening test*. London: Psychological Corporation.

Nicolson, R.I. & Fawcett, A.J. (2011). Dyslexia, dysgraphia, procedural learning and the cerebellum. *Cortex: A Journal Devoted to the Study of the Nervous System and Behavior, 47*(1), 117–127.

Nunes, T., Bryant, P. & Bindman, M. (1997). Morphological spelling strategies: Developmental stages and processes. *Developmental Psychology, 33*, 637–649.

Oakhill, J. & Garnham, A. (1988). *Becoming a skilled reader*. New York: Blackwell Press.

Oettingen, G. (1995). Cross-cultural perspectives on self-efficacy. In A. Bandura (Ed.), *Self-efficacy in changing societies* (pp. 149–176). New York: Cambridge University Press.

Ofiesh, N. & Mather, N. (2012). Resilience and the child with learning disabilities. In S. Goldstein & R.B. Brooks (Eds.), *Handbook of resilience in children* (pp. 329–348). New York, NY: Springer Science.

Olofsson, A. & Lundberg, I. (1985). Evaluation of long-term effects of phonemic awareness training in kindergarten: Illustrations of some methodological problems in evaluation research. *Scandinavian Journal of Psychology, 16*, 21–34.

Olson, R.K. (2004). Genetic and environmental causes of reading disabilities: Results from the Colorado Learning Disabilities Research Center. In M. Turner & J. Rack (Eds.), *The study of dyslexia* (pp. 23–33). New York: Kluwer Academic/Plenum Pubs.

Olson, R.K., Kliegl, R. & Davidson, B.J. (1983). Dyslexic and normal readers' eye movements. *Journal of Experimental Psychology: Human Perception and Performance, 9*, 816–825.

Oney, B. Peter, M. & Katz, L. (1997). Phonological processing in printed word recognition: Effects of age and writing system. *Scientific Studies of Reading, 1*, 65–83.

Orton, S.T. (1937). *Reading, writing and speech problems in children*. New York: Norton.

Osmond, J. (1993). *The reality of dyslexia*. London: Cassell.

Pajares, F. (1996). Self-efficacy beliefs in academic settings. *Review of Educational Research, 66*(4), 543–578.

Pajares, F. & Schunk, D.H. (2001). Self-beliefs and school success: Self-efficacy, self-concept, and school achievement. In R. Riding & S. Rayner (Eds.), *Perception* (Vol. 11, pp. 239–266). London: Ablex Publishing.

Park, L.E. & Crocker, J. (2013). Pursuing self-esteem: Implications for self-regulation and relationships. In V. Zeigler-Hill (Ed.), *Self-esteem* (pp. 43–59). New York: Psychology Press.

Patel, T.K., Snowling, M.J. & de Jong, P.F. (2004). A cross-linguistic comparison of children learning to read in English and Dutch. *Journal of Educational Psychology, 96*, 785–797.

Pavlidis, G.Th. (1981). Sequencing, eye movements and the early objective diagnosis of dyslexia. In G. Pavlidis & T.R. Miles (Eds.), *Dyslexia research and its applications to education* (pp. 99–163). London: Wiley.

Perfetti, C.A. (1985). *Reading ability*. Oxford, UK: Oxford University Press.

Perfetti, C.A. & Roth, S. (1981). Some of the interactive processes in reading and their role in reading skill. In A. Lesgold & C. Perfetti (Eds.), *Interactive processes in reading* (pp. 269–297). Hillsdale, NJ: LEA.

Pickering, S.J. & Gathercole, S.E. (2001). *Working memory test battery for children*. London: Psychological Corporation.

Posner, M.I., Walker, J.A., Friedrick, F.J. & Rafal, R.D. (1984). Effects of parietal injury on covert orienting of visual attention. *Journal of Neuroscience, 4*, 1863–1874.

Pressley, M. & McCormick, C.B. (1995). *Cognition, teaching and assessment*. New York: HarperCollins.

Pringle Morgan, W. (1896). A case of congenital word blindness. *Lancet*, 1378.

Prochnow, J.E., Tunmer, W.E. & Chapman, J.W. (2013). A longitudinal investigation of the influence of literacy-related skills, reading self-perceptions, and inattentive behaviours on the development of literacy learning difficulties. *International Journal of Disability, Development and Education, 60*(3), 185–207.

Pumfrey, P.D. & Reason, R. (1991). *Specific learning difficulties (dyslexia): Challenges and responses*. Abingdon, UK: Routledge.

Puolakanaho, A., Ahonen, T., Aro, M., Eklund, K., Leppänen, P.H., Poikkeus, A.M., Tolvanen, A., Torppa, M. & Lyytinen, H. (2007). Very early phonological and language skills: Estimating individual risk of reading disability. *Journal of Child Psychology and Psychiatry, 48*, 923–931.

Raberger, T. & Wimmer, H. (2003). On the automaticity/cerebellar deficit hypothesis of dyslexia: Balancing and continuous rapid naming in dyslexic and ADHD children. *Neuropsychologia, 41*, 1493–1497.

Rack, J.P., Snowling, M.J., Hulme, C. & Gibbs, S. (2007). No evidence that an exercise-based treatment programme (DDAT) has specific benefits for children with reading difficulties. *Dyslexia, 13*, 97–104.

Rack, J.P., Snowling, M.J. & Olson, R.K. (1992). The nonword reading deficit in developmental dyslexia: A review. *Reading Research Quarterly, 27*, 29–53.

Raman, I., Baluch, B. & Besner, D. (2004). On the control of visual word recognition: Changing routes versus changing deadlines. *Memory & Cognition, 32*, 489–500.

Ramus, F., Pidgeon, E. & Frith, U. (2003). The relationship between motor control and phonology in dyslexic children. *Journal of Child Psychology and Psychiatry, 44*, 712–722.

Rastle, K., Davis, M.H. & New, B. (2004). The broth in my brother's brothel: Morpho-orthographic segmentation in visual word recognition. *Psychonomic Bulletin & Review, 11*, 1090–1098.

Raven, J. (1976). *Coloured progressive matrices*. Oxford, UK: Oxford Psycholinguistics Press Ltd.

Ravid, D. & Schiff, R. (2004). Learning to represent vowels in written Hebrew: Different factors across development. *First Language, 24*, 185–208.

Rayner, K. & Pollatsek, A. (1989). *The psychology of reading*. Hillsdale, NJ: LEA.

Reid, G. (2009). *Dyslexia: A practitioner's handbook* (4th ed.). Chichester, UK: Wiley/Blackwell.

Reid, G., Elbeheri, G. & Everatt, J. (2015). *Assessing children with specific learning difficulties: A teacher's practical guide*. Abingdon, UK: Routledge.

Reid, G. & Green, S. (2011). *100+ ideas for children with dyslexia*. London: Continuum Publications.

Reynolds, D.E., Nicolson, R.I. & Hambley, H. (2003). Evaluation of an exercise-based treatment for children with reading difficulties. *Dyslexia, 9*, 48–71.

Riding, R. & Cheema, I. (1991). Cognitive styles: An overview and integration. *Educational Psychology, 11*, 193–215.

Robins, R.W., Hendin, H.M. & Trzesniewski, K.H. (2001). Measuring global self-esteem: Construct validation of a single-item measure and the Rosenberg Self-Esteem Scale. *Personality and Social Psychology Bulletin, 27*(2), 151–161.

Robinson, H.M. (1972). Visual and auditory modalities related to methods for beginning reading. *Reading Research Quarterly, 8*(1), 7–39.

Robinson, W.P. & Tayler, C.A. (1991). Correlates of low academic attainment in three countries: England, France and Japan. *Análise Psicológica, 9*, 277–290.

Rosenberg, M. (1979). *Conceiving the self*. New York: Basic Books.

Rosenberg, M., Schoenbach, C., Schooler, C. & Rosenberg, F. (1995). Global self-esteem and specific self-esteem: Different concepts, different outcomes. *American Sociological Review, 60*(1), 141–156.

Rutter, M. (1987). Psychosocial resilience and protective mechanisms. *American Journal of Orthopsychiatry, 57*(3), 316.

Sadeghi, A. & Everatt, J. (2015). Influence of language background on English reading comprehension skills: Cross-language transfer effects. In L.T. Wong & A. Dubey-Jhaveri (Eds.), *English language education in a global world: Practices, issues and challenges* (pp. 69–80). New York: Nova Science Publishers.

Sadeghi, A., Everatt, J. & McNeill, B. (2014). Factors related to reading comprehension weaknesses in Persian speaking primary school children. *Asian Pacific Journal of Developmental Differences, 1*(2), 172–189.

Saiegh-Hadded, E. (2005). Correlates of reading fluency in Arabic: Diglossic and orthographic factors. *Reading and Writing, 18*, 559–582.

Sala, G. & Gobet, F. (2017). Working memory training in typically developing children: A meta-analysis of the available evidence. *Developmental Psychology, 53*(4), 671685.

Scarborough, H.S. (1990). Very early language deficits in dyslexic children. *Child Development, 61*, 1728–1743.

Scarborough, H.S. (1998). Predicting the future achievement of second graders with reading disabilities: Contributions of phonemic awareness, verbal memory, rapid naming, and IQ. *Annals of Dyslexia, 48*, 115–136.

Schiff, R. & Ravid, D. (2004). Vowel representation in written Hebrew: Phonological, orthographic and morphological contexts. *Reading and Writing, 17*, 241–265.

Schmeck, R.R. (Ed.). (1988). *Learning strategies and learning styles.* New York: Plenum Press.

Schneider, W., Küspert, P., Roth, E., Visé, M. & Marx, H. (1997). Short- and long-term effects of training phonological awareness in kindergarten: Evidence from two German studies. *Journal of Experimental Child Psychology, 66*, 311–340.

Schonell, F.J. (1950). *Diagnostic and attainment testing.* London: Oliver Boyd.

Schoon, I. (2006). *Risk and resilience: Adaptations in changing times.* Cambridge, UK: Cambridge University Press.

Schrank, F., Mather, N. & McGrew, K. (2014). *Woodcock-Johnson IV tests of achievement.* Rolling Meadows, IL: Riverside.

Schulte-Korne, G., Bartling, J., Deimel, W. & Remschmidt, H. (2004). Visual evoked potentials elicited by coherently moving dots in dyslexic children. *Neuroscience Letters, 357*, 207–210.

Schwaighofer, M., Fischer, F. & Buhner, M. (2015). Does working memory training transfer? A meta-analysis including training conditions as moderators. *Educational Psychologist, 50*, 138–166.

Scruggs, T.E. & Mastropieri, M.A. (1990). The case for mnemonic instruction: From laboratory research to classroom applications. *Journal of Special Education, 24*, 7–32.

Selikowitz, M. (1993). *Dyslexia and other learning difficulties.* Oxford, UK: Oxford University Press.

Semrud-Clikerman, M., Guy, K., Griffin, J.D. & Hynd, G.W. (2000). Rapid naming deficits in children and adolescents with reading disabilities and attention deficit hyperactivity disorder. *Brain and Language, 74*, 70–83.

Seymour, P.H.K. (1990). Developmental dyslexia. In M.W. Eysenk (Ed.), *Cognitive psychology: An international review* (pp. 135–195). Chichester, UK: John Wiley & Sons.

Seymour, P.H.K., Aro, M. & Erskine, J.M. (2003). Foundation literacy acquisition in European orthographies. *British Journal of Psychology, 94*, 143–174.

Share, D.L. (1996). Word recognition and spelling processes in specific reading disabled and garden-variety poor readers. *Dyslexia, 2*, 167–174.

Share, D.L. (2008). On the Anglocentricities of current reading research and practice: The perils of overreliance on an 'Outlier' orthography. *Psychological Bulletin, 134*, 584–615.

Shavelson, R.J., Hubner, J.J. & Stanton, G.C. (1976). Self-concept: Validation of construct interpretations. *Review of Educational Research, 46*(3), 407–441.

Shaywitz, S.E. (2003). *Overcoming dyslexia*. New York: Random House.

Shaywitz, S.E., Escobar, M.D., Shaywitz, B.A., Fletcher, J.M. & Makugh, R. (1992). Evidence that dyslexia may represent the lower tail of a normal distribution of reading ability. *New England Journal of Medicine, 326*, 145–150.

Shaywitz, S.E., Mody, M. & Shaywitz, B.A. (2006). Neural mechanisms in dyslexia. *Current Directions in Psychological Science, 15*(6), 278–281.

Siegel, L., Share, D. & Geva, E. (1995). Evidence for superior orthographic skills in dyslexics. *Psychological Science, 6*, 250–254.

Simpson, J. & Everatt, J. (2005). Reception class predictors of literacy skills. *British Journal of Educational Psychology, 75*, 171–188.

Skottun, B.C. (2000). On the conflicting support for the magnocellular deficit theory of dyslexia. *Trends in Cognitive Sciences, 4*, 211–212.

Smith, F. (1994). *Understanding reading* (5th ed.). Hillsdale, NJ: LEA.

Smith, L. & Nelson, C. (2006). World Englishes and issues of intelligibility. In B. Kachru, Y. Kachru & C. Nelson (Eds.), *The handbook of world Englishes* (pp. 428–445). Oxford, UK: Blackwell.

Smythe, I. (Ed.). (2001). *The dyslexia handbook 2001*. Reading, UK: British Dyslexia Association.

Smythe, I. (2002). *Cognitive factors underlying reading and spelling difficulties: A cross linguistic study* (PhD thesis, University of Surrey, UK).

Smythe, I. (2010). *Dyslexia in the digital age*. London: Continuum.

Smythe, I. & Everatt, J. (2009). Checklist for adults with dyslexia. In I. Smythe (Ed.), *Employment and dyslexia handbook 2009* (pp. 15–17). Bracknell, UK: British Dyslexia Association.

Smythe, I., Everatt, J., Al-Menaye, N., He, X., Capellini, S., Gyarmathy, E. & Siegel, L. (2008). Predictors of word level literacy amongst Grade 3 children in five diverse languages. *Dyslexia, 14*, 170–187.

Snowling, M.J. (2000). *Dyslexia* (2nd ed.). Oxford, UK: Blackwell.

Snowling, M.J. (2013). Early identification and interventions for dyslexia: A contemporary view. *Journal of Research in Special Educational Needs, 13*(1), 7–14.

Snowling, M.J. & Hulme, C. (Eds.). (2005). *The science of reading: A handbook.* Malden, MA: Blackwell Publishing.

Snowling, M.J. & Melby-Lervåg, M. (2016). Oral language deficits in familial dyslexia: A meta-analysis and review. *Psychological Bulletin, 142*, 498–545.

Snowling, M.J., Adams, J.W., Bishop, D.V.M. & Stothard, S.E. (2001). Educational attainments of school leavers with a preschool history of speech–language impairments. *International Journal of Language and Communication Disorders, 36*(2), 173–183.

Snowling, M., Dawes, P., Nash, H. & Hulme, C. (2012). Validity of a protocol for adult self-report of dyslexia and related difficulties. *Dyslexia, 18*(1), 1–15.

Solity, J. (2000). The early reading research: Applying psychology to classroom practice. *Educational and Child Psychology, 17*, 46–55.

Solity, J., Deavers, R., Kerfoot, S., Crane, G. & Cannon, K. (2000). The early reading research: The impact of instructional psychology. *Educational Psychology in Practice, 16*, 109–129.

Sparks, R.L., Patton, J. & Murdoch, A. (2014). Early reading success and its relationship to reading achievement and reading volume: Replication of '10 years later.' *Reading and Writing: An Interdisciplinary Journal, 27*(1), 189–211.

Specht, K., Hugdahl, K., Ofte, S., Nygard, M., Bjornerud, A., Plante, E. & Helland, T. (2009). Brain activation on pre-reading tasks reveals at-risk status for dyslexia in 6-year-old children. *Scandinavian Journal of Psychology, 50*, 79–91.

Spencer, K. (2000). Is English a dyslexic language? *Dyslexia, 6*, 152–162.

Spieleberger, C.D. (1973). *State-trait anxiety inventory for children.* Palo Alto, CA: Consulting Psychologists Press.

Spinelli, D., Angelelli, P., De Luca, M., Di Pace, E., Judica, A. & Zoccolotti, P. (1997). Developmental surface dyslexia is not associated with deficits in the transient visual system. *Neuroreport, 8*, 1807–1812.

Sprenger-Charolles, L., Siegel, L.S. & Bechennec, D. (1997). Beginning reading and spelling acquisition in French: A longitudinal study. In C. Perfetti, L. Rieben & M. Fayol (Eds.), *Learning to spell: Research, theory, and practice across language* (pp. 339–359). Hillsdale, NJ: Erlbaum.

Spring, C. & Capps, C. (1974). Encoding speed, rehearsal and probed recall of dyslexic boys. *Journal of Educational Psychology, 66*, 780–786.

Stackhouse, J. & Snowling, M. (1992). Barriers to literacy development in two cases of developmental verbal dyspraxia. *Cognitive Neuropsychology, 9*, 273–299.

Stackhouse, J. & Wells, B. (1997). *Children's speech and literacy difficulties: A psycholinguistic framework*. London: Whurr.

Stanley, G., Smith, G.A. & Howell, E.A. (1983). Eye movements and sequential tracking in dyslexic and control children. *British Journal of Psychology, 74*, 181–187.

Stanovich, K.E. (1980). Toward an interactive–compensatory model of individual differences in the development of reading fluency. *Reading Research Quarterly, 16*, 32–71.

Stanovich, K.E. (1986). Matthew effects in reading: Some consequences in individual differences in the acquisition of literacy. *Reading Research Quarterly, 21*, 360–364.

Stanovich, K.E. (1988). Explaining the differences between the dyslexic and the garden-variety poor reader: The phonological-core variable-difference model. *Journal of Learning Disabilities, 21*, 590–604.

Stanovich, K.E. & Siegel, L.S. (1994). Phenotypic performance profile of children with reading disabilities: A regression-based test of the Phonological-Core Variable-Difference Model. *Journal of Educational Psychology, 86*, 24–53.

Stanovich, K.E., Siegel, L.S. & Gottardo, A. (1997). Converging evidence for phonological and surface subtypes of reading disability. *Journal of Educational Psychology, 89*, 114–127.

Stanovich, K.E., West, R.F., & Feeman, D.J. (1981). A longitudinal study of sentence context effects in second-grade children: Tests of the interactive–compensatory model. *Journal of Experimental Child Psychology, 32*, 185–199.

Stein, J.F. (2001). The magnocellular theory of developmental dyslexia. *Dyslexia, 7*, 12–36.

Stein, J.F., Riddell, P. & Fowler, M.S. (1987). Fine binocular control in dyslexic children. *Eye, 1*, 433–438.

Stein, J.F., Riddell, P. & Fowler, M.S. (1989). Disordered right hemisphere function in developmental dyslexia. In C. von Euler, I. Lundberg & G. Lennerstrand (Eds.), *Brain and reading* (pp. 139–157). New York: Stockton Press.

Stein, J. & Walsh, V. (1997). To see but not to read: The magnocellular theory of dyslexia. *Trends in Neuroscience, 20*, 147–152.

Stordy, B.J. & Nicholl, M.J. (2000). *The LCP solution: The remarkable nutritional treatment for ADHD, dyslexia and dyspraxia*. New York: Ballantine Books.

Stroop, J.R. (1935). Studies of interference in serial verbal reactions. *Journal of Experimental Psychology, 18*, 643–662.

Stuart, M. & Coltheart, M. (1988). Does reading develop in a sequence of stages? *Cognition, 30*, 139–181.

Studdert-Kennedy, M. (2002). Deficits in phoneme awareness do not arise from failures in rapid auditory processing. *Reading and Writing, 15*, 5–14.

Swan, D. & Goswami, U. (1997). Picture naming deficits in developmental dyslexia: The phonological representations hypothesis. *Brain and Language, 56*, 334–353.

Swanson, H.L. (2015). Intelligence, working memory, and learning disabilities. In T.C. Papadopoulous, R.K. Parrila and J.R. Kirby (Eds.), *Cognitive, intelligence and achievement* (pp. 175–196). Boston: Elsevier.

Swanson, H.L., Trainin, G., Necoechea, D.M. & Hammill, D.D. (2003). Rapid naming, phonological awareness, and reading. A meta-analysis of the correlational evidence. *Review of Educational Research, 73*, 407–444.

Taibah, N.J. & Haynes, C.W. (2011). Contributions of phonological processing skills to reading skills in Arabic speaking children. *Reading and Writing, 24*, 1019–1042.

Tallal, P. (1980). Auditory temporal perception, phonics and reading disabilities in children. *Brain and Language, 9*, 182–198.

Tallal, P. (2000). Experimental studies of language learning impairments: From research to remediation. In D.V.M. Bishop & L.B. Leonard (Eds.), *Speech and language impairments in children: Causes, characteristics, intervention and outcome* (pp. 131–155). New York: Psychology Press.

Tallal, P., Miller, S.L., Jenkins, W.M. & Merzenich, M.M. (1997). The role of temporal processing in developmental language-based learning disorders: Research and clinical implications. In B.A. Blachman (Ed.), *Foundations of reading acquisition and dyslexia: Implications for early intervention*. Mahwah, NJ: LEA.

Tanaka, H., Black, J.M., Hulme, C., Stanley, L.M., Kesler, S.R., Whitfield-Gabrieli, S., Reiss, A.L., Gabrieli, J.D.E. & Hoeft, F. (2011). The brain basis of the phonological deficit in dyslexia is independent of IQ. *Psychological Science, 22*(11), 1442–1451.

Tannock, R. (2013). Specific learning disabilities in DSM-5: Are the changes for better or worse? *International Journal for Research in Learning Disabilities, 1*(2), 2–30.

Taouk, M. & Coltheart, M. (2004). The cognitive processes involved in learning to read Arabic. *Reading and Writing, 17*, 27–57.

Taylor, M.J., Batty, M., Chaix, Y. & Démonet, J.-F. (2003). Neurophysiological measures and developmental dyslexia: Auditory segregation analysis. *Current Psychology Letters: Behaviour, Brain & Cognition, 10*(1).

Thiede, K.W., Anderson, M.C.M. & Therriault, D. (2003). Accuracy of metacognitive monitoring affects learning of texts. *Journal of Educational Psychology, 95*(1), 66–73.

Thomson, M.E. (1988). Preliminary findings concerning the effects of specialised teaching on dyslexic children. *Applied Cognitive Psychology, 2*, 19–33.

Thomson, M. (2009). *The psychology of dyslexia* (2nd ed.). Chichester, UK: Wiley/Blackwell.

Torgesen, J.K. (1982). The learning disabled child as an inactive learner: Educational implications. *Topics in Learning and Learning disabilities, 2*, 45–52.

Torgesen, J.K. (2005). Recent discoveries on remedial interventions for children with dyslexia. In M.J. Snowling & C. Hulme (Eds.), *The science of reading: A handbook* (pp. 521–536). Malden, MA: Blackwell Publishing.

Torgesen, J.K. & Davis, C. (1996). Individual difference variables that predict response to training in phonological awareness. *Journal of Experimental Child Psychology, 63*, 1–21.

Torgesen, J.K., Morgan, S. & Davis, C. (1992). The effects of two types of phonological awareness training on word learning in kindergarten children. *Journal of Educational Psychology, 84*, 364–370.

Trautwein, U., Lüdtke, O., Köller, O. & Baumert, J. (2006). Self-esteem, academic self-concept, and achievement: How the learning environment moderates the dynamics of self-concept. *Journal of Personality and Social Psychology, 90*(2), 334.

Treiman, R., Cassar, M. & Zukowski, A. (1994). What types of linguistic information do children use in spelling? The case of flaps. *Child Development, 65*, 1310–1329.

Tunmer, W. & Chapman, J. (2012). The simple view of reading redux: Vocabulary knowledge and the independent components hypothesis. *Journal of Learning Disabilities, 45*, 453–466.

Tunmer, W. & Greaney, K. (2010). Defining dyslexia. *Journal of Learning Disabilities, 43*, 229–243.

Uhry, J.K. & Clark, D.B. (2005). *Dyslexia: Theory and practice of remedial instruction* (3rd ed.). Baltimore: York Press.

Underwood, G. & Batt, V. (1996). *Reading and understanding*. Oxford, UK: Blackwell.

Uppstad, P.H. & Tønnessen, F.E. (2007). The notion of phonology in dyslexia research: Cognitivism – and beyond. *Dyslexia, 13*, 154–174.

Van Beinum, F.J., Schwippert, C.E., Been, P.H., van Leeuwen, T.H. & Kuijpers, C.T.L. (2005). Development and application of a /bAk/-/dAk/ continuum for testing auditory perception within the Dutch longitudinal dyslexia study. *Speech Communication, 47*, 124–142.

Van Bergen, E., de Jong, P.F., Maassen, B. & van der Leij, A. (2014). The effect of parents' literacy skills and children's preliteracy skills on the risk of dyslexia. *Journal of Abnormal Child Psychology, 42*(7), 1187–1200.

Vanderbilt-Adriance, E. & Shaw, D.S. (2008). Conceptualizing and re-evaluating resilience across levels of risk, time, and domains of competence. *Clinical Child and Family Psychology Review, 11*(1–2), 30–58.

Vargo, F.E., Grosser, G.S. & Spafford, C.S. (1995). Digit span and other WISC-R scores in the diagnosis of dyslexia in children. *Perceptual and Motor Skills, 80*, 1219–1229.

Vaughn, S. & Fuchs, L. (2003). Redefining learning disabilities as inadequate response to instruction: The promise and potential problems. *Learning Disabilities Research and Practice, 18*, 137–146.

Veii, K. & Everatt, J. (2005). Predictors of reading among Herero-English bilingual Namibian school children. *Bilingualism: Language and Cognition, 8*, 239–254.

Vellutino, F.R. (1987). Dyslexia. *Scientific American, 256*, 20–27.

Vellutino, F.R., Fletcher, J.M., Snowling, M.J. & Scanlon, D.M. (2004). Specific reading disability (dyslexia): What have we learned in the past four decades? *Journal of Child Psychology and Psychiatry, 45*, 2–40.

Vellutino, F.R., Scanlon, D.M., Sipay, E., Small, S., Pratt, A., Chen, R. & Denckla, M. (1996). Cognitive profiles of difficult to remediate and readily remediated poor readers: Towards distinguishing between constitutionally and experientially based causes of reading disability. *Journal of Educational Psychology, 88*, 601–638.

Vellutino, F.R., Scanlon, D.M., Small, S. & Fanuele, D.P. (2006). Response to intervention as a vehicle for distinguishing between children with and without reading disabilities: Evidence for the role of kindergarten and first grade intervention. *Journal of Learning Disabilities, 39*, 157–169.

Vinegrad, M. (1994). A revised adult dyslexia checklist. *Educare, 48*, 21–23.

Voight, R.G., Llorente, A.M., Jensen, C.L., Fraley, J.K., Berretta, M.C. & Heird, W.C. (2002). A randomized double-blind, placebo-controlled trial of docosahexaneoic acid supplementation in children with attention-deficit/hyperactivity disorder. *Journal of the American Academy of Child and Adolescent Psychiatry, 41*, 139.

Wagner, R.K. & Torgesen, J.K. (1987). The nature of phonological processing and its causal role in the acquisition of reading skills. *Psychological Bulletin, 101*, 192–212.

Wagner, R.K., Torgesen, J.K. & Rashotte, C.A. (1994). Development of reading-related phonological processing abilities: New evidence of bidirectional causality from a latent variable longitudinal study. *Developmental Psychology, 30*, 73–87.

Wagner, R.K., Torgesen, J.K., Rashotte, C.A., Hetch, S.A., Barker, T.A., Burgess, S.R., Donahue, J. & Garon, T. (1997). Changing relations between phonological processing abilities and word-level reading as children develop from beginning to skilled readers: A 5-year longitudinal study. *Developmental Psychology, 33*, 468–479.

Wagner, R., Torgesen, J., Rashotte, C. & Pearson, N. (2013). *Comprehensive test of phonological processing: Examiners manual* (2nd ed.). Austin, TX: Pro-ed.

Wechsler, D. (1992). *The Wechsler intelligence scale for children III*. Sidcup, UK: Psychological Corporation

Wechsler, D. (2005). *Wechsler individual achievement test* (2nd ed.). London: Psychological Corporation.

Wechsler, D. (2008). *Wechsler adult intelligence scale* (4th ed.). San Antonio, TX: Pearson.

Weedon, C. & Reid, G. (2003). *Special needs assessment profile (SNAP)*. London: Hodder.

Weeks, S., Brooks, P. & Everatt, J. (2002). Differences in learning to spell: Relationships between cognitive profiles and learning responses to teaching methods. *Educational and Child Psychology, 19*, 47–62.

Werner, E.E. (2000). Protective factors and individual resilience. In J.P. Shonkoff & S.J. Meisels (Eds.), *Handbook of early childhood intervention* (pp. 115–132). New York: Cambridge University Press.

Wilkins, A. (2005). *Reading through colour*. Chichester, UK: Wiley.

Wilkins, A.J., Evans, B.J.W., Brown, J.A., Busby, A.E., Wingfield, A.E., Jeanes, R.J. & Bald, J. (1994). Double-masked placebo-controlled trial of precision spectral filters in children who use coloured overlays. *Ophthalmic and Physiological Optics, 14*, 365–370.

Wilson, K.M. & Trainin, G. (2007). First-grade students' motivation and achievement for reading, writing, and spelling. *Reading Psychology, 28*(3), 257–282.

Wimmer, H. (1993). Characteristics of developmental dyslexia in a regular writing system. *Applied Psycholinguistics, 14*, 1–33.

Wimmer, H., Landerl, K. & Schneider, W. (1994). The role of rhyme awareness in learning to read a regular orthography. *British Journal of Developmental Psychology, 12*, 469–484.

Wimmer, H., Mayringe, H. & Landerl, K. (1998). Poor reading: A deficit in skill automatization or a phonological deficit? *Scientific Studies of Reading, 2*, 321–340.

Wimmer, H., Mayringer, H. & Raberger, T. (1999). Reading and dual-task balancing: Evidence against the automatization deficit explanation of developmental dyslexia. *Journal of Learning Disabilities, 32*, 473–478.

Winner, E., von Karolyi, C., Malinsky, D., French, L., Seliger, C., Ross, E. & Weber, C. (2001). Dyslexia and visual-spatial talents: Compensation vs deficit model. *Brain and Language, 76*, 81–110.

Wise, B.W., Ring, J. & Olson, R. (1999). Training phonological awareness with and without explicit attention to articulation. *Journal of Experimental Child Psychology, 72*, 271–304.

Wolf, M. & Bowers, P.G. (2000). Naming speed processes and developmental reading disabilities: An introduction to the special issue on the double-deficit hypothesis. *Journal of Learning Disabilities, 33*, 322–324.

Wolf, M., Miller, L. & Donnelly, K. (2000). Retrieval automaticity, vocabulary elaboration, orthography (RAVE-O): A comprehensive fluency-based reading intervention programme. *Journal of Learning Disabilities, 33,* 375–386.

Wolf, M. & O'Brien, B. (2001). On issues of time, fluency and intervention. In A. Fawcett (Ed.), *Dyslexia: Theory and good practice* (pp. 124–140). London: Whurr.

Wolf, M., Pfeil, C., Lotz, R. & Biddle, K. (1994). Towards a more universal understanding of the developmental dyslexias: The contribution of orthographic factors. In V.W. Berninger (Ed.), *The varieties of orthographic knowledge* (pp. 137–171). Dordrecht: Kluwer Academic.

Wolff, P.H., Michel, G.F. & Ovrut, M. (1990). Rate and timing precision of motor co-ordination in developmental dyslexia. *Developmental Psychology, 26,* 349–359.

Woolfolk-Hoy, A.E. (2006). *Educational psychology* (10th ed.). Boston: Allyn & Bacon.

World Federation of Neurology. (1968). *Report of research group on dyslexia and world illiteracy.* Dallas, TX: WFN.

Ygge, J., Lennerstrand, G., Axelsson, I. & Rydberg, A. (1993). Visual functions in Swedish population of dyslexic and normally reading children. *Acta Ophthalmology, 71,* 1–9.

Zabell, C. (2003). *Individual differences in dyslexia* (PhD thesis, University of Surrey, UK).

Zabell, C. & Everatt, J. (2002). Surface and phonological subtypes of adult developmental dyslexia. *Dyslexia, 8,* 160–177.

Ziegler, J., Bertrand, D., Tóth, D., Csépe, V., Reis, A., Faísca, L., Saine, N., Lyytinen, H., Vaessen, A. & Blomert, L. (2010). Orthographic depth and its impact on universal predictors of reading: A cross-language investigation. *Psychological Science, 21,* 551–559.

Ziegler, J.C. & Goswami, U. (2005). Reading acquisition, developmental dyslexia, and skilled reading across languages: A psycholinguistic grain size theory. *Psychological Bulletin, 131,* 3–29.

Zimmerman, B.J. (2000). Self-efficacy: An essential motive to learn. *Contemporary Educational Psychology, 25*(1), 82–91.

INDEX